Patterns Plus

A Short Prose Reader with Argumentation

Tenth Edition

Mary Lou Conlin

Cuyahoga Community College

WADSWORTH
CENGAGE Learning

Australia • Brazil • Japan • Korea • Mexico • Singapore • Spain • United Kingdom • United States

WADSWORTH
CENGAGE Learning

Patterns Plus: A Short Prose Reader with Argumentation, **Tenth Edition**

Mary Lou Conlin

Director, Developmental English and College Success: Annie Todd

Development Editor: Maggie Barbieri

Associate Editor: Janine Tangney

Editorial Assistant: Melanie Opacki

Marketing Manager: Kirsten Stoller

Marketing Coordinator: Ryan Ahern

Marketing Communications Manager: Martha Pfeiffer

Content Project Manager: Rosemary Winfield

Art Director: Jill Ort

Print Buyer: Betsy Donaghey

Text Permissions Manager: Margaret Chamberlain-Gaston

Production Service: S4Carlisle Publishing Services

Cover Designer: Hanh Luu

Cover Image: Siri Stafford / Gettyimages (stones), Eastcott Momatiuk / Gettyimages (sand dunes)

Compositor: S4Carlisle Publishing Services

For product information and technology assistance, contact us at **Cengage Learning Customer & Sales Support, 1-800-354-9706.**

For permission to use material from this text or product, submit all requests online at **www.cengage.com/permissions** Further permissions questions can be e-mailed to **permissionrequest@cengage.com**

Library of Congress Control Number: 2009934816

ISBN-13: 978-0-495-80252-5
ISBN-10: 0-495-80252-2

Wadsworth
20 Channel Center Street
Boston, MA 02210
USA

Cengage Learning is a leading provider of customized learning solutions with office locations around the globe, including Singapore, the United Kingdom, Australia, Mexico, Brazil and Japan. Locate your local office at **international.cengage.com/region.**

Cengage Learning products are represented in Canada by Nelson Education, Ltd.

For your course and learning solutions, visit **www.cengage.com.**

Purchase any of our products at your local college store or at our preferred online store **www.cengagebrain.com.**

Printed in the United States of America
2 3 4 5 6 7 14 13 12 11 10

Contents

10   Argumentation and Persuasion   249

PARAGRAPHS

ESSAYS

Thematic Contents

Animals and Humans

The following readings discuss animal and human behavior under different situations and challenges.

Childhood

In the following readings, the writers share memories, lessons learned, risks taken in childhood and youth, and the significance of early parental involvement with one's children.

Communication

In the following readings, the writers consider the many ways we communicate and fail to communicate effectively.

Education and Learning

What we've learned and what we have yet to learn are considered in the
     following selections.

Expectations and Reality

In the following readings, the writers show us that expectations,
     whether positive or negative, may not be realized or may turn
     out differently than anticipated.

The Family

The following readings consider the positive and not-so-positive aspects
of family life.

Food for Thought

The following readings consider things we like to eat and drink, and things
we maybe shouldn't eat or drink.

The Individual in Society

The readings included in this section deal with the experiences, roles, and
responsibilities of individuals and with the effect of society on their lives.

The Natural Environment

The following selections consider our impact on the environment and its
impact on us.

Progress

The following readings consider the memorable but sometimes questionable
   effects of the discoveries, inventions, and decisions made in the name
   of progress—as well as our lack of progress in solving some of society's
   problems.

Racial, Ethnic, and Cultural Issues

African American, Italian, Japanese, Hispanic, Jewish, Chinese,
   and Muslim issues as well as cultural and class concerns are
   addressed in the following selections.

Values

Values associated with a particular culture, race, society, sight, food, piece
   of clothing, language, and even color are considered in the following
   readings.

The Working World

The nature of work, the definition of work, and the effects of not working are
    considered in the following readings.

Writing-across-the-Curriculum
Contents

Business

 Communication

 Computer Science and Information Systems

 Economics

 Education

Geography and Geology

History

Law and Public Policy

Media Studies

Medical Science and Health

Political Science

Psychology

Sociology

Women's Studies

Preface

Patterns Plus: A Short Prose Reader with Argumentation provides students with an understanding of the thinking process, organizational principles, and rhetorical strategies involved in producing clear and effective writing. In this ninth edition, students are introduced to the uses of freewriting and brainstorming in defining ideas for their writing and to the process of collaborative writing. The study apparatus provides complete and clear explanations of the various rhetorical modes, and the paragraph and essay-length readings provide students with examples of how the modes can be used in organizing and developing their ideas.

New to the Tenth Edition

Patterns Plus, tenth edition, provides students with a variety of models for their own writing and with readings that stimulate lively and thoughtful classroom discussions. Features that are new to this edition include the following:

- New readings by Nathalie Fiset, Jon Birger, and Leonard Pitts, jr.
- New collaborative writing assignments
- New Internet-based writing assignments (look for the globe icon)
- A revised Thematic Table of Contents
- A revised Writing across the Curriculum Table of Contents

An Overview of Patterns Plus

Chapter 1, an introductory chapter, describes the basics of the writing process and the construction of paragraphs and essays. In chapters 2 through 10, the various techniques used in developing the main idea of a paragraph and the thesis of an essay are explained: narration, description, and the expository modes of examples, classification and division, comparison and contrast, process, cause and effect, definition, and argumentation and persuasion. These are the traditional rhetorical modes—the strategies for development that have proved effective in providing starting points for student writers. Chapter 11, Combining the Strategies, contains student and professional essays that illustrate the ways writers combine various modes of development within a single essay.

Professional and student selections in *Patterns Plus* were chosen specifically to build students' confidence by showing them that the writing of short, effective compositions is within their reach. Selections range from simple, accessible paragraphs to longer, more challenging essays. The student writings that are included throughout the text will make students aware of the level of skill they can realistically expect to achieve.

The breadth of reading selections also allows the instructor a wide choice of topics—from serious and timely discussions related to global warming, cell phones in the classroom, and the legal drinking age to the lighthearted challenges of washing your hands or bathing a cat.

Apparatus

Patterns Plus offers a full range of study apparatus:

- Headnotes provide author information and a context for each reading selection to help students understand and enjoy the selection.
- Words to Know define unfamiliar words and clarify allusions that might be unfamiliar or regional.
- Getting Started questions prepare students to think critically about the topic presented in the reading selection or about topics for their own writing.
- Exercises promote comprehension and critical skills:

    Questions about the Reading are designed to stimulate thinking about the selection's meaning—expressed and implied—and to help students gain fuller understanding of the writer's message.

    Questions about the Writer's Strategies ask students to discuss the writer's thesis statement, mode of development, point of view, figurative language—or whatever strategy is particularly appropriate to a given selection—and thereby promote critical and analytical thinking.

    Writing Assignments are related to the topic and development mode of the reading selection and are designed to encourage the student to generate ideas that can be developed into paragraphs and essays.

- The Thematic Table of Contents groups the readings in the text by such themes as "Animals and Human," Childhood," "Communication," "Education and Learning," "Expectations and Reality," "The Family," "Food for Thought," "The Individual in Society," "The Natural Environment," "Progress," "Racial, Ethnic, and Cultural Issues, " "Values," and "The Working World."

- The Writing across the Curriculum Table of Contents arranges the readings by academic discipline, such as biology, education, and history.
- The Glossary provides definitions of all writing-process, rhetorical, and literary terms that are boldfaced throughout the chapter introductions and end-of-selection questions.

Support for Instructors

The *Instructor's Resource Manual for Patterns Plus* offers instructors a wide variety of supplemental materials:

- Part One supplies teaching suggestions that will allow flexibility in determining course content and structure.
- Part Two contains questions and their answers about the content of each chapter. The questions can be used as quizzes or to generate class discussion.
- Part Three provides suggested answers to the reading comprehension and Writer's Strategies questions that appear at the end of each reading selection in chapters 2 through 10.
- Part Four offers suggested questions and answers for the extra readings in chapter 11.
- Part Five includes a list of the reading levels according to the Fry and Dale-Chall readability formulas. Reading levels are arranged by chapter and by grade.

Acknowledgments

I would like to thank my good friends Ruth Silon, Cuyahoga Community College, for sharing her student's essay, "Students," and Kim Flachmann, California State University, Bakersfield, for providing "An Intruder in the House," by her student Carol Adams.

I am further indebted to the following persons for their helpful suggestions for revisions and new reading selections for this tenth edition of this text:

Jana Carter, Montana State University, Great Falls
Beth Maxfield, Henderson State University;
Karen O'Donnell, Finger Lakes Community College
Everest Onuoha, Roxbury Community College
Jim Schwartz, Wright State University

Finally, I thank the people at Cengage Learning who worked with me on this, my twenty-fourth textbook, especially Maggie Barbieri and Annie Todd. Working with the staff at Cengage Learning has been a great joy.

Mary Lou Conlin

1

The Basics of Writing: Process and Strategies

Of all the arts in which the wise excel, Nature's chief masterpiece is writing well.
—John Sheffield, Duke of Buckinghamshire 1648–1721

THIS BOOK TELLS you about the process and strategies that you can use to produce effective writing. It includes many paragraphs and essays—by both student and professional writers—that you can read and study as models for your own writing. By understanding and following the process involved in writing, by learning the strategies writers use to communicate their ideas, and by practicing in paragraphs and essays of your own, you can develop the skill and confidence needed to write effectively on many different subjects.

Purpose and Audience

Understanding the writing process and learning a variety of writing strategies will help you when you write in school (and afterward), for different **purposes**, to different types of **audiences**, and for varied **occasions**. Your purpose might be to persuade (perhaps in a memo recommending a new procedure at work), to instruct (in a description of how to do a lab assignment), or to inform (in a note to your teacher explaining your absence from class). Your audience, or reader, may be fellow students or friends, and the occasion may be an informal activity; your audience may be your employer, and the occasion a formal report. In any case, you will need to make choices—as you work through the process of prewriting, drafting, rewriting, revising, and editing your work—about the writing strategies that will most effectively explain your ideas.

As a student, you will often have tests and assignments that require you to write either a **paragraph** or an **essay.** Although such compositions

1

may differ in their length and content, a paragraph and an essay are alike in two important ways. First, each one should have a **main idea.** Second, the main idea should be fully explained or developed. In this book, you will learn the ways that many writers go about finding a main idea and the strategies that they use to explain or develop it.

Finding a Main Idea

If you are like most writers, you may find it difficult to come up with a main idea of your own. You may stare out the window, get something to eat, play a game on your computer, or in some other way put off starting to write. When you find yourself stalling, you may find it helpful to do some prewriting exercises to generate ideas. One method is to sit down and write without stopping for five or ten minutes. This is called **freewriting**, and its primary purpose is to get you started with writing.

As the term implies, "freewriting" is often disorganized and lacks a clear focus. Your freewriting might look like this:

> Need to wash my car. May rain though. What to write about? Maybe last night's ball game. What's that guy doing in his yard? He just mowed it yesterday. Ball game was great—all those homers and extra innings— exciting. Glad I went. Need to go to the store. Out of bread. What'll I get for dinner?

When you look over your freewriting, you can see that you wrote about the baseball game you saw last night. You could write about the exciting game.

Sometimes your instructor will suggest a topic to focus your freewriting. For example, suppose that your instructor asks you to write a paragraph describing the room you are in. Your freewriting might then look like this:

> Looks like rain. Wonder if I closed my bedroom windows. What can I say about this classroom except that it's pretty much like all college classrooms. Seats with writing arms, blackboard, teacher's desk, tan walls with lots of dents in them. Have to pick Chad up from the day-care center at 4. Hope he won't be crabby like he was yesterday. What should I say about this classroom?

When you read your freewriting, underline anything that strikes you as interesting or important. Your freewriting may trigger an idea that will focus your description. For example, you may notice that your classroom is like all classrooms, except that the walls have lots of dents. Choosing this as a main idea, you might then write a paragraph like this:

Main idea

⌈ The classroom is like all college classrooms except for the
⌊ many dents in its walls. Like all classrooms, it has thirty
chairs with writing arms, lined up in five rows with six
chairs in each row; a blackboard that still has the assignment
on it from the previous class and needs a good washing; the
professor's desk, with a podium on it to hold his oft-used
lecture notes; and tan, finger-marked walls. But for some
unknown reason, chairs have been shoved hard and often
against the walls, which have more and deeper dents than

Main idea
restated

⌈ those in other classrooms. Only its dented walls make this
⌊ classroom different from all college classrooms. → COMMON
SENCE.

Suppose, however, that the assignment is to (collaborate) with one
or more of your classmates in writing an essay about the environment.
Collaboration means working with others on a project—in this case,
writing an essay about the environment. After the members of your collaborative group are chosen, you will need to meet to discuss the assignment, determine each person's responsibilities, and schedule the project.
One member of your group may emerge as the leader, or your group
may elect a leader. The leader is responsible for coordinating the project
and for seeing that each member of the group meets the schedule that is
set for drafting, revising, and editing the assignment.

Next, each person might want to do some freewriting to get started,
but then all group members will want to do some **brainstorming**
together. Brainstorming, like freewriting, is simply a way of putting your
thoughts on paper to help you choose a main idea and develop supporting evidence for a paragraph or an essay. You will need to focus your
thinking on words and ideas that relate to the environment, with one of
you writing down what each person contributes. Your group's list might
look like this:

trees	water
pollution	diapers
landfills	food
harmful	resources
paper	waste disposal
flowers	cars, airplanes—noise
smog	cars, exhaust
plastics	wasting resources—oil, coal, water, land

After your group finishes the brainstorming list, you will need to
look for relationships among the words and ideas. For instance, your
group could decide that the items can be clustered into two groups or
categories—(1) things that the environment provides and (2) things
that can harm or damage the environment.

Environment provides:	Environment damaged by:
trees	waste disposal—diapers, plastics
flowers	cars—exhaust fumes, noise
food	airplanes—noise
resources—water, oil, coal	wasting resources—water, oil, coal, trees

Based on these categories, your group may decide that the main idea for the group's essay could be "We depend on our environment for food, water, and other resources, but we are damaging our environment in several ways." Your group could then decide to **classify** the *ways* in which we are damaging our food, water, and other resources. After reviewing your brainstorming list and talking it over, your group might decide that the classifications could be *polluting, poisoning,* and *wasting*. You could say, "We are *polluting* the land and our water supply with waste disposal, *poisoning* the air with the exhaust from cars and airplanes, and *wasting* our resources by the overuse of paper and oil."

You might then decide to assign responsibility for providing supporting details for each of the classifications to different members of the group. Thus, someone could be responsible for providing **examples** to support "polluting the land and our water supply with waste disposal"; someone else for "poisoning the air with the exhaust from cars and airplanes"; and someone else for "wasting our resources by the overuse of paper and oil."

Stating the Main Idea

The main idea of a paragraph is called the **topic**. This topic is usually stated in a sentence, called a **topic sentence**. The topic sentence usually expresses a general rather than a specific idea, and it may be placed anywhere within the paragraph. However, you will find that it generally helps to keep your writing clear and focused if you state your main idea at the *beginning* of the paragraph. In the sample paragraph that follows, the main idea (or topic) of the paragraph is stated in the first sentence, followed by the supporting examples. This is called general-to-specific, or **deductive**, order.

Topic sentence   <u>History does seem to repeat itself, even in the way that college students behave.</u> In the 1840s, students protested and acted in violent ways. Students at Yale University, for example, objected to their mathematics course and burned their books in the streets. Some captured their tutor and kept him tied up all night, and others shot a cannon through the tutor's bedroom window. In the 1940s and 1950s, students were a fun-loving, game-happy lot. They swallowed live goldfish, took part in dance marathons, and held contests to see how many people could crowd into a phone booth. The more daring males broke into women's rooms in "panty-raids" and festooned their own rooms with the ill-gotten silks. In the 1960s, students repeated the activities of the 1840s. They objected to their courses, littered the campuses with their books and papers, and locked teachers inside college buildings. They protested against all forms of social injustice, from war to the food in the cafeteria. The more violent threw rocks at the police, and a few planted bombs in college buildings. In the 1970s, students repeated the fun and games of the forties and fifties. They held contests to see how many people could squeeze into a phone booth. They had dance marathons. The more daring ran naked across campuses, in a craze called "streaking." The slightly less daring did their streaking with brown paper bags over their heads. <u>Yes, history does seem to repeat itself, even in the sometimes violent and sometimes fun-and-games behavior of the students on college campuses.</u>

Topic restated

In the following paragraph, the writer has stated the topic in the first and second sentences.

Topic sentence

<u>In the nineties and the early 1900s, gold teeth were as much a part of the fashion scene as peg-top trousers, choker collars, and chatelaine watches. There were, of course, certain practical reasons for this popularity.</u> From the viewpoint of the average dentist, gold-shell crowns provided a simple method of securely anchoring artificial teeth; at the same time they covered ugly, broken-down, and discolored natural teeth, as well as much inferior dental work. And to the patient, gold seemed to represent the most in value received.

Charles I. Stoloff,
Natural History (February 1972)

As you become more experienced, you may sometimes find it effective to place the topic sentence at the *end* of the paragraph. In the following paragraph, the writer has stated the topic in the last sentence. This is called specific-to-general, or **inductive**, order.

We think of an ideal society as being a community—whatever its size—in which the people, the environment, and the institutions are in harmony. No nation, ours included, has ever achieved such a society. In fact, most Americans would say that it is not really possible to establish an ideal society. But strangely enough, we keep trying. Time after time, a group of people will drop out of the mainstream of American society to try another "life style" based on the group's concept of an ideal society. Most of these groups have believed in holding their property in common—that is, they believed in a communistic or communal concept of property. Most of the groups have also used the word *family* to refer to all members of the group, rather than to a mother, father, and their children as the family unit. <u>But the groups have differed widely in their attitudes toward sex, marriage, and other values and seldom lasted for very long as a consequence.</u>

Topic sentence

As you study the student and professional writings that follow, you will find that writers do not always state the main idea of their paragraphs and essays outright. Instead, they may prefer to suggest or to **imply** the idea. Notice that the writer must provide enough clues to allow the careful reader to **infer** (determine) the main idea. In the following paragraph, for example, the writer implies the idea that the man saw the berries reflected rather than actually floating in the water. The writer provides the clues the reader needs to infer the main idea by saying that the man struck the bottom of the river when he dived in and that he then looked up and saw the berries hanging over him.

> While walking along the river, he saw some berries in the water. He dived down for them, but was stunned when he unexpectedly struck the bottom. There he lay for quite a while, and when he recovered consciousness and looked up, he saw the berries hanging on a tree just above him.
>
> Paul Radin,
> *"Manbozho and the Berries"*

If you experiment with implying your main idea, be sure to give the reader enough clues to determine your meaning.

In a longer piece of writing, such as an essay, the main idea is called the **thesis** (rather than the topic). The thesis is usually stated in one or more sentences called the **thesis statement.** Like the topic sentence of a paragraph, the thesis statement is often placed near the beginning of an essay. In the essay that follows, the thesis is stated in the opening sentence.

Thesis

<u>A safe city street must have three main qualities.</u>

Topic sentence

First, there must be a clear demarcation between what is public space and what is private space. Public and private spaces cannot ooze into each other as they do typically in suburban settings or in projects.

Topic sentence

Second, there must be eyes upon the street, eyes belonging to those we might call the natural proprietors of the street. The buildings on a street equipped to handle strangers and to insure the safety of both residents and strangers must be oriented to the street. They cannot turn their backs or blank sides on it and leave it blind.

Topic sentence

And third, the sidewalk must have users on it fairly continuously, both to add to the number of effective eyes on the street and to induce the people in buildings along the street to watch the sidewalks in sufficient numbers. Nobody enjoys sitting on a stoop or looking out a window at an empty street. Almost nobody does such a thing. Large numbers of people entertain themselves, off and on, by watching street activity. . . .

Jane Jacobs,
Death and Life of Great American Cities
(New York: Random House, 1961)

In addition to noting the thesis statement, notice that each paragraph has its own topic sentence. The topic sentences support and clarify the thesis. The topic sentences are supported, in turn, by the specifics in each paragraph.

Experienced writers may place the thesis statement in later paragraphs or at the end of the essay. They may, indeed, only imply the thesis. For your own writing, the important point to remember is that an effective essay has a clear thesis statement, just as a well-made paragraph has a topic sentence. When you are reading, your task is to discover the writer's thesis. When you are writing, your task is to make your own thesis as clear as possible to your reader. And your best strategy, initially, is to *state your thesis at or near the beginning of your essay.*

Developing the Main Idea

The second important way in which paragraphs and essays are alike is that their main ideas must be explained or **developed** by the writer. The strategies used by writers to develop their ideas include

narration	process
description	cause and effect
examples (illustrations)	definition
classification and division	argumentation and persuasion
comparison and contrast	

These strategies for developing the main idea are called **modes of development.** Although they have different characteristics, the modes of development have a common purpose—to provide the reader with the specific information needed to **support** or clarify the main idea. As stated earlier, the main idea is a general statement; the development provides the details to support or explain the main idea.

In developing a paragraph, the writer usually (1) begins with a topic sentence, (2) develops the main idea (topic) by a series of related sentences that explain the idea fully, and (3) concludes with a sentence that restates or summarizes the main idea. Look at the following paragraph diagram and compare it with the example paragraph about the classroom on page 3. Notice that the example paragraph begins with a topic sentence; develops the main idea (topic) with the sentences about the chairs, blackboard, desk, and walls; and then concludes by restating the topic sentence.

Paragraph

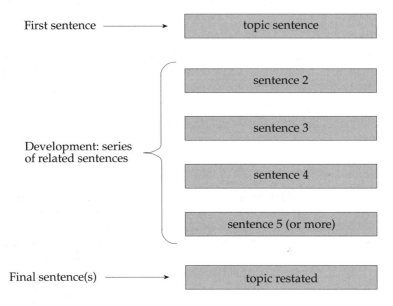

Next, compare the paragraph diagram with the essay diagram that follows. Notice that in developing the essay, the writer starts with a thesis statement, which is generally part of the introduction and may make up the whole first paragraph. Then the writer develops the thesis in a series of related paragraphs, called the **body** of the essay. Usually, each paragraph has its own topic sentence. The conclusion, which may restate the thesis or summarize the essay's important points, is usually found in the final paragraph.

Essay

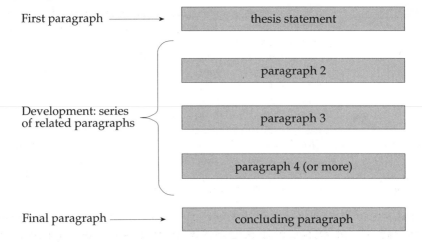

Now look at the following essay developed by a group of students for the environment assignment. Notice that the thesis is stated in the first paragraph, which is called the **introduction** of the essay. The thesis is developed, or supported, by the next three paragraphs that make up the body of the essay. In these paragraphs, each classification of the ways in which the environment is being damaged has been used as the topic for a body paragraph, and items from the brainstorming lists (see page 3) have been used as examples to develop the topics. The final paragraph, called the conclusion or concluding paragraph, restates the thesis and sums up the main points of the essay.

Thesis statement (introduction)

Modern conveniences have made our lives easier but often at the expense of our environment. Science and society, which have been quick to create and adopt new consumer goods, have been slow in creating and adopting practices to protect the environment from the same consumer goods. As a result, just through everyday living, we are damaging the environment that we depend on and wasting our resources.

Development (body paragraph)

For one thing, we pollute the land and our water supply with the by-products of modern life. We fill our garbage dumps and landfills with throwaway plastic products and "disposable" diapers that will not disintegrate for hundreds of years, if ever. Industries accidentally or willfully spill oil and chemicals into the ground or streams and pollute our water supply.

Development (body paragraph)

For another thing, we poison the air with exhaust from the cars and airplanes that have become an important part of our lives. In some areas, the exhaust from cars creates smog that poisons our lungs and causes respiratory ailments. Air pollution also causes acid rain that, in turn, destroys rivers, lakes, woods, and farm crops.

Development (body paragraph)

Finally, we are wasting our resources shamefully. For example, we use far more water than we need to in brushing our teeth and taking showers. Even something as "harmless" as letting dripping faucets go unrepaired wastes a lot of valuable water. We water our lawns through automatic sprinkler systems that run even in rainstorms. We also waste oil by driving millions of cars hundreds of millions of needless miles each year and by keeping our houses warmer than we need to. We are even dangerously close to depleting our "renewable" resources. We cut down our forests with abandonment in order to eat from paper plates, drink from paper cups, and carry products home from the store.

Thesis and important points restated (concluding paragraph)

Yes, we have come to depend on technology to fulfill our needs, but we still need our natural environment. Unless we start developing technology to protect our natural world, it may soon pollute and poison us.

The essay has also been developed by using **classification, examples, cause and effect,** and **persuasion** as modes of development. The *classifications* are the *ways* in which we are damaging the environment—polluting, poisoning, and wasting. *Examples* are filling waste dumps with plastics and diapers, spilling oil and chemicals, allowing cars and airplanes to exhaust fumes, using too much water to brush our teeth and water our lawns, driving needlessly, overheating our houses, and using paper products. In turn, the examples are *causes* of three *effects*—pollution, poisoning, and wasting. The smog created by car exhaust is also a *cause* of lung and respiratory ailments (*effects*). The essay also seeks to persuade readers to stop damaging the environment.

Notice, too, the use of the words *for one thing, for another thing,* and *finally* at the beginning of paragraphs 2, 3, and 4. These are called **transitional** words, and their purpose is to help the reader identify the connection among the ideas in a composition and to move the reader along from one idea to another.

Although the modes of development are often combined as they are in the students' collaborative essay, a single mode of development will often be dominant in a composition. For instance, if you are writing a **descriptive** essay, that does not mean you cannot use **examples** to illustrate your description, but it does mean that most of the paragraphs will be descriptive. Or you might write a **cause-and-effect** essay in which you **narrate** a series of events that constitute a cause and another event that is the effect. In general, however, you will learn to be comfortable with the modes of development if you first study them individually, and this text is organized so you can do that. You will see that chapters 2 through 10 deal with a single mode of development and bring together paragraphs and essays in which that mode dominates. Chapter 11 contains essays that combine the modes, even though one mode may still dominate.

Before each paragraph or essay, you will find a note that tells you something about the reading, definitions of words that might be unfamiliar to you, and a question that either will help you think about the reading or will provide a writing idea. Following each reading selection are questions about the reading, questions about the writer's strategies, and suggestions for your own writing assignments.

The Glossary at the back of the book defines and explains the technical terms that you will learn to use. These terms are boldfaced throughout the text. If you encounter a boldfaced term and cannot recall what it means, turn to the Glossary to refresh your memory.

The ability to state an idea and to develop it so that it is clear to your reader is essential to all forms of composition. The writing strategies covered in this text will help you develop those abilities. However, to produce an effective piece of writing you will generally need to follow this process:

- **Prewriting** (freewriting, brainstorming), to get started and to define your idea
- **Drafting,** to learn what your idea is about
- **Rewriting,** to clarify your idea and to improve or add to the strategies used to develop it
- **Revising,** to improve the organization and content
- **Revising,** to polish the organization and content
- **Editing,** to improve word choices and sentences and to correct punctuation and spelling

Your instructor may also want you to keep a journal as a way to record your thoughts and experiences, to keep you writing, and perhaps to give you ideas for writing. Your instructor may also want you to compile a portfolio—a collection of all your drafts and revisions—as part of your course and to demonstrate your writing progress. Some instructors may want you to collaborate with your classmates on various writing assignments. Still other instructors may give you the option of submitting your drafts by computer and receiving their corrections and suggestions the same way. In any event, you should expect to draft, rewrite, revise, and edit all of your writing assignments until they are clear and convincing to your reader. You can then apply your skills to the many kinds of writing that will be required now, at school, and later, in your career.

2

Narration

Have you ever seen a bad car accident, a fire, or a robbery? Have you had an especially sad or happy experience that made a lasting impression on you or made a difference in your life? If you later mention one of these **events** to friends, they will probably want to know more about it. What individual **incidents** made up the event? How did it happen? At what time? Where did it take place? On the spot, you become a narrator or storyteller and try to give a clear and lively account of the event. Thus, you are already familiar with **narration,** one of the modes of development that writers frequently use to illustrate and explain their ideas. The purpose of narration is to interest the reader in a story that illustrates a particular idea clearly.

Narration is frequently used to tell about personal experiences. You have a variety of personal experiences every day. Your car won't start, you miss the bus, and then you are late for your class. Such experiences, although important to you, will not necessarily make for an effective narrative. For a narrative to be effective, the writer needs to describe an experience that has some unusual meaning or significance for both the writer and the reader. Usually, an experience is significant because it taught you—and may teach your reader—something new, something you never before realized about life. For example, in the following paragraph, the writer tells about a personal experience that taught him about being responsible, not only for making decisions but also for accepting the consequences of those decisions.

> As I was growing up, my father and I often disagreed about how I should spend my time. He began telling me, "If you get yourself into it, you'll have to get yourself out." But

Topic sentence	I learned what it meant to be responsible for the consequences of my decisions only after I went to a weekend
Incident 1	party when I should have studied for a math exam. I needed a good grade on the exam to stay eligible to play basketball.
Incident 2	The consequences of my decision to go to the party were clear when I got my exam back with a notice that I was on academic probation. I spent two semesters of almost steady
Incident 3	studying before I was back in good standing. Now, whenever I have a difficult decision to make, I remind myself,
Topic restated: significance of narrative	"If you get yourself into it, you'll have to get yourself out." It was a tough lesson, but I learned that making a decision means taking the responsibility for its consequences.

Effective narrative writing, like all good writing, is carefully organized. Since a narrative describes events, its organization must be governed by some form of time **order.** The writer often tells about events in the order in which they took place. This method of organization, called **chronological order,** ensures that the sequence of the incidents will be logical.

In the following sample paragraph, the writer uses narration to give a factual account of an event—the discovery of Wheaties. Notice that this writer has chosen to explain the different incidents in a simple chronological order.

Topic sentence	Like gravity and penicillin, Wheaties was discovered by accident. In 1921, a health clinician named Minnenrode, in
Incident 1	Minneapolis, was mixing up a batch of bran gruel for his patients when he spilled some on a hot stove. He heard it
Incident 2	crackle and sizzle, and had a taste. Delicious, he thought. He
Incident 3	took his cooled gruel to the Washburn Crosby Company, which in 1928 would merge with three mills to become
Incident 4	General Mills. Favorably impressed, Washburn Crosby gave Minnenrode use of a laboratory. Alas, his flakes crumbled
Incident 5	too easily and turned to dust in a box. Exit Minnenrode, enter George Cormack, Washburn Crosby's head miller.
Conclusion	Cormack tested 36 varieties of wheat. He cracked them, he steamed them, he mixed them with syrup, he cooked them, he dried them, he rolled them. Finally he found the perfect flakes.

Steve Wulf,
"The Breakfast of Champions"

Notice the **details** in this paragraph. In addition to re-creating the incidents that are significant to his topic, the writer uses descriptive words to tell what happened. Minnenrode "spilled" the gruel, heard it "crackle" and "sizzle," and found that the flakes "turned to dust in a box." By using words that provide descriptive detail, the writer adds variety and interest to his narrative. (**Description,** a mode of development in its own right, is the subject of chapter 3.)

Notice, too, that this paragraph contains only the incidents or details that contribute directly to the story. Avoiding irrelevant incidents and details is essential to effective narrative writing. Perhaps you have heard some long-winded person tell a story and found yourself wishing that the person would skip some of the trivial details. You should keep this in mind when you are writing and limit yourself to the details that are *essential* to the main idea of your narrative. In the following essay, for example, the writer does not include any incidents that happened before the robbery. He concentrates on those incidents and details that explain his actions and reactions only during key moments. As you read the essay, think about the details the writer provides and try to form an image of the scene in your mind.

Thesis statement	Recently I was unfortunate enough to be in a store when 1 a robbery took place. <u>I learned from that experience that a pointed gun makes people obey.</u>
Incidents arranged as they occurred in time	I had stopped at the store on my way home from work to 2 get a loaf of bread. I was at the checkout counter when a man standing nearby pulled out a gun and yelled, "Everyone on the floor and away from the cash register!"
Frozen in place	My first reaction was fear. Around me, people dropped to 3 the floor. But <u>I felt frozen where I stood.</u>
Gun pointed	As I hesitated, the <u>robber pointed his gun</u> at me and 4 yelled again, "On the floor!" Then I felt angry. I was bigger and stronger than he was. I was sure I could put *him* on the floor in a fair fight.
Sank to the floor	But the gun, small enough to be cradled in the palm of my 5 hand, was bigger and stronger than I was. <u>I sank obediently to the floor.</u>
Robbery took place	All of us watched silently as the <u>robber scooped money</u> 6 out of the cash register into a paper bag. Then he ran out the door and jumped into a car that was waiting, and the car raced away.
After robbery	<u>Everyone stood up</u> and started talking. A clerk called the 7 police, who asked if anyone could describe the robber or the car. No one could.
Dialogue— Significance of narrative restated	Then one man, blustering defensively, told the clerk 8 just what I was thinking: "Listen. Tell them when a gun is pointed at me, it's all I'm looking at. One look and I'm going to do whatever I'm told."

Look at each paragraph in this essay. The first paragraph is an introduction in which the main idea or thesis of the essay is stated. Each successive paragraph deals with an incident or a set of incidents in the narrative. Each incident contributes key information to the essay and moves the story forward in time. The final paragraph concludes the narrative by restating the main idea of the essay.

As you can see, the narrative mode is used for more than just retelling what happened. In addition to reporting the action, narrative writing often explains the *reactions*—emotions and thoughts—of the narrator and others involved. At other times, the writer may leave it to the reader to determine the narrator's feelings and reactions.

In this and other ways, the writer establishes a particular **point of view** for the essay. Point of view involves three elements—**person, time, and tone.** The essay may be written in the **first person** (*I/we*), **second person** (*you*), or **third person** (*he/she/it/they*). The time in which the essay is set may be the past, present, or future. The tone is the attitude (serious, humorous, angry, sad) that the writer adopts.

In a narrative essay, the point of view creates the context for the incidents described—that is, who saw or experienced the events, when the events occurred, and how the writer felt about the events. Narration is generally written from the first- or third-person point of view—that is, from the point of view of the person who observed or was a party to the event. Usually, too, the person—the narrator—is kept consistent throughout the narrative, although writers may sometimes use different narrators to express another view or opinion of an event.

Because narration deals with an event or personal experience that has already happened, it is usually written in the past tense. Experienced writers may change the verb tense from the present to the past in what is called a "flashback"—but in general, the tense should be kept consistent.

In narration and the other modes of development, an important factor in point of view is whether the writer is being objective or subjective. An **objective** essay presents the **facts**—the basics of what occurred or what is being described—without including the writer's own interpretations or personal opinions of those facts. The writer tries to portray the subject of the essay as truly as possible and does not try to influence how the reader will react. A **subjective** essay, by contrast, expresses how the writer feels and may try to get the reader to feel a certain way. It may state an opinion or reveal the writer's emotions, or it may present facts in a way that allows the reader to draw a conclusion favored by the writer. The Wheaties story is an example of objective writing; it presents the facts without interpreting them. The other two examples are written more subjectively, expressing the writers' own feelings about and interpretations of the events described.

Often, writers give clues that indicate that they are being subjective. Phrases like "in my opinion" or "I felt" or "I learned" signal a subjective interpretation. (Just because an essay is written in the first person does not mean that it is entirely subjective, however.) As you will see in some of the selections in this text, writers may not always tell you when they are being subjective. Some writers may even take an objective tone when they are being quite subjective—perhaps, for instance, by presenting certain facts about a subject but not others. No matter what mode of development is used in an essay, you should try to find out just how subjective or objective the writer is being.

Narrative writing is called **nonfiction** if the story or event is true and actually happened. All of the preceding examples are nonfictional accounts. This kind of factual narrative is found in biography, history, and newspaper writing. Narrative is also the predominant mode used in short stories and novels. If a story is not true or did not actually occur, it is called **fiction.**

In fiction and nonfiction narrative writing, writers use **dialogue** as a "technique" to re-create what characters or people in the narrative said. In the essay on the store robbery, notice that the writer often tells you exactly what was said and encloses the statement using quotation marks to let you know that he is quoting word-for-word conversation. Quoted dialogue can help the writer accurately express the incidents in a narrative and can add variety and color. To practice working with dialogue, listen to your friends talking with one another and see if you can reproduce something like their conversation in dialogue in your own narratives.

Writers use narration to tell about personal experiences, about other people's lives and experiences, and about factual or historical events, such as the discovery of Wheaties. Narration adds interest, suspense, and clarity to writing, as you will find in the reading selections that follow. Consequently, it is a writing skill well worth mastering.

The questions and assignments at the ends of the readings in this chapter will help you to recognize and apply the principles of narration. They will give you practice with the concepts of chronological order, narrative detail, subjective and objective writing, and dialogue.

The Movie House

John Updike

Our childhood memories are often laced with terror. This paragraph from John Updike's memoir of life in a small town is filled with details that provide a vivid description of just how exciting it is to be terrified.

Words to Know

glowered   scowled, stared angrily
indulgent   not strict, tolerant
supersensory   beyond or above awareness of senses, supernatural

Getting Started

Can you recall a frightening incident from your childhood that haunts you to this day?

It was two blocks from my home; I began to go alone from the age of six. My mother, so strict about my kissing girls, was strangely indulgent about this. The theater ran three shows a week, for two days each, and was closed on Sundays. Many weeks I went three times. I remember a summer evening in our yard. Supper is over, the walnut tree throws a heavy shadow. The fireflies are not out yet. My father is off, my mother and her parents are turning the earth in our garden. Some burning sticks and paper on our ash heap fill the damp air with low smoke; I express a wish to go to the movies, expecting to be told no. Instead, my mother tells me to go into the house and clean up; I come into the yard again in clean shorts, the shadows slightly heavier, the dew a little wetter; I am given eleven cents and run down Philadelphia Avenue in my ironed shorts and fresh shirt, down past the running ice-plant water, the dime and the penny in my hand. I always ran to the movies. If it was not a movie with Adolphe Menjou, it was a horror picture. People turning into cats—fingers going stubby into paws and hair being blurred in with double exposure—and Egyptian tombs and English houses where doors creak and wind disturbs the curtains and dogs refuse to go into certain rooms because they sense something supersensory. I used to crouch down into the seat and hold my coat in front of my face when I sensed a frightening scene coming, peeking through the buttonhole to find out when it was over. Through the buttonhole Frankenstein's monster glowered; lightning flashed; sweat poured over the bolts that held his face together. On the way home, I ran again, in terror now. Darkness had come, the first show was from seven to nine, by nine even the longest summer day was ending. Each porch along the street seemed to be a tomb crammed with shadows, each shrub seemed to shelter a grasping arm. I ran with a frantic high step, trying to keep my ankles away from the reaching hands. The last and worst terror was our own porch; low brick walls on either side concealed possible cat people. Leaping high, I launched myself at the door and, if no one was in the front of the house, fled through suffocating halls past gaping doorways to the kitchen, where there was always someone working, and a light bulb burning. The icebox. The rickety worn table, oilcloth-covered, where we ate. The windows solid black and fortified by the interior brightness. But even then I kept my legs away from the dark space beneath the table.

Questions about the Reading

1. Did the writer enjoy horror movies as a young boy? How can you tell?
2. What gives this paragraph a breathless, frightened quality? Try to identify specific **details** that contribute to this quality.
3. As a young boy, the writer spent many hours at the movies. Does he ever mention being there with friends? What does the writer **imply** about his social experiences in this paragraph?

Questions about the Writer's Strategies

1. Is the main idea of the paragraph directly stated? If so, in which sentence(s)? If not, state the main idea in a sentence of your own.
2. What is the **point of view** in the narrative? Could another point of view be used? Using the first two sentences of the paragraph as an example, explain how you could change the point of view.
3. If you had never seen a horror movie, what **details** in the paragraph would give you an idea of what one would be like?
4. In what ways is this paragraph **subjective**? In what ways is it **objective**?

Writing Assignments

1. Recall the most frightening episode from your childhood. Write a narrative paragraph describing the feelings you experienced.
2. Write a narrative paragraph that describes the neighborhood in which you grew up. Try to include details that will help the reader **infer** the size and type of town.
3. Think of an activity that you loved as a child. Write a narrative paragraph in the **third person** that describes a child participating in that activity.

The Hunt

Lesley Stern

In this paragraph, the writer conveys the tension and suspense felt by the narrator as he observes a prowler who enters his bedroom and ransacks the closet. Lesley Stern is the author of The Scorsese Connection *and* The Smoking Book *and coeditor of* Falling for You: Essays on Cinema and Performance.

Words to Know

accretions   accumulations, collections

dissipate   ease, lessen

voluminous   large, huge

Getting Started

How would you feel and what would you do if an intruder entered your bedroom at night?

The door edges open and in the crack light flickers. A figure moves into the room, a dark silhouette. The figure turns into the light and he sees: it is her. Only her, a figure as familiar as his own body. The tension begins to dissipate, but slowly, uneasily. It is as though knots have formed through his being from tip to toe. He holds his breath and watches as she moves across the room, easing the wardrobe door open, carefully trying to avoid the habitual squeak. I must oil the hinges, he thinks. With her back to the bed, shielding the flashlight beam, she scrambles among old clothes piled at the back of the wardrobe; she burrows into the bottom of voluminous coat pockets, turns shirts inside out, baggy jeans upside down. He knows that she will already have gone through the house searching in jars, behind books in the bookcase, at the back of untidy drawers filled with junk. It happens once a year or so: the evil spirit comes upon her in the night, and she invades her own house, excavating the accretions of daily living, wanting desperately to find a remnant of the past, a sign of life. "Not much to ask," she'd say if pushed, "a little thing." That thing which is so simply and satisfyingly itself: a cigarette.

Questions about the Reading

1. Where is the narrator when the event takes place?
2. Who is the "intruder" who enters the room?
3. What does the "intruder" do?
4. Is this the first time the "intruder" has acted as she does?
5. Why does the intruder act this way?

Questions about the Writer's Strategies

1. What is the main idea of the paragraph?
2. Is the main idea stated or implied?
3. Is the paragraph objective, subjective, or both?
4. What order does the writer use?
5. What is the point of view of the paragraph? Does it change? If so, where and why?

Writing Assignments

1. Write a narrative paragraph about an experience you had that was scary.
2. Write a narrative paragraph about a happy event you are anticipating.

3. Use the Internet to find out more about the writer, and make an entry in your journal about Lesley Stern's birthplace, education, occupation, and honors.

Why Harlem Is Not Manhattan

John L. Jackson

A young black man insists that Harlem is not part of Manhattan.

Words to Know

distinction   difference
Dominican   a country (Dominican Republic in the West Indies)
queue   line or file of waiting people
scissored   cut

Getting Started

Has anyone ever made you feel "different" or "left out" because of where you live?

Standing at the end of a too-long line of customers inside a too-crowded fast food restaurant in northern Manhattan, I listened attentively as Dexter, a twenty-three-year-old black man, argued across the shiny McDonald's countertop with the Dominican cashier who was trying patiently to take his order. Dressed in white, gray, and black fatigues, with neatly coifed dreadlocks down to his shoulders and two-summers-old Air Jordans on his feet, Dexter held up that queue by waving a color-ful coupon in the palm of his right hand. Scissored out from an insert in that Sunday's local newspaper, the coupon redeemed a ninety-nine-cent Big Mac in every part of New York City (so read the fine print) "except the borough of Manhattan," where Big Macs, with this very same square of paper, were discounted to $1.39 instead. Well, hearing the cashier, Pam, make that borough-specific distinction several times, Dexter became increasingly annoyed. He crossed and uncrossed his arms with emphatic gestures. He sighed audibly and repeatedly. Squeezing a dollar bill and a dime in his outstretched left hand (the ten cents was "for tax," he declared numerous times), Dexter made his case: "This is Harlem," he stated with electrified finality, "not Manhattan! If they meant Harlem, if they meant Harlem, they should have written Harlem! Harlem is not Manhattan! So, I'm paying $1.10 for my Big Mac."

Questions about the Reading

1. Where does the event take place?
2. Who is the person the event is about?
3. What does he look like?
4. What does he want?
5. Do you think his demand is justified? Why or why not?

Questions about the Writer's Strategies

1. What is the point of view of the narrative?
2. Is the narrative objective or subjective?
3. What order does the writer use in the narrative?
4. What "technique" does the writer use to clarify Dexter's demand and emphasize his frustration?

Writing Assignments

1. Write a narrative paragraph about an experience you or an acquaintance has had redeeming a coupon at the grocery store.
2. Write a narrative paragraph about an unusual or exciting event that happened in your city or neighborhood.

Geography

Elizabeth Bishop

It is often obvious when a writer is using narration as a mode of development. But narration can also be subtle. In this paragraph, notice how Elizabeth Bishop uses sensory details—what she sees, hears, and feels—to add appeal and color to an unspectacular event.

Words to Know

recitation   a student's oral delivery of prepared materials

Getting Started

What was your favorite or least favorite subject in grade school?

Only the third and fourth grades studied geography. On their side of the room, over the blackboard, were two rolled-up maps, one of Canada and one of the whole world. When they had a geography lesson, Miss Morash pulled down one or both of these maps, like window shades. They were on cloth, very limp, with a shiny surface, and in pale colors— tan, pink, yellow, and green—surrounded by the blue that was the ocean. The light coming in from their windows, falling on the glazed, crackly surface, made it hard for me to see them properly from where I sat. On the world map, all of Canada was pink; on the Canadian, the provinces were different colors. I was so taken with the pull-down maps that I wanted to snap them up, and pull them down again, and touch all the countries and provinces with my own hands. Only dimly did I hear the pupils' recitations of capital cities and islands and bays. But I got the general impression that Canada was the same size as the world, which somehow or other fitted into it, or the other way around, and that in the world and Canada the sun was always shining and everything was dry and glittering. At the same time, I knew perfectly well that this was not true.

Questions about the Reading

1. Was the writer herself in the third or fourth grade? How do you know?
2. Was the writer paying attention to the geography lesson? Explain your answer.

3. What type of essay do you think this paragraph comes from? What do you think the writer's purpose was in composing the essay?

Questions about the Writer's Strategies

1. What is the **main idea** of this paragraph? Is there a **topic sentence**? If so, where is it located? If not, where is the main idea expressed?
2. What makes this a narration paragraph? What are the incidents? What is the main event?
3. What else does the writer do besides narrating what happened?

Writing Assignments

1. Recall a situation from your childhood or even from later years in which you used your imagination to keep yourself interested during what might seem a boring event. Write a narrative paragraph describing the situation and your mental reaction.
2. Pick an event that you think *nobody* would be interested in. In a paragraph, try to narrate the event in a way that will hold your reader's interest. Try to think of active, colorful words to enhance your narrative, and feel free to use humor if you like.
3. Write a paragraph about your favorite or least favorite subject in grade school, and tell why it was your favorite or least favorite subject.

The Memorial Service

Christopher Malinowski (student)

In his essay, Christopher Malinowski gives us a picture of a traditional memorial service and of the people who are there to light a candle in memory of a deceased loved one. One person in particular, in contrast to the others, speaks the name of her deceased loved one clearly and moves quickly to light her candle.

Words to Know

stammers   speaks hesitantly

stricken   struck, affected

Getting Started

Do you have a tradition that you follow related to the birth of a child, a marriage, a graduation, or some other event?

As my brother and I sit in the church pew, we watch people slowly file into the church for the All Souls Day Memorial Service. After a brief opening blessing, we see a microphone being passed slowly through the trembling hands of people. They say the name of a deceased person whom they wish others to pray for and light their candles in the flame of the burning Easter Candle, but they are stricken with so much grief that saying the name through choking tears is a struggle. As we listen, another gentleman stammers out the name of one person who had been dear to him during life. As he moves slowly to the candle, he stumbles as if the person he had loved mattered more than where he walked. As he walks back, I try following him with my eyes but lose sight as he moves behind a crowd of people. I soon realize that I am like the people in the congregation who try to follow the person throughout their lives, but lose sight of him or her when they least expect to. Then the microphone passes to an elderly woman whom my brother and I recognize instantly as my mother's secretary, Mary. However, she has become more than a mere secretary to my brother, our parents, and me. She has been a dear friend to all of us, someone to count on, my Confirmation Sponsor, and my former loving babysitter, who lost her husband during the past year from sickness and old age. She says his name into the microphone clearly. After finishing, she strides to light her candle. She doesn't see my brother and me as she reaches up to touch her candlewick to the large Easter Candle. Unknowingly, she lights our lives also.

Questions about the Reading

1. What is the event that the writer and his brother are attending?
2. What is the procedure that is followed during the event? Why?
3. What does the writer mean when he says he's "like the people in the congregation who try to follow the person throughout their lives, but lose sight of him or her when they least expect to"?
4. Who is the person who makes the greatest impression on the writer? Why?

Questions about the Writer's Strategies

1. What is the main idea of the paragraph?
2. What is the point of view of the paragraph?
3. What order does the writer use?

Writing Assignments

1. Write a narrative paragraph in which you explain a tradition you follow in observing some holiday.
2. Write a narrative paragraph about learning to drive a car, registering for classes, taking a bus to school, or asking someone for a date.

Learning to Write

Russell Baker

Russell Baker is a Pulitzer Prize winner noted for his humorous writing. Although this passage from his autobiographical book Growing Up *is lighthearted, we learn in the end that Baker is earnestly describing an event of serious, almost touching, personal importance.*

Words to Know

antecedent   the word to which a pronoun refers
listless   without energy, boring
prim   formal and neat, lacking humor
reminiscence   memory of a past experience

Getting Started

Can you describe an experience that changed the way you thought about yourself?

When our class was assigned to Mr. Fleagle for third-year English I anticipated another grim year in that dreariest of subjects. Mr. Fleagle was notorious among City students for dullness and inability to inspire. He was said to be stuffy, dull, and hopelessly out of date. To me he looked to be sixty or seventy and prim to a fault. He wore primly severe eyeglasses, his wavy hair was primly cut and primly combed. He wore prim vested suits with neckties blocked primly against the collar buttons of his primly starched white shirts. He had a primly pointed jaw, a primly straight nose, and a prim manner of speaking that was so correct, so gentlemanly, that he seemed a comic antique.

I anticipated a listless, unfruitful year with Mr. Fleagle and for a long time was not disappointed. We read *Macbeth.* Mr. Fleagle loved *Macbeth* and wanted us to love it too, but he lacked the gift of infecting others with his own passion. He tried to convey the murderous ferocity of Lady Macbeth one day by reading aloud the passage that concludes

> . . . I have given suck, and know
> How tender 'tis to love the babe that milks me.
> I would, while it was smiling in my face,
> Have plucked my nipple from his boneless gums. . . .

The idea of prim Mr. Fleagle plucking his nipple from boneless gums was too much for the class. We burst into gasps of irrepressible snickering. Mr. Fleagle stopped.

"There is nothing funny, boys, about giving suck to a babe. It is the—the very essence of motherhood, don't you see."

He constantly sprinkled his sentences with "don't you see." It wasn't a question but an exclamation of mild surprise at our ignorance. "Your pronoun needs an antecedent, don't you see," he would say, very primly. "The purpose of the Porter's scene, boys, is to provide comic relief from the horror, don't you see."

Late in the year we tackled the informal essay. "The essay, don't you see, is the . . ." My mind went numb. Of all forms of writing, none seemed so boring as the essay. Naturally we would have to write informal essays. Mr. Fleagle distributed a homework sheet offering us a choice of topics. None was quite so simpleminded as "What I Did on My Summer Vacation," but most seemed to be almost as dull. I took the list home and dawdled until the night before the essay was due. Sprawled on the sofa, I finally faced up to the grim task, took the list out of my notebook, and scanned it. The topic on which my eye stopped was "The Art of Eating Spaghetti."

This title produced an extraordinary sequence of mental images. Surging up out of the depths of memory came a vivid recollection of a night in Belleville when all of us were seated around the supper table—Uncle Allen, my mother, Uncle Charlie, Doris, Uncle Hal—and Aunt Pat served spaghetti for supper. Spaghetti was an exotic treat in those days. Neither Doris nor I had ever eaten spaghetti, and none of the adults had enough experience to be good at it. All the good humor of Uncle Allen's house reawoke in my mind as I recalled the laughing arguments we had that night about the socially respectable method for moving spaghetti from plate to mouth.

Suddenly I wanted to write about that, about the warmth and good feeling of it, but I wanted to put it down simply for my own joy, not for Mr. Fleagle. It was a moment I wanted to recapture and hold for myself. I wanted to relive the pleasure of an evening at New Street. To write it as I wanted, however, would violate all the rules of formal composition I'd learned in school, and Mr. Fleagle would surely give it a failing grade. Never mind. I would write something else for Mr. Fleagle after I had written this thing for myself.

When I finished it the night was half gone and there was no time left to compose a proper, respectable essay for Mr. Fleagle. There was no choice next morning but to turn in my private reminiscence of Belleville. Two days passed before Mr. Fleagle returned the graded papers, and he returned everyone's but mine. I was bracing myself for a command to report to Mr. Fleagle immediately after school for discipline when I saw him lift my paper from his desk and rap for the class's attention.

"Now boys," he said, "I want to read you an essay. This is titled 'The Art of Eating Spaghetti.'"

And he started to read. My words! He was reading *my words* out loud to the entire class. What's more, the entire class was listening. Listening attentively. Then somebody laughed, then the entire class was laughing, and not in contempt and ridicule, but with openhearted enjoyment. Even Mr. Fleagle stopped two or three times to repress a small prim smile.

I did my best to avoid showing pleasure, but what I was feeling was pure ecstasy at this startling demonstration that my words had the power to make people laugh. In the eleventh grade, at the eleventh hour as it were, I had discovered a calling. It was the happiest moment of my entire school career. When Mr. Fleagle finished he put the final seal on my happiness by saying, "Now that, boys, is an essay, don't you see. It's—don't you see—it's of the very essence of the essay, don't you see. Congratulations, Mr. Baker."

Questions about the Reading

1. Why did the writer not want to write an essay? What discovery changed his mind?
2. Why did eating spaghetti so delight the people at the supper table?
3. What comment does the writer make on the role of formal rules in writing?
4. What is your opinion of Mr. Fleagle? How did it change during the course of reading the essay?
5. What was the significance of the essay's main event for the writer?

Questions about the Writer's Strategies

1. What is the **main idea** of this essay?
2. At what point in the essay did you begin to figure out what the main idea would be?
3. What **order** does the writer use in describing the **incidents** in his narrative?
4. Is this essay written **objectively** or **subjectively**? Cite examples from the essay to help explain your answer.

Writing Assignments

1. Write a narrative essay about the most important event you experienced in grade or middle school. Use **chronological order** to describe the event and the incidents leading up to it.
2. Write a narrative essay on one of the following events in your own life: leaving high school, learning to read a novel, using a computer for the first time, learning to have confidence, learning not to jump to conclusions, or controlling your temper. Try to indicate the significance that the event has had for you since it took place.

Daughter's Doll Teaches Mom Lesson on Race

Connie Schultz

Mothers may usually know best, but Connie Schultz, a reporter for the Cleveland (Ohio) Plain Dealer and Pulitzer Prize winner, learned that when it came to choosing a doll, her daughter had a perfectly logical reason for the one she wanted. (Connie Schultz, "Daughter's Doll Teaches Mom Lesson on Race" © 2000 The Plain Dealer. All rights reserved. Reprinted with permission.)

Words to Know

balked refused
furrowed wrinkled, rutted
nuzzling caressing with the nose
venue location, site

Getting Started

What was your favorite plaything as a child, and why did you like it?

Sometimes our kids teach us lessons we thought we were teaching them. 1

That's how Addy made her way into our family's life five years ago. 2

Addy is an American Girl doll. She is based on the main character in 3 a series of books about a slave girl whose family escaped to freedom in the 1800s.

Addy is black. My daughter is white. But from the moment Cait read 4 her first sentence about Addy, she was convinced she and that slave girl were practically twins. And since her father and I had recently separated, it didn't take much lobbying on Cait's part to get exactly what she wanted from this mother steeped up to her furrowed brow in guilt: An Addy doll. An almost-$100 Addy doll, to be precise.

That Christmas morning, my then 8-year-old daughter greeted her 5 new friend with squeals of delight. Not only did she get Addy, she and Addy got matching nightgowns, which Cait quickly snatched up before running off to her bedroom.

A few minutes later, there they were: Addy and Cait, cheek to cheek 6 and dressed in matching white, ruffly nightgowns. "Don't we look alike,

Mommy?" Cait said, her face beaming as she wrapped her arms around her doll.

I looked at my blue-eyed daughter, as pale as a calla lily, squeezing 7
her doll with the creamy brown skin and big dark eyes, and wondered what she could be thinking. Tread gently here, I told myself.

"How do you and Addy look alike?" I asked.   8

Cait just smiled as she brushed back Addy's hair. "Oh, you know," 9
she said, nuzzling the doll's cheek. But I didn't know, and I felt left out, blinded to the bigger picture only my daughter seemed to see.

For the next two months, Cait took Addy everywhere she went. You 10
can learn a lot about strangers by their reaction to a pretty black doll in a white girl's arms. One woman, who was white, glared at me as we stood in line at a McDonald's. "You *made* her buy that, didn't you?" she hissed, shaking her head as she looked at Cait clutching Addy to her chest. "There is no way she would have asked for a doll like that."

A young black woman working at a local drugstore stared at Cait and 11
Addy and then politely leaned in to whisper to me. "Did she want that doll?" When I nodded my head, she winced. "Why?"

"We're a lot alike," piped up Cait. I looked at the bewildered woman, 12
shrugged my shoulders and smiled.

I thought of Addy recently after talking to a mother with two adopted 13
sons from Korea. For years, Linda has sent her boys to a camp for Korean children adopted by Americans. "I thought it was a good idea," she said. "All year long they are with kids who don't look like them, who didn't come from Korea, and everything I had heard and read said this is a good thing to do."

One of her sons, however, balked last year, announcing he did not 14
want to go to that camp again. Her 10-year-old did this in what is all children's venue of choice for serious conversations: In the car, while his mother was driving.

Linda was surprised, but undeterred. "Don't you like to be some place 15
where everyone is like you?" Her son's response so startled her she nearly ended up on a tree lawn: "Isn't the important thing supposed to be liking who you are and not being like everyone else?"

Linda smacked her forehead in recounting this conversation. "You 16
know, you raise them to believe certain things, to get beyond the issues of race and gender and all that, but then you're blown away when you realize they're there, all your lessons took, and *you're* the one who isn't getting it."

At that point I was required to welcome Linda into the Clueless 17
Mothers Club, of which I am president. Then I told her about Addy, and how I finally found out why Cait wanted the doll in the first place.

"Addy and I are so alike," Cait said yet again as I tucked them into 18 bed one night. "How so?" I asked. Cait reached up and touched my face. "Addy had to leave with her mom, just like you and me."

I froze. For eight years I had been teaching my daughter that it's 19 what's on the inside that counts. Obviously, only one of us had been listening.

And you know what? Cait was right. She and Addy, they're so alike. 20 They're practically twins.

Questions about the Reading

1. When did Cait get Addy, the black doll?
2. Why did Cait want Addy?
3. How did people react to Cait having Addy?
4. What did Linda's Korean son tell her when she asked why he didn't want to go back to camp?
5. What is the lesson the writer learned?

Questions about the Writer's Strategies

1. Where is the main idea (thesis) of the essay? Is it stated more than once? If so, where?
2. What is the order the writer uses in the essay?
3. What technique does the writer use to re-create what Addy, Linda, and the writer said?
4. Is the essay objective or subjective?

Writing Assignments

1. Write a narrative essay telling about your favorite plaything as a child and explaining why it was your favorite.
2. Write a narrative essay telling about why you wanted to learn to drive a car and the first time you drove someplace by yourself.

The Farm

M. L. Simpson

A young girl remembers her visits to a farm before and during the drought of the 1930s.

Words to Know

yowling mournful crying, wailing

Getting Started

When you were a child, was there a place you really wanted to visit or a favorite place you liked to go?

I was five years old and had never been to a farm so I was really excited when my Mother told me we were going to take my Grandmother to see Aunt Mamie and her husband, Uncle Will. It would be an all-day drive from our house to their farm in Iowa so my Mother packed a picnic lunch, my Dad loaded our suitcases in the car, and we left early one cool late-summer morning.

As we drove along the roads my grandmother played games with me counting cows, horses, and other animals we saw in the green fields. I used my newly-learned reading skills to read all the Burma Shave signs and the signs painted on barn roofs to her and my mother. We also counted license plates we saw from other states, although there weren't but a few of those. We stopped at a small town along the road and had our picnic under the leafy green branches of a large tree in the town square.

The roads got bumpier and my Grandmother suddenly said "There's their windmill! Their road is right past it!" We pulled into the farm in the late afternoon and my Uncle and Aunt rushed out to meet us while their two dogs ran around barking at us. As soon as I got out of the car, Uncle Will swung me up on his shoulders, a perch I would occupy for most of the next three days as he showed me the wonders of a working farm.

There were cows to be brought in from the green pastures, water to be pumped into troughs for the cows and horses to drink, eggs to be gathered from the hen house, and ripe corn to be picked from the stalks. That was one of the best times because after the bushel basket was filled with ears of corn, Uncle Will sat me on top of it and carried me back to the house. There was Aunt Mamie's garden to explore too, and when she said we would fix some potatoes for dinner, I looked around the kitchen but didn't see any. She just gave me a tool that looked like a big fork, took me out to her garden, and showed me where to dig. To my surprise, I dug up a potato! I had never known that the potatoes I ate almost every day grew underground.

The other wonderful surprise she showed me was a litter of baby kittens and told me I could take one home if my Mother said I could! Somehow, maybe because I lived in a city, I had thought a farm was a desolate place with nothing much there, but looking at the corn and wheat growing in the fields and the water filling the troughs and kitchen sink, it seemed like there was plenty of everything on a farm, from food to kittens. When I told Uncle Will how I had imagined a farm, he said "Honey, this is the land of plenty!"

One of the best nights was when the neighbors from miles around came for a party. A few families came in cars but most came in horse-drawn wagons. Everyone brought food—lots of it—and, along with talk of the crops coming in that the men would help each other harvest and take to market, there was singing and a fiddle player. As the sun began to set, everyone packed up, got in their cars or hitched up their horses to their wagons, and went home.

It was six or seven years later before I went to the farm again with my Mother and Grandmother. This time it was because my Aunt had died.

We still packed a lunch to take in the car and when we stopped in the same town to eat the tree we had sat under had turned brown and the grass was brown and brittle. It was blazing hot, so we ate in a hurry to be on our way again. There was at least shelter from the sun inside the car, and if we had the windows open a little, some air movement.

When we were about to pull in the yard, Mother said to close all the car windows and, after we stopped she told me to wait until the dust settled before opening the car door. Uncle Will waited on the porch of the house but dust kicked up from his feet as he came to the car, and no dogs came to greet us. There weren't any cows or horses drinking at the troughs either. When I looked out the car window I saw tumbleweeds stirring up dust as they blew across brown empty fields.

Neighbors had already gathered, but not for an evening of pleasure. They had brought food, too, but there weren't any wonderful cakes or puddings this time. It seemed that everyone had also brought whatever they would want to drink—even water. I had never been to a funeral in the country but it soon became clear that all the neighbors were prepared to spend the night "protecting" Aunt Mamie who was "laid out" in her own bed.

When it turned dark, candles were lit around her bed and the neighbors took turns "keeping watch." I went to bed in a room next door but sleep didn't come because Aunt Mamie's cats sat on the fence outside her bedroom and kept yowling. When I asked why they were yowling I was told that they wanted her to feed them but there wasn't any food for them unless they caught a mouse or a rat someplace.

The next day everyone got in their cars or wagons and followed the wagon with Aunt Mamie's casket in it to a cemetery. Dust was everywhere, swirling ahead and around us. The sun burned down on us while the minister spoke briefly of her life and her contributions to others. When it was over, Uncle Will rode back to the farm with us. As we drove past the brown empty fields, I told him how different everything looked from when I was there before when everything was green and that I remembered picking corn with him and being carried on the bushel basket. He shook his head, sighed a bit, and said, "Well, we won't be picking corn anytime soon, honey, the land of plenty has dried up!"

Questions about the Reading

1. Why was the little girl excited about going to the farm?
2. What did the little girl do during the ride to the farm?
3. When did the girl's visits to the farm take place? What had changed at the farm between her visits?

Questions about the Writer's Strategies

1. What is the main idea (thesis) of the essay? Is it stated or implied?
2. What is the point of view of the essay?
3. What order does the writer use?

Writing Assignments

1. Write a narrative essay in which you explain visits you have made to a particular place at different times—either a few years apart or at different seasons of the year.
2. Imagine that you want to plant a vegetable garden. Write a narrative essay in which you explain what you planted, how you planted it, and what you have to do to take care of it and make it grow.

A Little Nebraska

Sarah Smith (student)

On a football game Saturday, the population of Lincoln, Nebraska, doubles. People come from all over the state to fill the University of Nebraska stadium to overflowing, and throughout the state, work comes to a stop while the rest of the population watches the game on television.

Words to Know

falter   hesitate, stumble

irreplaceable   cannot be replaced

pretentious   showy, false

Getting Started

Have you ever arranged your work or school schedule around some favorite activity or television program?

T he small town of Imperial, Nebraska, has one grocery store. The store 1
has four carts, three baskets, and two checkout lanes manned by one
checker and one bag-boy. On this particular Saturday afternoon, four
people can be found inside. Walking slowly down each aisle is a grandmother and a 13-year-old girl. The grandmother's age shows in her face
and her walk, leaning on the cart for support. Her cotton white hair is
held neatly in place with an old hair pin; she is wearing a lovely flower-
patterned summer dress and a pair of comfortable white sneakers. In the
same way, the girl's youth is evident in her walk and manner, she takes
long strides down the aisles. The girl's hair is held up in a high ponytail
and covered with a baseball cap. She is wearing a red Huskers T-shirt
and holey jeans. She listens to her grandmother's instructions and gath-
ers all items that are dictated. She is becoming more and more anxious
as time ticks on.

Far across the state in the capital city of Lincoln, 78,000 people stand 2
singing the national anthem in Memorial Stadium. As the marching
band sounds out "Hail Varsity," the Huskers rush the field. The roar of
the stadium becomes almost deafening, as team members feed on the
crowd's energy. The game begins with a kickoff to the visiting team and
the Huskers stopping them at the 20-yard line. On the sideline stands a
nineteen-year-old boy from Imperial, Nebraska. He is wearing a team
jersey, an issued pair of white pants, and an ankle brace on his left leg.

He stands watching the plays intently. He holds his breath at kickoff, and cheers for his friends and teammates.

In Imperial, the girl and grandmother walk slowly to their car. The 3 girl's arms carry two big, brown bags. Her patience is almost gone now, and it is visible in her manner that her grandmother is holding her hostage. She had tried to explain earlier that day that this is the opening game of the season. It is the first chance she has to see the local small town boy, her cousin, in play, and she can't miss a moment of the game. The entire town is indoors glued to their TV screens, and here she is carrying groceries. Seemingly unaware of the dire situation, the grandmother slowly unlocks the car doors, "Place the bags in the back seat, Sweetie. Mind the eggs, now." Their house is approximately two miles in distance from the store. However, at the speed the grandmother drives they will arrive in ten minutes. She can barely see over the steering wheel and believes in stopping at every intersection. The possibility of being hit on this day is almost impossible, yet her driving continues as normal.

In the stadium the sea of red is on its feet cheering the winning team. 4 The Huskers have stopped the opposing team from scoring and have run the ball for a touchdown. The boy watches as the kicker stands poised for the snap. He questions how many times back home he had done the same thing. He begins to think of his small town and the people in it. He knows today they will all be focused on the game. There will be fewer cars than usual on the streets and the local bar will be filled to the brim with customers who have no satellite dish to pick the game up at home. He hopes that one girl in particular is watching, his favorite 13-year-old cousin. Her admiration for him inspired him to come as far as he had, and he knew, whether he had played today or not, she would still be his biggest fan.

The girl is now running to the TV set to find the correct station. The 5 groceries are sitting on the kitchen counter and the grandmother is carefully placing each item in its proper place. "Don't sit so close to the television," calls out the grandmother. "So much fuss over one little game." The grandmother does not understand the obsession with football. The girl's parents had been the same way before they died and she seemed to have it in her blood. After her parents died three years ago, the girl had come to live with her grandmother. The grandmother knew how to deal with the loss of her daughter. She had lost her husband ten years ago. "It's a part of life," she always said. Somehow the two of them had made it this far. Today she just was not in a football mood. The idea of rearranging one's day to fit a football schedule seemed a little pretentious. She felt assured that the game would turn out the way all Husker games do, with a win, so why the fuss about catching every moment?

Three years ago the boy had almost lost his chance to be at this game. 6
That was his junior year in high school, and he started for the varsity
team. He played defense on the opening game and in the last quarter he
almost lost his carrier. He landed on the bottom of a tackle and felt his
ankle pop. The doctors told him the injury was serious. The ankle was
broken, and if he did not give it time to heal, he might never play again.
It seemed like the end of the world, until his cousin moved in with his
grandmother. A car accident had claimed the life of her parents. Spending time with her made a busted ankle seem minor. She was ten years old
and full of energy. She knew she had lost something irreplaceable and
yet it did not stop her. If she could continue, he knew he could too.

The girl does not hear her grandmother's instructions to move from the 7
set. She is looking intently for a glimpse of her cousin. He had been her
comfort and her friend when her parents died. Her grandmother helped,
but her cousin was never too busy for her and never made her feel like a
little kid. She felt needed when she visited him and told him no busted
ankle could stop him. She felt special just knowing he was her friend.

The boy's thoughts return to the game when it suddenly takes a major 8
twist. Something goes wrong in the play. The snap is dropped. There is
a mad dash to recover the fumble. In all of the confusion the kicker goes
down hard on his right knee. He is injured. The boy is now the only
kicker. The coach approaches him, "I hope you're ready, Son. You better
get warmed up."

The girl watches it all and begins to jump and cheer with the news. 9
She will see her hero play today. He is all the world to her and now the
world can see how great he is. "Grandma," she calls out. "He's going to
play." She is disappointed in the first half. The opposing team's defense
does not allow the Huskers to cross the 50-yard line. The girl does not
lose hope, and during half-time she says a prayer for her hero to have
the courage to do his job.

The boy's chance arrives in the third quarter. The Huskers come in 10
with new energy and run the ball for a touchdown in the first three minutes of the game. The boy's heart is pounding as he runs in to take his
turn at the extra point. The world around him seems to hold its breath.
He signals for the snap and is shocked as the ball flies above the setter's
head. The timing is off and the kick goes to the left. It hits the goal post
and bounces off into the stands. The band plays on and the crowd seems
to ignore the disaster.

In Imperial the girl is yelling at the TV, "Get rid of the snapper. I could 11
do better than that guy." The grandmother's interest has been sparked
and she joins the girl on the couch. The girl reminds her of the boy's high
school stats and the many times he has come through for his team in a
tight situation. He will not falter now.

The feel of the game has become urgent in the fourth quarter. The Husk- 12 ers are behind by two points and there are three minutes left in the game. The Huskers are playing defense. The stadium is alive with the chants of the fans. The opposing team approaches the line of scrimmage and the quarterback calls out the play. He goes back for a pass but is sacked by a Nebraska lineman. The Huskers take over at their own 40-yard line. The crowd is yelling insanely and the band continuously plays "There Is No Place Like Nebraska." The offense wastes no time pushing their way down the field. The Huskers call a time out to decide the next play.

The set in the living room switches to a commercial. "Ahhhh, I hate 13 it when they do that!" The girl is pacing around the room. The grandmother sits holding a bowl of popcorn, "Would you kindly sit down. You're making me more nervous than the game." She can't believe how caught up she has become. The girl laughs and takes a seat. She grabs a handful of popcorn and waits for the game to resume.

Wild cheers and music fill the stadium. With 30 seconds on the clock 14 the Huskers will attempt a field goal. The ball is on a 35-yard line. The boy's mind is racing, his heart is pounding, and his palms are sweating. He takes a deep breath, says a prayer, "God bless this kick," and waits for the snap. All goes well; he kicks the ball and watches in what seems slow motion as the ball sails beautifully between the goal posts. The stadium explodes with excitement. The fans give each other hugs and high-fives as if they were on the field themselves. His teammates and TV crews bombard the boy. He jumps and cheers and can almost not believe this dream come true.

In Imperial the whole town is alive with cheers and congratulations. 15 The bartender takes out his trumpet and plays the Huskers fight song. The girl and grandmother shout aloud and hug each other. The grandmother says she is proud of that boy and she can't wait to tell him. The girl replies, "I knew he could do it the whole time." Inside she thinks of how much fun the next game is going to be.

Questions about the Reading

1. Why was the girl in a hurry to get home from the grocery store?
2. Why are there "fewer cars than usual on the streets" of the town on this Saturday?
3. Why is the girl living with her grandmother? What is her grandmother's attitude toward the football game? Does her attitude change?
4. What happened to the boy when he played football in high school?

Questions about the Writer's Strategies

1. What is the thesis of the essay? Is it stated or implied?
2. The writer shifts the point of view between the thoughts and actions of the girl and those of the boy. Why do you think she does this? Do you think this shift is necessary to the story?
3. What details does the writer use to help the reader understand the excitement and sounds of the football game?

Writing Assignments

1. Write a narrative essay about a sports event in which you competed.
2. Write a narrative essay about an important school sports event you attended with some friends.
3. *Working Together* Divide your group into two groups. Have each group watch an important football, baseball, or basketball game on television. Then write a narrative essay together using the viewpoints of the opposing teams.

3

Description

DESCRIPTION PROVIDES THE reader with a "word picture" of a specific person, the flavor of a special place, or the look of a particular object. To help the reader visualize the object, the writer chooses key details to develop the description: a certain liveliness in a person's eyes, the movement of ocean waves, the design of a favorite chair.

We saw in chapter 2 that writers use descriptive words to add color and vividness to the details they describe. The specific descriptive words the writer chooses depend on the particular **impression**, or image, the writer wants to create. For example, the writer can create the impression of a person who is likable by describing the person's face as "friendly" and "good natured." The writer can create the opposite impression by using such descriptive words as *shifty* or *scowling.* In the following paragraph, the writer develops an effective impression of a chair by the buildup of details and descriptive words that re-create the object for the reader.

Detail:
location

Detail:
appearance

Detail:
appearance

The chair was the one piece of furniture I wanted to take with me when I closed up my parents' house for the final time. To look at it, <u>sitting in the same kitchen corner</u> where it had been for fifty years, you'd wonder how it could be my favorite chair. It was nothing but a <u>straight-backed wooden</u> chair, its <u>seat scratched</u> here and there from the soles of a small boy's shoes. The only thing unusual about it was the <u>intricate design</u> carved into its back. But the carving was what made the chair meaningful to me. I had sat in that chair many times as punishment for errors in my ways. I suppose my mother thought it was defiance that led me to sit cross-legged on the seat with my back to her in the kitchen. But it

Detail:
decoration of
chair

was not defiance. Rather, in that position my eyes and then
my fingers could <u>trace</u> the <u>intertwining leaves and flowers</u> of
the design carved in the back of the chair. Each time I sat there
I seemed to see lines and shapes I hadn't seen before: <u>a heart-</u>
<u>shaped leaf, a budding rose, a blade of grass</u>. Perhaps that chair
had something to do with my lasting interest in well-made
antique furniture. Who knows? I do know that when I drove
away on that last day, the chair, <u>carefully wrapped</u> in several
old quilts, lay <u>tenderly cradled</u> on the back seat of my car.

Notice that the chair is described only as being a straight-backed
wooden chair with a scratched seat and a design carved into its back.
However, the writer creates the dominant impression that the chair—in
spite of being associated with childhood punishment—remained beautiful to him and probably influenced his lifelong interest in fine woods and
antiques. The words *intricate, trace, intertwining, heart-shaped,* and *budding*
describe and help the reader picture the design in the back of the chair.
And in the last sentence, the phrases *carefully wrapped* and *tenderly cradled*
convey indirectly the writer's feelings about the chair. The reader must
be given enough detail not only to picture an object but also to understand what touched or moved the writer to single it out.

In descriptive writing, you will often find stylistic devices that help
convey both the essential qualities of the subject and its significance to
the writer. Consider the following paragraph.

> A baseball weighted your hand just so, and fit it. Its red stitches, its good
> leather and hardness like skin over bone, seemed to call forth a skill both
> easy and precise. On the catch—the grounder, the fly, the line drive—you
> could snag a baseball in your mitt, where it stayed, snap, like a mouse
> locked in its trap, not like some pumpkin of a softball you merely halted,
> with a terrible sound like a splat. You could curl your fingers around
> the baseball, and throw it in a straight line. When you hit it with a bat it
> cracked—and your heart cracked, too, at the sound. It took a grass stain
> nicely, stayed round, smelled good, and lived lashed in your mitt all
> winter, hibernating.
>
> Annie Dillard,
"An American Childhood"

In this paragraph, the writer uses a **figure of speech** called a **simile**
to help enhance the description of the baseball. A simile takes items that
are considered unlike and then compares them in a way that shows an
unexpected similarity. Usually, a simile uses *like* or *as* to establish the
connection between the items. For example, three similes in this paragraph are "like skin over bone," "like a mouse locked in its trap," and
"not like some pumpkin of a softball."

A figure of speech related to the simile is the **metaphor**, which also
compares unlike items but does so without directly stating the connection

with *like* or *as*. Metaphors may be used to express an idea that is rather abstract, as in "the *scales* of justice." But they can be used for other effects, too, and they may only be **implied** by the use of a certain verb—"The swimmer *waddled* across the sand."

Read the paragraph that follows. What is the metaphor for the matron and for the electric car? Is there another metaphor?

> In 1900, electric cars were a common sight on city streets. They were high, boxy, and heavy—those early electric cars—and they couldn't get up much speed. Nor could they be driven very far before the battery had to be recharged. So by the 1930s, the electric car was a curiosity piece that now and then sailed out of a carriage house, usually with a stern-faced matron at the steering tiller. Car and driver were somehow suited to each other: heavily built, elegantly appointed, and quietly majestic. They were quality products. They didn't guzzle fuel, raise their voices above a murmur, or create a public problem as they floated across the streets. But they both disappeared in favor of slim-lined, stripped-down models that drink high-powered fuels, make noise in the streets, and create a public nuisance. Now maybe only a few people would like to see that old-style matron come back. But these days, most of us would like to have a car that didn't use gas, was really quiet, and didn't pollute the environment. That's why our engineers have worked to solve the battery problem: so we can have electric cars again.

Personification, another figure of speech, attributes human qualities or abilities to animals or objects. For example, after Red Riding Hood observes that the wolf has big teeth, the wolf answers, "The better to eat you with, my dear!"

Exaggeration, which is called **hyperbole**, is also used. "I could have danced all night" might be possible for a few people, but for most of us, it would be hyperbole.

The organization of a description also contributes to its effectiveness. The writer may arrange the details in **order of importance**, usually moving from the less important to the more important details. The details in the paragraph on page 45–46 are arranged so that they build to the most significant point—the deeper meaning of the chair to the writer. The writer may choose to arrange the details according to space, called **spatial order**. When a description is organized according to space, the writer takes a physical position in a room or at a scene and then describes what can be seen from that position, using some consistent order such as moving from left to right, from foreground to background, or from top to bottom.

In creating a description, the writer must identify the important characteristics of the object or scene being described and then find the words—nouns and verbs, as well as adjectives and adverbs—that best express these characteristics. In the essay that follows, the student describes the house in which she is living. Notice that she describes the house in **spatial order**—first from the outside and then as she walks through its rooms. Notice, too, that the descriptive details provide the reader with an image of both the house and its owner.

View of the outside of the house	It's really not a striking house, nor is it an old charming house. It is, in fact, very plain—just like the houses on each side of it. As I climb up the hilly driveway, its <u>whiteness</u> stares blankly back at me, reminding me that I am not the owner but just a temporary, unwanted trespasser. There are
Details: preciseness of the landscaping	flowers lining the driveway, which push their faces toward the sun as they lie in their bed <u>perfectly spaced</u>, not too close and not too far apart, <u>perfectly coordinated</u> to reflect all the colors of the spectrum. Through the windows of the house nothing
Thesis statement	but my reflection can be seen. They are like the house, clean and tinted, allowing no one a look in, keeping life in the house shut off from the rest of the world, uninviting of intrusion, only interested in cleanliness, only leading the people inside to a feeling of loneliness.
Entering the house	<u>Upon entering the house</u> the smell of Pinesol and disinfectant engulfs my nostrils and shoots directly to my brain,
Details: cleanliness and coldness of kitchen	anesthetizing any emotions that might surface. Like the windows, the kitchen floor reflects the <u>cleanliness</u> of the house with its <u>spotless white surface, scrubbed and shined</u>, casting off reflections from the <u>bright lights</u> overhead. There is wallpaper on the walls of the kitchen, but it is <u>void of any pattern</u> and lends <u>very little color</u> to the <u>whiteness</u> of the room. Only
	items of importance for the duties of the kitchen are displayed, all in their properly appointed places, with the appropriate covers placed over them to hide them from prying eyes. The only personality the kitchen portrays is a cold, calculating, suspicious one, wary of intruders who may cause unnecessary filth to enter.
Moving to dining room	<u>Around the corner from the kitchen lies the dining room</u>.
Details: formality and whiteness of room	An <u>elegant, dark, formal table</u> sits in the center of the room, the surface of which is smooth as glass under my fingertips. A <u>white centerpiece</u> is carefully placed at the table's center, with two <u>white candles that have never been</u> lit standing erect
	at the centerpiece's ends. The chairs around the table are hard, providing support for the back but lending the body no comfort. Above hangs a crystal chandelier—expensive, elegant, giving the room an artificial brightness. It is made up of many dangling, teardrop-shaped crystals, all <u>cleaned and polished</u>, and is the only object in the dining room that speaks clearly of conspicuous consumption. The drapes covering the tinted windows are a dark color and <u>keep out the sun of the day</u>. This room is <u>often cleaned, often walked through</u>, but <u>never used</u>.
Entering the living room	<u>Having walked through the dining room, I enter the living room</u>. Although this is the only room in the house where the

Paragraph numbers: 1, 2, 3, 4

Details: impersonality of living room

family can all converge to spend time together, it is not a cheerful place. The walls are <u>white</u>, like the rest of the house, with the same drapery as the dining room, and the couch and loveseat are velvet, <u>stiff, uncomfortable, and well maintained</u>. A television set is placed in the corner but <u>lies blank with disuse</u>. The <u>air of coldness</u> here seems to hold tension though at the same time it gives the impression of ossification.

I have heard it said that a person's home is a reflection of   5
that person, a sentiment that, with few exceptions, is true of this home. <u>Cleanliness</u> is a priority of the owner, and socializing with people in this house is considered a nuisance that only causes more work because of the dirt that people carry in with them. The walls are kept white because it looks clean and repainting is made easy. And the smell of disinfectant pleases the owner, as it proves to the few who do enter that

Thesis related and conclusion

the house is clean. This house, the place I am calling home for this period of my life, offers me no comfort but does provide shelter and quiet. And with the <u>dark stillness</u> in its rooms, I can think, read, and plan my escape.

Carol Adams (student),
"An Intruder in the House"

In the introduction to chapter 2, you learned about the difference between writing **objectively** and **subjectively**. Notice, in the previous essay, that although the writer's style is objective, her choice of specific descriptive details and words supports her subjective, negative opinion of the house and its owner.

When brainstorming for a description, it may help to begin by listing all the features of the subject that come to mind and all the details that seem related to those features.

Descriptive details are often combined with other modes of development. The following paragraphs, for example, are from a narrative essay about a young man's visit to the Mexican town that he had left soon after he was born. Notice his descriptions of the people and the Spanish architecture of the town.

Description: Spanish architecture

On my arrival at Morelia airport, I was greeted by the   1
most attractive architecture I had ever seen. All the buildings had a very strong Spanish influence. Was it possible I had taken the wrong plane and landed somewhere in Spain?

People and their clothing

No, indeed; it was Morelia, and what a town! Its people   2
were very plain and small-townlike. I was amused by some very oddly dressed people who wore white cotton clothing. On their heads the men wore straw hats, and the women wore large Spanish scarves called mantillas. I asked a ticket agent about the oddly dressed people. He explained that they were the native people, known as Tarascos. They were the founders of the land, and even today they are very traditional in their beliefs and ways.

I took a taxi to El Hotel Virrey de Mendoza, located in   5
the middle of the town square. The hotel was made of hewn
stone that was cut and shaped into the most captivating
three-story building I had ever seen. It was built in the traditional Spanish style, with a central open patio completely
surrounded by the building. My room had a spacious view of
the town square and its cathedral. The cathedral was built in
the seventeenth century in a baroque style that was popular
in Europe. Beside the cathedral was the municipal palace and
other government buildings, all in Colonial Spanish style.
The feeling I had from the view was that I was back in the
days when Spanish viceroys ruled the land, and the Catholic
priests taught religion to the native inhabitants.

Architectural features — (marginal note beside paragraph)

Arturo E. Ramirez (student),
"Back to Where the Seed Was Planted"

Descriptive words and phrases are essential to effective writing. They can make an object concrete for the reader by describing how it looks, sounds, tastes, smells, or feels. Such sensory details can create a distinct impression or **image** of that which is described and thus help the reader visualize the writer's ideas. You will find specific descriptive words and details in all the paragraphs and essays that follow. As you read, notice that experienced writers select revealing details because, as with the incidents in narrative writing, these details produce the most effective description. In your own writing, select—as the writers of the reading selections do—the most essential qualities of whatever you describe.

A Perfect Dog

John Grogan

> *In this paragraph from* Marley and Me, *John Grogan describes Shaun, a dog he had when he was young—a dog that is very different from his dog Marley.*

> ## Words to Know
> **effortlessly**   without difficulty, easily
> **hazard**   danger, risk

> ## Getting Started
> Have you ever had a dog or cat that was especially hard to train?

I brought him home in a cardboard box and named him Shaun. He was one of those dogs that give dogs a good name. He effortlessly mastered every command I taught him and was naturally well behaved. I could drop a crust on the floor and he would not touch it until I gave the okay. He came when I called him and stayed when I told him to. We could let him out alone at night, knowing he would be back after making his rounds. Not that we often did, but we could leave him alone in the house for hours, confident he wouldn't have an accident or disturb a thing. He raced cars without chasing them and walked beside me without a leash. He could dive to the bottom of our lake and emerge with rocks so big they sometimes got stuck in his jaws. He loved nothing more than riding in the car and would sit quietly in the backseat beside me on family road trips, content to spend hours gazing out the window at the passing world. Perhaps best of all, I trained him to pull me through the neighborhood dog-sled-style as I sat on my bicycle, making me the hands-down envy of my friends. Never once did he lead me into hazard.

Questions about the Reading

1. What would Shaun do if his master dropped a "crust on the floor"?
2. What are the behaviors that the writer tells us gave his dog Shaun "a good name"?

3. What did the writer train Shaun to do that made the writer "the envy" of his friends?
4. How did Shaun behave when he was riding in the car?

Questions about the Writer's Strategies

1. What is the main idea of the paragraph?
2. What is the point of view (person, time, tone) of the paragraph?
3. What is the order the writer uses in the paragraph?
4. Is the paragraph objective or subjective?

Writing Assignments

1. Write a descriptive paragraph about a dog, cat, hamster, or other pet you have had.
2. Write a descriptive paragraph about a special friend, a relative, or an elementary school teacher you had.

The Hiroshima Museum

Barbara Kingsolver

> *In this selection from her book* High Tide in Tucson, *Barbara Kingsolver describes her visit to the Peace Memorial Museum in Hiroshima and the items displayed there that speak silently of the impact of an atomic bomb.*

Words to Know

artifacts   objects of historical importance
histrionic   emotional, theatrical, dramatic
hypocenter   surface beneath the center of a nuclear explosion
ideological   reflective of an idea, belief, or culture
saki   wine made from rice

Getting Started

How do you feel when you look at paintings and exhibits in a museum?

Since that day, I've had the chance to visit another bomb museum of a different kind: the one that stands in Hiroshima. A serene building set in a garden, it is strangely quiet inside, with hushed viewers and hushed exhibits. Neither ideological nor histrionic, the displays stand entirely without editorial comment. They are simply artifacts, labeled: china saki cups melted together in a stack. A brass Buddha with his hands relaxed into molten pools and a hole where his face used to be. Dozens of melted watches, all stopped at exactly eight-fifteen. A white eyelet petticoat with great, brown-rimmed holes burned in the left side, stained with black rain, worn by a schoolgirl named Oshita-chan. She was half a mile from the hypocenter of the nuclear blast, wearing also a blue short-sleeved blouse, which was incinerated except for its collar, and a blue metal pin with a small white heart, which melted. Oshita-chan lived for approximately twelve hours after the bomb.

Questions about the Reading

1. Why do you think the displays in the museum "stand entirely without editorial comment"?

2. What do the exhibits tell you about the effect of an atomic bomb?
3. Why do you think the museum visitors are "hushed"?
4. What is the significance of all the watches being "stopped at exactly eight-fifteen"?

Questions about the Writer's Strategies

1. What is the main idea of the paragraph? Is it stated or implied? State the main idea in your own words.
2. What order does the writer use to describe the artifacts in the museum? Why do you think she chose that order?
3. Is the paragraph objective or subjective or both? Support your answer with examples.
4. What descriptive details does the writer give about Oshita-chan and her clothing? Do the details provide an image of what happened to Oshita-chan?

Writing Assignments

1. Write a narrative paragraph in which you describe your feelings during a visit to a museum.
2. Write a narrative paragraph in which you describe a visit to a city you had never been to before.
3. Visit an elder-care center, a church other than your own, or a day-care center for preschoolers, and write a narrative paragraph describing the place.

The Ravine

Quincy Stott (student)

In this paragraph, Quincy Stott describes a place where he, his brother, and their cousins played and tells us why it was a special place for them.

Words to Know

billowing   surging, rising
crevasse   deep crack or hole
verdant   immature, young
vibrant   quivering, moving

Getting Started

Did you and your friends have a favorite place to play when you were young?

Past the small concrete patio behind our house was a typical yard that suffered from crab grass and a chain-link fence. Behind the fence was a dirt alley that would fill with billowing dust when cars or trucks drove by too quickly. But beyond that was green—the vibrant, verdant green of trees and tall pasture grass that created a stark contrast to the dull, brown exterior of our neighborhood. Tall, soaring branches erupted out of the small, canal-shaped cavity in the otherwise dreary landscape behind our backyard. A small, murky stream quietly trickled down the u-shaped crevasse and separated our house from farmland. This place, which my brother and I affectionately called the "Ravine," was the staple environment for most of our free time from spring to summer, and then autumn. Sometimes we would even escape the narrow confines of our house in the winter to play in the magnificent outdoors just a few feet away. In the spring, the trees of the Ravine sprouted leaves. They were small and underdeveloped— merely buds on the branches. During the summer months, they changed into lush green leaves and rustled quietly in hot and muggy summer breezes. In autumn, the leaves turned yellow and orange, slowly fell, and carpeted the crackly, dead underbrush with their lively color. This was the place where my brother, our cousins, and I had some of our best times as children. The Ravine was a fantastic place to play when we were young because we grew closer as family and matured as individuals.

Questions about the Reading

1. Where is the Ravine located?
2. What separated the writer's house from farmland? What did the writer and his brother call this place?
3. When did the writer and his brother play in this place? What was the place like in the different seasons of the year?
4. Why was the Ravine a fantastic place to play?

Questions about the Writer's Strategies

1. What is the main idea of the paragraph? Is it stated or implied? If stated, identify the sentence or sentences that state the idea. If implied, state the main idea in your own words.
2. What is the point of view (person, time, tone) of the paragraph?
3. What are the descriptive details the writer uses to describe the yard, the alley, and the stream that separated his house from farmland?
4. What are the descriptive details the writer uses to contrast the area past the dirt alley with his neighborhood?

Writing Assignments

1. Write a paragraph in which you describe an outdoor place where you and your friends played when you were young.
2. Write a paragraph describing a place that is special to you.

The Attic

Stephen King

In this paragraph from his book On Writing, *Stephen King describes his boyhood bedroom.*

Words to Know

boa constrictor   long tropical snake that strangles prey in its coils
whose   a "swooshing" sound
45s   small phonograph records popular in the 1940s and 1950s

Getting Started

What details in this description indicate Stephen King's future as a science fiction writer?

My room in our Durham house was upstairs, under the eaves. At night I would lie in bed beneath one of those eaves—if I sat up suddenly, I was apt to whack my head a good one—and read by the light of a gooseneck lamp that put an amusing boa constrictor of shadow on the ceiling. Sometimes the house was quiet except for the whose of the furnace and the patter of rats in the attic; sometimes my grandmother would spend an hour or so around midnight yelling for someone to check Dick—she was afraid he hadn't been fed. Dick, a horse she'd had in her days as a schoolteacher, was at least forty years dead. I had a desk beneath the room's other eave, my old Royal typewriter, and a hundred or so paperback books, mostly science fiction, which I lined up along the baseboard. On my bureau was a Bible won for memorizing verses in Methodist Youth Fellowship and a Webcor phonograph with an automatic changer and a turntable covered in soft green velvet. On it I played my records, mostly 45s by Elvis, Chuck Berry, Freddy Cannon, and Fats Domino. I like Fats; he knew how to rock, and you could tell he was having fun.

Questions about the Reading

1. Why would Stephen King's grandmother yell in the night?
2. What kind of books does the writer read?

3. Where is the writer's bedroom located?
4. What would happen to the writer if he sat up suddenly in bed?

Questions about the Writer's Strategies

1. What is the main idea of the paragraph?
2. Is the main idea stated or implied?
3. What are the details the writer uses to describe his bedroom?
4. What is the *personification* in the paragraph?

Writing Assignments

1. Write a paragraph in which you describe your bedroom.
2. Write a paragraph in which you describe a person in your family.

My Father

James Baldwin

In this paragraph, James Baldwin describes his father as a man of beauty but of bitterness of spirit.

Words to Know

emanated   came from

intolerable   unbearable

mementos   souvenirs

unabating   never ending or ceasing

Getting Started

Have you ever met a person you admired but who also intimidated you?

$\mathbf{H}$e was, I think, very handsome. I gather this from photographs and from my own memories of him, dressed in his Sunday best and on his way to preach a sermon somewhere, when I was little. Handsome, proud, and ingrown, "like a toenail," somebody said. But he looked to me, as I grew older, like pictures I had seen of African tribal chieftains: he really should have been naked, with war paint on and barbaric mementos, standing among spears. He could be chilling in the pulpit and indescribably cruel in his personal life and he was certainly the most bitter man I have ever met; yet it must be said that there was something else in him, buried in him, which lent him his tremendous power and, even, a rather crushing charm. It had something to do with his blackness, I think—he was very black—with his blackness and his beauty, and with the fact that he knew that he was black but did not know that he was beautiful. He claimed to be proud of his blackness but it had also been the cause of much humiliation and it had fixed bleak boundaries to his life. He was not a young man when we were growing up and he had already suffered many kinds of ruin; in his outrageously demanding and protective way he loved his children, who were black like him and menaced, like him; and all these things sometimes showed in his face when he tried, never to my knowledge with any success, to establish contact with any of us. When he took one of his children on his knee to play, the child always became fretful and began to cry; when he tried to help one of us with our homework the absolutely unabating tension which emanated from him caused our minds and our tongues to become paralyzed, so that he, scarcely knowing why, flew into a rage and the child, not knowing why, was punished. If it ever entered his head to bring a surprise home for his children, it was, almost unfailingly, the wrong surprise. I do not remember, in all those years, that one of his children was ever glad to see him come home. From what I was able to gather of his early life, it seemed that this inability to establish contact with other people had always marked him and had been one of the things which had driven him out of New Orleans. There was something in him, therefore, groping and tentative, which was never expressed and which was buried with him. One saw it most clearly when he was facing new people and hoping to impress them. But he never did, not for long. We went from church to smaller and more improbable church, he found himself in less and less demand as a minister, and by the time he died none of his friends had come to see him for a long time. He had lived and died in an intolerable bitterness of spirit and it frightened me to see how powerful and overflowing this bitterness could be and to realize that this bitterness now was mine.

Questions about the Reading

1. What was the profession of the writer's father?
2. Was his father successful in his profession?
3. What does the writer think his father looked like?
4. How did the writer's father treat his children?
5. Do you think the writer loves, admires, fears, or dislikes his father? Support your answer with statements from the paragraph.

Questions about the Writer's Strategies

1. What is the main idea of the paragraph? Is it stated or implied? If stated, where in the paragraph?
2. What are the similes in the paragraph?
3. What order does the writer use in describing his father?
4. Why do you think he chose this order?

Writing Assignments

1. Write a paragraph describing a person you admire and respect.
2. Write a paragraph describing a person you dislike and do not respect.
3. Use the Internet to learn about James Baldwin and write an entry in your journal about his career.

Hush, Timmy—
This Is Like a Church

Kurt Anderson

In this essay, Kurt Anderson, a writer for Time *magazine, describes the Viet Nam Veterans Memorial in Washington, DC, and the behavior of the people who visit it.*

Words to Know

catharsis   relief, purification
contemplative   thoughtful
liturgical   public worship
mandarins   officials, authorities
rambunctious   boisterous, noisy, unruly
sanctum   holy place
stigmatized   branded, disgraced
vertex   highest point

Getting Started

Do you know someone who has a bad temper?
Is there a place that makes you feel sad or happy?

The veteran and his wife had already stared hard at four particular 1 names. Now the couple walked slowly down the incline in front of the wall, looking at rows of hundreds, thousands more, amazed at the roster of the dead. "All the names," she said quietly, sniffling in the early-spring chill. "It's unreal, how many names." He said nothing. "You have to see it to believe it," she said.

Just so. In person, close up, the Viet Nam Veterans Memorial—two 2 skinny black granite triangles wedged onto a mount of Washington sod—is some kind of sanctum, beautiful and terrible. "We didn't plan that," says John Wheeler, chairman of the veterans' group that raised the money and built it. "I had a picture of seven-year-olds throwing a Frisbee around on the grass in front. But it's treated as a spiritual place." When Wheeler's colleague Jan Scruggs decided there ought to be a monument, he had only vague notions of what it might be like. "You don't set out and *build* a national shrine," Scruggs says. "It *becomes* one."

Washington is thick with monuments, several of them quite affecting. 3 But as the Viet Nam War was singular and strange, the dark, dreamy, redemptive memorial to its American veterans is like no other. "It's more solemn," says National Park Service Ranger Sarah Page, who has also worked at the memorials honoring Lincoln, Washington and Jefferson. "People give it more respect." Lately it has been the most visited monument in the capital: 2.3 million saw it in 1984, about 45,000 a week, but it is currently drawing 100,000 a week. Where does it get its power—to console, and also to make people sob?

The men who set up the Viet Nam Veterans Memorial Fund wanted   4 something that would include the name of every American killed in Viet Nam, and would be contemplative and apolitical. They conducted an open design competition that drew 1,421 entries, all submitted anonymously. The winner, Maya Ying Lin, was a Chinese-American undergraduate at Yale: to memorialize men killed in a war in Asia, an Asian female studying at an old antiwar hotbed.

Opposition to Lin's design was intense. The opponents wanted some-   5 thing gleaming and grand. To them, the low-slung black wall would send the same old defeatist, elitist messages that had lost the war in the '60s and then stigmatized the veterans in the '70s. "Creating the memorial triggered a lot of old angers and rage among vets about the war," recalls Wheeler, a captain in Viet Nam and now a Yale-trained government lawyer. "It got white hot."

In the end, Lin's sublime and stirring wall was built, 58,022 names   6 inscribed. As a compromise with opponents, however, a more conventional figurative sculpture was added to the site last fall (at a cost of $400,000). It does not spoil the memorial, as the art mandarins had warned. The three U.S. soldiers, cast in bronze, stand a bit larger than life, carry automatic weapons and wear fatigues, but the pose is not John Wayne-heroic: these American boys are spectral and wary, even slightly bewildered as they gaze southeast toward the wall. While he was planning the figures, sculptor Frederick Hart spent time watching vets at the memorial. Hart now grants that "no modernist monument of its kind has been as successful as that wall. The sculpture and the wall interact beautifully. Everybody won." Nor does Lin, his erstwhile artistic antagonist, still feel that Hart's statue is so awfully trite. "It captures the mood," says Lin. "Their faces have a lost look." Out at the memorial last week, one veteran looked at the new addition and nodded: "That's us."

But it is the wall that vets approach as if it were a force field. It is at the   7 wall that families of the dead cry and leave flowers and mementos and messages, much as Jews leave notes for God in the cracks of Jerusalem's Western Wall. Around the statue, people talk louder and breathe easier, snap vacation photos unselfconsciously, eat Eskimo Pies and Fritos. But near the wall, a young Boston father tells his rambunctious son, "Hush, Timmy—this is like a church." The visitors' processionals do seem to have a ritual, even liturgical quality. Going slowly down toward the vertex, looking at the names, they chat less and less, then fall silent where the names of the first men killed (July 1959) and the last (May 1975) appear. The talk begins again, softly, as they follow the path up out of the little valley of the shadow of death.

For veterans, the memorial was a touchstone from the beginning, and   8 the 1982 dedication ceremony a delayed national embrace. "The actual act of being at the memorial is healing for the guy or woman who went to Viet Nam," says Wheeler, who visits at least monthly. "It has to do with the felt presence of comrades." He pauses. "I always look at Tommy Hayes' name. Tommy's up on panel 50 east, line 29." Hayes, Wheeler's West Point pal, was killed 17 years ago this month. "I know guys," Wheeler says, "who are still waiting to go, whose wives have told me, 'He hasn't been able to do it yet.'" For those who go, catharsis is common. As Lin says of the names, chronologically ordered, "Veterans can look at the wall, find a name, and in a sense put themselves back in time." The war has left some residual pathologies that the memorial cannot leach away. One veteran killed himself on the amphitheatrical green near the wall. A second, ex-Marine Randolph Taylor, tried and failed in January. "I regret what I did," he said. "I feel like I desecrated a holy place."

The memorial has become a totem, so much so that its tiniest imper-   9 fections make news. Last fall somebody noticed a few minute cracks at the seams between several of the granite panels. The cause of the hairlines is still unknown, and the builders are a little worried.

Probably no one is more determined than Wheeler to see the memo-   10 rial's face made perfect, for he savors the startlingly faithful reflections the walls give off: he loves seeing the crowds of visitors looking simultaneously at the names and themselves. "Look!" he said the other day, gesturing at panel 4 east. "You see that plane taking off? You see the blue sky? No one expected that."

Questions about the Reading

1. About how many people a week visited the Viet Nam Veterans Memorial in 1984?
2. How many people a week were visiting the memorial at the time the essay was written (1985)?
3. What did the men who set up the Viet Nam Veterans Memorial Fund want the memorial to include?
4. Who won the contest for the design of the memorial? Why was her design controversial?

5. How many names were inscribed on the wall?
6. What differences are there between people's behavior at the wall and their behavior at the sculpture?

Questions about the Writer's Strategies

1. What is the main idea (thesis) of the essay?
2. Is the main idea directly stated or implied?
3. What is the point of view (person, time, tone) of the essay?
4. What is the impression of the memorial that the writer creates?
5. Is the essay objective, subjective, or both?

Writing Assignments

1. Write a descriptive essay about a place you visited that made you feel particularly sad.
2. Write a descriptive essay about a place you visited that made you feel particularly happy.

3. Use the Internet to research the following historical monuments: the Statue of Liberty in New York City; the Lincoln Memorial in Washington, DC; and Mount Rushmore in Keystone, South Dakota. Write an essay describing each monument, who or what it represents, and when and by whom it was built or created. Include a list of the web addresses you use.

   To find helpful Web sites, use a search engine—such as Google (**http://www.google.com**), or Yahoo! (**http://www.yahoo.com**), and type in keywords, such as "Statue of Liberty" or "national monuments."

The Monster

Deems Taylor

In this essay, Deems Taylor describes a totally unpleasant man. In each paragraph, he piles detail upon detail until we find ourselves wondering, "How bad can one man be?" Then we read the next paragraph and we find out—he gets worse. Near the end, though, Taylor identifies his subject and offers some possible explanations—some surprising ones—for the "monster's" bad nature.

Words to Know

arrogance   overbearing pride
Beethoven   a German composer
burlesquing   mocking
callous   unfeeling
conceit   an elaborate or exaggerated opinion of oneself
delusions   false beliefs
harangue   a long, pompous speech
infidelities   unfaithfulness
libretto   the text of an opera
mania   an intense enthusiasm, craze
monologue   a long speech by one person
Plato   a Greek philosopher
rajah   a prince in India
royalties   money paid to a composer out of the proceeds from a
  performance
scrupulous   conscientious, principled
synopsis   outline of a story
trilogy   a group of three works
volubility   ready, fluent speech

Getting Started

Do you know someone who has a bad temper?

He was an undersized little man, with a head too big for his body—a   1
sickly little man. His nerves were bad. He had skin trouble. It was agony
for him to wear anything next to his skin coarser than silk. And he had
delusions of grandeur.

He was a monster of conceit. Never for one minute did he look at the   2
world or at people, except in relation to himself. He was not only the

most important person in the world, for himself; in his own eyes he was the only person who existed. He believed himself to be one of the greatest dramatists in the world, one of the greatest thinkers, and one of the greatest composers. To hear him talk, he was Shakespeare, and Beethoven, and Plato, rolled into one. And you would have had no difficulty in hearing him talk. He was one of the most exhausting conversationalists that ever lived. An evening with him was an evening spent in listening to a monologue. Sometimes he was brilliant; sometimes he was maddeningly tiresome. But whether he was being brilliant or dull, he had one sole topic of conversation: himself. What *he* thought and what *he* did.

He had a mania for being in the right. The slightest hint of disagreement, 3 from anyone, on the most trivial point, was enough to set him off on a harangue that might last for hours, in which he proved himself right in so many ways, and with such exhausting volubility, that in the end his hearer, stunned and deafened, would agree with him, for the sake of peace.

It never occurred to him that he and his doing were not of the most 4 intense and fascinating interest to anyone with whom he came in contact. He had theories about almost any subject under the sun, including vegetarianism, the drama, politics, and music; and in support of these theories he wrote pamphlets, letters, books . . . thousands upon thousands of words, hundreds and hundreds of pages . . . He not only wrote these things, and published them—usually at somebody else's expense—but he would sit and read them aloud, for hours, to his friends, and his family.

He wrote operas; and no sooner did he have the synopsis of a story, 5 but he would invite—or rather summon—a crowd of his friends to his house and read it aloud to them. Not for criticism. For applause. When the complete poem was written, the friends had to come again, and hear *that* read aloud. Then he would publish the poem, sometimes years before the music that went with it was written. He played the piano like a composer, in the worst sense of what that implies, and he would sit at the piano before parties that included some of the finest pianists of his time, and play for them, by the hour, his own music, needless to say. He had a composer's voice. And he would invite eminent vocalists to his house, and sing them his operas, taking all the parts.

He had the emotional stability of a six-year-old child. When he felt 6 out of sorts, he would rave and stamp, or sink into suicidal gloom and talk darkly of going to the East to end his days as a Buddhist monk. Ten minutes later, when something pleased him, he would rush out of doors and run around the garden, or jump up and down on the sofa, or stand on his head. He could be grief-stricken over the death of a pet dog, and he could be callous and heartless to a degree that would have made a Roman emperor shudder.

He was almost innocent of any sense of responsibility. Not only did he 7 seem incapable of supporting himself, but it never occurred to him that he was under any obligation to do so. He was convinced that the world owed him a living. In support to this belief, he borrowed money from everybody who was good for a loan—men, women, friends, or strangers. He wrote begging letters by the score, sometimes groveling without shame, at others loftily offering his intended benefactor the privilege of contributing to his support, and being mortally offended if the recipient declined the honor. I have found no record of his ever paying or repaying money to anyone who did not have a legal claim upon it.

What money he could lay his hand on he spent like an Indian rajah. 8 The mere prospect of a performance of one of his operas was enough to set him running up bills amounting to ten times the amount of his prospective royalties. On an income that would reduce a more scrupulous man to doing his own laundry, he would keep two servants. Without enough money in his pocket to pay his rent, he would have the walls and ceiling of his study lined with pink silk. No one will ever know— certainly he never knew—how much money he owed. We do know that his greatest benefactor gave him $6,000 to pay the most pressing of his debts in one city, and a year later had to give him $16,000 to enable him to live in another city without being thrown into jail for debt.

He was equally unscrupulous in other ways. An endless procession of 9 women marched through his life. His first wife spent twenty years enduring and forgiving his infidelities. His second wife had been the wife of his most devoted friend and admirer, from whom he stole her. And even while he was trying to persuade her to leave her first husband he was writing to a friend to inquire whether he could suggest some wealthy woman—*any* wealthy woman—whom he could marry for her money.

He was completely selfish in his other personal relationships. His 10 liking for his friends was measured solely by the completeness of their devotion to him, or by their usefulness to him, whether financial or artistic. The minute they failed him—even by so much as refusing a dinner invitation—or began to lessen in usefulness, he cast them off without a second thought. At the end of his life he had exactly one friend left whom he had known even in middle age.

He had a genius for making enemies. He would insult a man who 11 disagreed with him about the weather. He would pull endless wires in order to meet some man who admired his work and was able and anxious to be of use to him—and would proceed to make a mortal enemy of him with some idiotic and wholly uncalled-for exhibition of arrogance and bad manners. A character in one of his operas was a caricature of one of the most powerful music critics of his day. Not content with burlesquing him, he invited the critic to his house and read him the libretto aloud in front of his friends.

The name of this monster was Richard Wagner. Everything I have said 12 about him you can find on record—in newspapers, in police reports, in the testimony of people who knew him, in his own letters, between the lines of his autobiography. And the curious thing about this record is that it doesn't matter in the least.

Because this undersized, sickly, disagreeable, fascinating little man 13 was right all the time. The joke was on us. He *was* one of the world's greatest dramatists; he *was* a great thinker; he *was* one of the most stupendous musical geniuses that, up to now, the world has ever seen. The world did owe him a living. People couldn't know those things at the time, I suppose; and yet to us, who know his music, it does seem as though they should have known. What if he did talk about himself all the time? If he talked about himself for twenty-four hours every day for the span of his life he would not have uttered half the number of words that other men have spoken and written about him since his death.

When you consider what he wrote—thirteen operas and music dra- 14 mas, eleven of them still holding the stage, eight of them unquestionably worth ranking among the world's great musico-dramatic masterpieces— when you listen to what he wrote, the debts and heartaches that people had to endure from him don't seem much of a price. Edward Hanslick, the critic whom he caricatured in *Die Meistersinger* and who hated him ever after, now lives only because he was caricatured in *Die Meistersinger*. The women whose hearts he broke are long since dead; and the man who could never love anyone but himself has made them deathless atonement, I think, with *Tristan und Isolde.* Think of the luxury with which for a time, at least, fate rewarded Napoleon, the man who ruined France and looted Europe; and then perhaps you will agree that a few thousand dollars' worth of debts were not too heavy a price to pay for the *Ring* trilogy.

What if he was faithless to his friends and to his wives? He had one 15 mistress to whom he was faithful to the day of his death: Music. Not for a single moment did he ever compromise with what he believed, with what he dreamed. There is not a line of his music that could have been conceived by a little mind. Even when he is dull, or downright bad, he is dull in the grand manner. There is a greatness about his worst mistakes. Listening to his music, one does not forgive him for what he may or may not have been. It is not a matter of forgiveness. It is a matter of being dumb with wonder that his poor brain and body didn't burst under the torment of the demon of creative energy that lived inside him, struggling, clawing, scratching to be released; tearing, shrieking at him to write the music that was in him. The miracle is that what he did in the little space of seventy years could have been done at all, even by a great genius. Is it any wonder he had no time to be a man?

Questions about the Reading

1. In what ways was Wagner conceited?
2. With what was he obsessed?
3. Was Wagner ever considerate of others? Give examples.
4. Why does the author say that "the joke was on us"?
5. Does Wagner's great talent justify his behavior?

Questions about the Writer's Strategies

1. What is the dramatic purpose for concealing the name of the composer until paragraph 12?
2. Is there any deliberate order to the presentation of *examples*? (See Glossary for *examples*.)
3. What effect do the detailed, numerous examples have on the way the reader views Wagner? Is the reader led to think there is anything positive about his behavior?

Writing Assignments

1. Do you know someone who is extremely good at what he or she does but is impossible to live with? Describe that person.
2. Describe your favorite singer or musician. What special qualities appeal to you?
3. Think of a movie, television, or sports personality whose personal behavior is disagreeable or in some way unacceptable. Describe the person's behavior and its influence on your enjoyment or admiration of that person's professional achievements.

Summer School

Jenny Cho (student)

A young woman begins a class in summer school with students she doesn't know, only to find that their intentions toward her are not as she thought.

Words to Know

excel do extremely well
stern severe, harsh
doodle scribble, draw pictures
icy unfriendly, cold

Getting Started

Have you ever misjudged a person or a situation?

It was 1980, and I was fifteen years old. I was brought up in a strict, 1 Korean American family and was supposed to excel at every subject in school. Although I was good at English, science, and social studies, I struggled all year with geometry. By the end of the school year, it was clear to me that I was not going to pass the course and would have to attend eight weeks of summer school.

Oh, and did I mention that I went to a small, all-girls, Catholic high 2 school that was fifteen miles from the town I lived in? The summer school class was held at the local public high school in my town, which had a reputation as being a rough place to go to school. So even before I got to my first day of class, I was terrified, thinking that I was going to a place roughly similar to prison.

My mother was angry with me that I had failed the course, so as pun- 3 ishment, she made me ride my bike to school. The bike was a pink, Sears bike with a banana seat and a big oval bar that went up way over my head on the back. When I arrived at the big brick school on the first day, I stood outside and took a good look. The building was low, flat, and brick with windows all across the front, one or two broken and taped up. To me, it looked more like a prison than a school. The parking lot on the side of the school was covered with blacktop that was cracked in places with green weeds shooting up between the cracks. I saw a few students going into the school, all in ripped jeans and concert T-shirts. I was wearing a white blouse and black pants that my mother had ironed before I left. I stood out like a sore thumb.

Our teacher went to my church and knew me. He was tall and stern- 4 looking but acknowledged me when I walked in, which convinced me that I would be beat up after school. Who wants to the teacher to know you from church? I sat down next to a boy who lived on block away from me—figuring that might be a safe bet—and cast my eyes down to the scarred, wooden desk. The kids around me looked rough, tough, and ready to rumble. I started working on the first problem that the teacher gave us and hoped for the best. The problems on the bright white sheet of paper looked like a jumble of black lines and words I didn't know, but I tried to figure out what I needed to do.

I handed in my paper just before the end of class, and the teacher held it 5 up for the class to see. My paper was a neat and clean sheet of paper. My classmates' papers were folded, torn, and ripped, with doodles covering most of the sheets. "See, class? This is what a paper is supposed to look like. Not like the messy junk you all just turned in!" Everyone turned and stared at me, and I knew my fate was sealed. I was Korean, nerdy, neat (according to the teacher), and a Catholic school kid.

After class, I gathered up my books and tried to avoid the icy stares of 6 the kids around me. A girl approached me and asked me where I went to school. I told her. She asked me why she hadn't seen me around town, and I told her that after school, I worked in my parents' store and didn't go out much. The other kids were staring at us as she spoke to me. Finally, she said, "Where did you learn how to write like that? Your handwriting is totally awesome!"

It turns out that the kids didn't want to beat me up. They just wanted to 7 know who I was and what I was all about. The kids weren't as different or tough as I thought they were. Knowing that made things easier. Although I didn't make any friends that summer, I realized that the students in my class were not as bad as I thought they were going to be.

Questions about the Reading

1. Why does Jenny Cho go to summer school?
2. How does she get to class every day?
3. Why does the teacher single her out in class?
4. How do the students react to Jenny?

Questions about the Writer's Strategies

1. What is the thesis of this essay? Is it stated or implied? If stated, identify the sentence or sentences in which it is stated. If implied, state the thesis in your own words.
2. To what does the writer compare the school building? Why? How are they similar?
3. What is the purpose of the concluding paragraph of this essay? Is it effective?

Writing Assignments

1. Have you ever been in a situation that you thought was going to be horrible but that turned out to be better than you expected? Describe.
2. Think about some first impressions that you've made on other people. Were they always correct? Sometimes? Describe a situation where your first impression of someone or something was completely incorrect and why.

Limbo

Rhonda S. Lucas (student)

A new experience, a change in our lives, can make us see familiar objects in a new light. And a new location can make an old possession—a piece of furniture, an article of clothing—look strange. Rhonda S. Lucas, a student at East Los Angeles College, discovered both these things one day as she sat in a garage full of packing boxes and old furniture. In this essay, she describes what she saw.

Words to Know

cryptic   secret, mystifying

dilapidated   fallen into a state of disrepair

elegy   a mournful poem or song, often lamenting the dead

futility   uselessness

irony   the use of words to convey the opposite of their literal meaning

limbo   an intermediate place or state; a region or condition of oblivion or neglect

tubular   having the form of a tube

Getting Started

If you had to leave your house tomorrow, what would you miss most about it?

My parents' divorce was final. The house had been sold and the day   1
had come to move. Thirty years of the family's life were now crammed into the garage. The two-by-fours that ran the length of the walls were the only uniformity among the clutter of boxes, furniture, and memories. All was frozen in limbo between the life just passed and the one to come.

The sunlight pushing its way through the window splattered against   2
a barricade of boxes. Like a fluorescent river, it streamed down the sides and flooded the cracks of the cold, cement floor. I stood in the doorway between the house and garage and wondered if the sunlight would ever again penetrate the memories packed inside those boxes. For an instant, the cardboard boxes appeared as tombstones, monuments to those memories.

The furnace in the corner, with its huge tubular fingers reaching out   3
and disappearing into the wall, was unaware of the futility of trying to warm the empty house. The rhythmical whir of its effort hummed the

elegy for the memories boxed in front of me. I closed the door, sat down on the step, and listened reverently. The feeling of loss transformed the bad memories into not-so-bad, the not-so-bad memories into good, and committed the good ones to my mind. Still, I felt as vacant as the house inside.

A workbench to my right stood disgustingly empty. Not so much as a   4
nail had been left behind. I noticed, for the first time, what a dull, lifeless green it was. Lacking the disarray of tools that used to cover it, now it seemed as out of place as a bathtub in the kitchen. In fact, as I scanned the room, the only things that did seem to belong were the cobwebs in the corners.

A group of boxes had been set aside from the others and stacked in   5
front of the workbench. Scrawled like graffiti on the walls of dilapi-dated buildings were the words "Salvation Army." Those words caught my eyes as effectively as a flashing neon sign. They reeked of irony. "Salvation—was a bit too late for this family," I mumbled sarcastically to myself.

The houseful of furniture that had once been so carefully chosen to   6
complement and blend with the color schemes of the various rooms was indiscriminately crammed together against a single wall. The uncoor-dinated colors combined in turmoil and lashed out in the greyness of the room.

I suddenly became aware of the coldness of the garage, but I didn't   7
want to go back inside the house, so I made my way through the boxes to the couch. I cleared a space to lie down and curled up, covering myself with my jacket. I hoped my father would return soon with the truck so we could empty the garage and leave the cryptic silence of parting lives behind.

Questions about the Reading

1. Why is the title of this essay "Limbo"? Between which two stages of life is the writer?
2. How does the writer feel about moving out of the house?
3. Why does the writer view the empty workbench as disgusting (para-graph 4)?
4. Why didn't she want to go back inside the house?
5. What does Lucas mean in the last line by the "cryptic silence" of the house?

Questions about the Writer's Strategies

1. Although she never says it, the writer is saddened by her parents' divorce and the subsequent need to move. What details does she use to convey this feeling?
2. In what ways is this an extremely subjective essay?
3. Give your impression of the writer's life before her parents' divorce. What methods does she use to suggest this impression?
4. What is the thesis statement in the essay? Which paragraphs are used to develop the thesis statement? Is there a concluding paragraph?
5. What is the purpose of the metaphor in the last sentence of paragraph 2? In which sentence of paragraph 3 is the metaphor repeated?

Writing Assignments

1. Write an essay describing your favorite room in the house where you live now or the one where you grew up. Try to use examples from your life to give meaning to the objects you describe.
2. Write an essay describing a walk through your neighborhood or another one with which you are familiar. Describe the things that most interest you or that you think you will remember best in the future.

4

Examples

AN EXAMPLE IS a specific instance or fact that is used to support an idea or a general statement. As you learned in chapter 1, the topic sentence states the main idea of a paragraph, and the thesis statement states the main idea of an essay. Both must be supported through a mode of development, which the writer selects. Writers frequently use **examples** to explain or illustrate a main idea, as in the following paragraph.

Topic sentence	As they had resolved to do, my siblings took any job they could find to survive. In Montreal, Luong went to work at a
Example	plastics factory, mixing resins, until he found a job in the city government. In California, Zuong began working at a hotel,
Example	while his wife Hao started assembling electronics components in a factory; they became self-sufficient so quickly that they never had to resort to welfare. In Australia, Phú took a
Example	job as a cleaning lady until she got a position in the post office. (My nephew Nam went back to school and, after
Example	taking a series of jobs, became a real estate agent.) Tuyet, in
Example	Paris, also started out as a cleaning lady for an office, and eventually found a position in a government agency.

Duong Van Mai Elliott, The Sacred Willow,
Oxford University Press, © 1999, p. 465

Some writers announce their strategy by the transitional words *for instance, to illustrate,* or *for example.* Other times, as in the sentences about the jobs the writer's siblings got, the writer expects the reader to notice that these are examples and that they support the topic of the paragraph.

To make a clear case, the writer usually needs to give several examples. The order in which the examples are presented may be **chronological**— that is, in sequence according to time. In other cases, **order of importance** may be more effective, with the most important or convincing example presented last. In still other cases, the writer may use an example at the beginning of the essay to capture the reader's interest and to illustrate the **thesis**, which is stated later. The selection that follows illustrates the use of an introductory example.

Example used to introduce essay

The red-and-white pickup bounced along a gravel road in   1
north-central Washington State. It was just past midnight on a summer Saturday last year. Two boys and two girls, recent graduates of Tonasket High School, had been "cruising" for a couple of hours, talking and laughing. At a sharp curve, the pickup somehow went off the road, rolled down the steep, rocky mountainside and twisted around a pine tree. All four occupants—none wearing a seat belt—were tossed out of the cab.

Driver Joe McDaniel escaped with cuts on his face and   2
arms. Josh Wheeler suffered bruises but was able to cradle Amy Burdick in his arms until help arrived. She died the next day. Katy Watson, a former cheerleader who had won a scholarship to college, was dead at the scene, with massive chest and back injuries.

Thesis statement

Motor-vehicle injury is the greatest threat to the lives of   3
adolescents in America. During the 1980s, over 74,000 teenagers were killed in such accidents, more than died from all diseases combined. On average, every two or three weeks the equivalent of a senior class at a typical high school is wiped out on our streets and highways. The National Safety Council (NSC) estimates that the financial toll is at least $10 billion annually for medical and insurance costs, property damage and lost wages resulting from accidents involving teen drivers.

Reader's Digest, June 1991

Examples in an essay can both illustrate and **support** the thesis. That is, if a writer makes a claim or a point in the **thesis statement** and then provides evidence in the form of actual situations that illustrate the thesis, it will help convince the reader that the thesis is valid. When you write, you should also search for examples as a way to test your thesis. For example, if you cannot think of a single specific example that supports your main idea, you will need to rethink your main idea. Or if you think of several examples that support your thesis, but also of several that work against it, you might want to revise your thesis and develop an **objective** essay presenting both sides of the issue.

In addition to providing concrete support for the thesis, examples can be used to enliven and clarify writing. In a description, for instance, examples can supply concrete details that add variety and interest. A single example may also be **extended** throughout an essay to illustrate the thesis, as in the following essay about the Kickapoo Indian Medicine Company. Notice, too, that minor examples are also used within the essay, as in paragraphs 2 and 3, to support the topic sentences of some paragraphs.

Thesis

Major extended example—from here to end of essay

By 1880 several hundred medicine shows were traveling in the United States, giving performances varying from simple magic acts to elaborate "med-presentations." Among the largest of such operations from 1880 to 1910 was the Kickapoo Indian Medicine Company, "The King of Road Shows." Founded by two veteran troupers, John E. "Doc" Healy and Charles H. "Texas Charlie" Bigelow, the Kickapoo Company maintained a large headquarters building, "The Principal Wigwam," in New Haven, Connecticut, and from there sent out shows, as many as twenty-five at a time, to cities and villages throughout the country.   1

Minor examples of *performers* who were hired

Doc Healy hired performers, both Indian and white—dancers, singers, jugglers, fire-eaters, acrobats, comedians, fiddlers—and Texas Charlie managed the medicine business and trained the "Doctors" and "Professors" who gave "Medical Lectures."   2

Minor examples of *distinctively garbed* troupe members

All troupe members were distinctively garbed. The Indians—including Mohawks, Iroquois, Crees, Sioux, and Blackfeet—billed as "all pure-blooded Kickapoos, the most noted of all Indian Medical People," were adorned with colored beads and feathers and loaded down with primitive weapons; they trailed great strings of unidentified hairy objects. Some lecturers wore western-style leather clothes and boots with silver-capped toes, others fancy silk shirts, frock coats, and high silk hats. One of the most colorful Kickapoo figures was smooth-talking Ned T. Oliver—"Nevada Ned, the King of Gold"—who wore an enormous sombrero from the brim of which dangled 100 gold coins, and a fancy suit loaded with buttons made of gold pieces.   3

The Kickapoo shows were presented under canvas at "Kickapoo Camps" during the summer and in opera houses and town halls in winter. On many nights the show was free to all, on others each adult was charged 10¢. The money poured in from medicine sales.   4

The wonder-working Kickapoo concoctions were "compounded according to secret ancient Kickapoo Indian tribal formulas" from "blood root, feverwort, spirit gum, wild poke berries, sassafras, slippery elm, wintergreen, white oak bark, yellow birch bark, dock root, sarsaparilla, and other Natural Products." The medicines were made in the Connecticut factory in vats so huge the "mixers" had to perch on ladders and wield long paddles. The leader of the Kickapoo line was Sagwa, which sold at 50¢ and $1 per bottle—"Sagwa, the wonderful remedy for catarrh, pulmonary consumption, and all ills that afflict the human body. It is made from roots, barks, gums, leaves, oils, and berries gathered by little   5

Kickapoo children from God's great laboratory, the fertile
fields and vast forests. Sagwa, Nature's own great secret
cure, now available to all mankind!"

Long after the Kickapoo Company was dissolved, a   6
woman who had worked in the medicine factory recalled
that one of the ingredients of Kickapoo Cough Syrup was
Jamaica rum. Could this "cure" have been the inspiration
for the "Kickapoo Joy Juice" Al Capp featured in his popular
comic strip?

Peggy Robbins,
"The Kickapoo Indian Medicine Company"

In this essay, the writer's use of concrete examples gives us a clear
picture of the Kickapoo medicine show. In addition, the great number
and the variety of minor examples give us a good idea of the crazy-quilt
nature of medicine shows in general.

When using examples in your own writing, **brainstorm** for possibilities (as described in chapter 1) and select those that illustrate your idea
most accurately. In choosing among possibilities, select those that you
sense your reader will respond to as convincing and colorful. Several
well-chosen examples will hold your reader's interest and add credibil-
ity to your main idea.

Distance Learning

Mary Lord

Computers and the Internet have opened up a new way of learning for people who need or want to add to their knowledge.

Words to Know

buffing   polishing, adding to
credentials   credit, authority

Getting Started

Does your college offer some courses through distance learning?

The old correspondence course has stormed into the high-tech age—and it's proving to be a big hit. As many as 4 million Americans are now buffing their professional credentials by padding over to their PCs and plugging into "distance learning." Need to get over your fear of public speaking? Front Range Community College near Denver will teach you the techniques over the Internet. (Note: There's no escaping four live on-campus presentations.) How about accounting? Great Britain's Open University, with nearly 150,000 students worldwide, offers a highly regarded curriculum. The University of Massachusetts at Dartmouth recently started an online course in writing for the World Wide Web.

Questions about the Reading

1. According to the writer, how many people are now taking courses by distance learning?
2. What is the special requirement for the public speaking course offered by Front Range Community College?
3. Which university offers an accounting course by distance learning?
4. Which university offers a distance-learning course in writing?

Questions about the Writer's Strategies

1. What is the main idea of the paragraph? Is it stated or implied? If stated, identify the sentence or sentences in which it is stated. If implied, state the main idea in your own words.

2. What is the order the writer uses in giving examples of distance-learning courses? Why do you think she uses that order?
3. If you were to change the order of the examples, how would you change them? Why?

Writing Assignments

1. If your college provides courses through distance learning, write a paragraph in which you give examples of such courses that are related to your major.
2. Write a paragraph in which you give examples of the advantages and disadvantages of taking a course through distance learning.

3. Use the Internet to find colleges in your state that offer courses in your major through distance learning. Write a paragraph in which you give examples of those courses.

The Digital Revolution

Ellen Cobb Wade

In a technological revolution, we have a lot to learn—not the least of which is how to program all those new devices we have. Here, the writer gives us an example of one of them—the digital clock radio—and its programmable options.

Words to Know

activate   start
formidable   fearful, difficult

Getting Started

What digital devices do you have?

T he digital revolution caused a lot of . . . confusion. A clock radio, for example, used to have a face and a slender hand that you'd set pointing to the time you wanted to get up. Nowadays, a clock radio is a formidable machine: programmable to the minute, it can wake you and your mate at different times, let one or both of you "snooze," [and] even activate the coffee maker. But just unplug the thing for a tenth of a second, and you'll be back studying the owner's manual as the display automatically blinks out 12:00—as though time were standing still.

Questions about the Reading

1. What can you set a digital clock radio to do?
2. What happens if the digital clock radio is unplugged?

Questions about the Writer's Strategies

1. What is the main idea of the paragraph? Is it stated or implied? State the main idea (topic) in your own words.
2. What is the point of view of the paragraph?

Writing Assignments

1. Write a paragraph in which you give examples of one or more of the digital devices you own or would like to own and the capabilities of each one.
2. Write a paragraph in which you give examples of the problems of programming a digital device you own or would like to own.

Boomtown, U.S.A.

Jeff Glasser

The small town of Bentonville, Arkansas, "booms" after three businesses move into the town.

Words to Know

titan person of great size or power

spurned rejected

Xanadu a place in Mongolia described in the poem "Kubla Khan" by Samuel Taylor Coleridge

Getting Started

Has the town or area in which you live been changed by unemployment, loss of a business, or development of a shopping center?

Sam Walton would not recognize the place. The famously unassuming Wal-Mart founder spurned foreign cars for his red Ford pickup, and he expected his employees to shun a "big showy lifestyle." But today in Mr. Sam's parking lot at Wal-Mart headquarters here, Mercedes Kompressor convertibles shine in the sun alongside BMW M3s. Not far away, Wal-Mart's chief executive and senior vice president live in splendor at Pinnacle, the area's first gated community and its most exclusive country club. Their neighbor, Red Hudson, a retired multimillionaire meat-packer, has built a 17,784-square-foot mansion there—complete with Italian marble and Minnesota stone—for a much-gossiped-about $10 million. Across the new Interstate 540 from Pinnacle, trucking titan J. B. Hunt is trying to erect his own Xanadu, with a dozen deluxe office and condominium towers, a hospital, and, in a first for the region, a skyline. "Everything's a poppin'," says the 74-year-old Hunt as he tools around the site in his tan GMC Sierra truck. "In the next five years, the weeds will be a city."

Questions about the Reading

1. Why would Sam Walton "not recognize the place"?
2. What is Red Hudson's business?
3. What is J. B. Hunt's business? Why is he called a "titan"?

4. What is the "first for the region"?
5. What does J. B. Hunt mean when he says, "In the next five years, the weeds will be a city"?

Questions about the Writer's Strategies

1. What is the main idea of the paragraph? State it in your own words.
2. What are the examples that support the main idea?
3. What is the metaphor in the paragraph?

Writing Assignments

1. Write a paragraph giving specific examples of the effect on your town of unemployment or loss of a business.
2. Interview some residents who were displaced by a building project in your town and write a paragraph using examples of how the displacement changed their lives.
3. These are the first two lines of the poem "Kubla Khan."

> In Xanadu did Kubla Khan
> A stately pleasure-dome decree

Write a paragraph explaining the relation of Xanadu to J. B. Hunt's building project.

Folk Art in the Barrios

Eric Kroll

In this paragraph, Eric Kroll describes the wall paintings in Santa Fe, New Mexico, that depict a bold and colorful Chicano history and that defy stereotypes.

Words to Know

Aztec   early people of Mexico

disproportionate   not in proportion, not actual size

Father Hidalgo   Miguel Hidalgo y Costilla (1753–1811), a Catholic priest who launched the revolution to free Mexico from Spanish rule

Pancho Villa   Mexican revolutionary leader

Getting Started

Have you ever looked at a painting of a famous person and thought that it wasn't accurate?

O̲n ten Santa Fe walls, the history of the Chicanos, both mythical and actual, is depicted in brilliant colors and disproportionate figures. Aztec medicine figures dance and gods protect peasants, all for the glory of the Chicano in the present. On some walls, the chains of bondage are being broken and the Lady of Justice, depicted as an Indian Maiden, watches over both Indians and Chicanos. On others, Pancho Villa and Father Hidalgo lead the Mexican peasants to freedom. But the clenched fist at the end of the grotesquely muscled arms is the most predominant image. It symbolizes unity, determination, ambition, and pride, all traits that Los Artes believe should be a part of Chicano psychology. The figures they paint are bold, upright, strong, and grasping, far from the stereotype of the Mexican-American with drooping moustache and floppy sombrero lying in the shade of a stucco building.

Questions about the Reading

1. On how many walls in Santa Fe are there paintings of Chicano history?
2. What is the purpose of the paintings?

3. What does the clenched fist in the paintings symbolize?
4. How do the figures in the paintings differ from the stereotype the author describes at the end of the paragraph?

Questions about the Writer's Strategies

1. What is the main idea (topic) of the paragraph?
2. What examples depict the freedom of Mexican peasants?
3. What is the metaphor for the traits that the artists believe the Chicanos should have?
4. What descriptive words are used for the figures in the paintings?
5. What descriptive words are used for the Mexican-American stereotype?

Writing Assignments

1. Write a paragraph in which you use examples to describe the behavior of a television personality.
2. Write a paragraph using examples to illustrate the traditions of different ethnic groups in your city.

3. Use the Internet to discover more about various kinds of folk art. Find a piece of folk art that interests you and write a descriptive paragraph about it.

Democracy (July 3, 1944)

E. B. White

If a concrete term like "poverty" (pg. 236) requires a few examples, what are you going to do about an abstract term like "democracy"? E. B. White— editor, essayist, humorist, and author of children's books—proves equal to the task. He offers a string of examples that will make you think about the subject in a way you never have before. This passage was written in 1944, when World War II was taxing this country to the fullest.

Words to Know
recurrent   repeated at intervals, occurring again

Getting Started
How would you define education?

We received a letter from the Writer's War Board the other day asking for a statement on "The Meaning of Democracy." It presumably is our duty to comply with such a request, and it is certainly our pleasure. Surely the Board knows what democracy is. It is the line that forms on the right. It is the don't in don't shove. It is the hole in the stuffed shirt through which the sawdust slowly trickles; it is the dent in the high hat. Democracy is the recurrent suspicion that more than half of the people are right more than half of the time. It is the feeling of privacy in the voting booths, the feeling of communion in the libraries, the feeling of vitality everywhere. Democracy is a letter to the editor. Democracy is the score at the beginning of the ninth. It is an idea that hasn't been disproved yet, a song the words of which have not gone bad. It is the mustard on the hot dog and the cream in the rationed coffee. Democracy is a request from a War Board, in the middle of the morning in the middle of a war, wanting to know what democracy is.

Questions about the Reading

1. Certain names and statements in the paragraph tell you that it was written at a particular time in history. When was it written? Explain which information you used to determine your answer.

2. What is the main idea (topic) of the paragraph?
3. What does the writer imply about the War Board in the last sentence of the paragraph?
4. What are the examples the author uses? Are some more effective than others?

Questions about the Writer's Strategies

1. *Parallelism* refers to the use of the same structure in successive sentences. Identify the sentences in the paragraph that are parallel in structure.
2. What is the *tone* of the paragraph? Support your answer by identifying the words and statements that you feel reveal the tone. (See Glossary for *tone*.)
3. Which *point of view* (first, second, or third person) does the writer use in the paragraph? (See Glossary for *point of view*.)
4. Although the writer explains democracy by using examples, could the paragraph be said to illustrate still another *mode of development*? If so, what is that mode? (See Glossary for *mode of development*.)

Writing Assignments

1. Use the same tone and person as in "Democracy" and define one of the following terms:

   • Justice
   • Freedom
   • Beauty
   • Selflessness
   • Generosity

2. Choose a familiar term and define it by using common examples of its meaning.
3. Suppose a college writes you and asks you for a statement on the meaning of education. Write a paper in which you answer the request.

The Social Meaning of T-shirts

Diana Crane

The T-shirt has become popular for expressing the wearer's support for an organization or a cause.

Words to Know

cachet   approval
coopted   used, taken

Getting Started

What T-shirts are in your closet, and what do they say about you?

The use of a specific type of clothing—the T-shirt—to communicate 1 other types of information began in the late 1940s, when faces and political slogans appeared on T-shirts and, in the 1960s, with commercial logos and other designs. Technical developments in the 1950s and 1960s, such as plastic inks, plastic transfers, and spray paint, led to the use of colored designs and increased the possibilities of the T-shirt as a means of communication. Approximately one billion T-shirts are purchased annually in the United States (McGraw 1996).

The T-shirt performs a function formerly associated with the hat, 2 that of identifying an individual's social location instantly. Unlike the hat in the nineteenth century, which signaled (or concealed) social class status, the T-shirt speaks to issues related to ideology, difference, and myth: politics, race, gender, and leisure. The variety of slogans and logos that appear on T-shirts is enormous. Much of the time, people consent to being coopted for "unpaid advertising" for global corporations selling clothes, music, sports, and entertainment in exchange for the social cachet of being associated with certain products (McGraw 1996). Some of the time, people use T-shirts to indicate their support for social and political causes, groups, or organizations to which they have made a commitment. Occasionally, the T-shirt becomes a medium for grassroots resistance. Bootlegged T-shirts representing characters on the television show *The Simpsons* appeared in response to T-shirts marketed by the network that produced the show (Parisi 1993). The bootlegged T-shirts represented the Simpson family as African Americans. Bart Simpson was shown as Rastabart, with dreadlocks and a red, green, and gold headband, as Rasta-dude Bart Marley, and as black Bart, paired with Nelson Mandela. Using clothing behavior as a means of making a statement, the T-shirts appeared to be intended as an affirmation of African Americans as an ethnic group and as a commentary on the narrow range of roles for black characters in the show. Victims of gender-related violence, such as rape, incest, battering, and sexual harassment, have used T-shirts as venues for statements about their experiences that are exhibited in clotheslines in public plazas (Ostrowski 1996). By contrast, some young men use T-shirts to express hostile, aggressive, or obscene sentiments denigrating women or to display pictures of guns and pistols (Cose 1993; *Time* 1992). Teens of both sexes use them as a means of expressing their cynicism about the dominant culture, particularly global advertising (Sepulchre 1994b).

The significance of the T-shirt in Western culture, as a means of social and political expression, is seen by comparing its roles in Western countries with the response to it in a nondemocratic country, the People's Republic of China (Barmé 1993). In 1991, a young Chinese artist created T-shirts bearing humorous statements, some of which could be interpreted as having mild political implications. The T-shirts were enormously successful with the public but were perceived as "a serious political incident" by the Chinese authorities. The artist was arrested and interrogated, and the T-shirts were officially banned. Thousands of them were confiscated and destroyed, although many Chinese continued to wear them.

Questions about the Reading

1. When did T-shirts begin to be used to communicate information?
2. What developments increased the use of T-shirts to communicate?
3. How does the use of the T-shirt to communicate differ from the use of the hat?
4. What "statement" did the Bart Simpson T-shirt seem to make?
5. What happened to the Chinese artist and the T-shirts he created? Why?

Questions about the Writer's Strategies

1. What is the thesis of the essay? State it in your own words.
2. What are the specific examples the writer uses to support her thesis?

3. What is each example meant to communicate?
4. Could the second paragraph be made into more than one paragraph? If so, how? What would be the topic sentence of each paragraph?

Writing Assignments

1. Write an essay using examples of each T-shirt you own that has lettering on it and explain what it "says" about you.
2. *Working Together*   Join with some classmates to write an essay using examples of the T-shirts each of you owns and explain what each T-shirt communicates about the wearer.

Each Game Was a Crusade

Mark Harris

*Jackie Robinson broke the color line in baseball in 1947 when he joined
the Brooklyn Dodgers. He was the first black player to wear the uniform
of a major league team. By the time he died a quarter-century later, all of
baseball and much of American life were integrated.*

Words to Know

anguish   pain, extreme discomfort

feint   pretend, fake

fortitude   courage, strength

incalculable   more than can be counted

innovators   inventors

manifestation   demonstration, showing, exhibition

nurtured   cultivated

shrewdest   most clever, most cunning

sustained   kept up

Getting Started

Think of a person who has made a contribution to society. What
did they do and how did they do it?

Sometimes on summer television when I watch a black fellow come 1
to bat during somebody's Game of the Day or Night or Week, I wonder
how much he knows about a recent fellow named Jackie Robinson.

Who was Jackie Robinson? I wondered if my students at the Univer- 2
sity of Pittsburgh knew, so I asked them to scribble me a little answer to
the question, "What does the name 'Jackie Robinson' mean to you?" For
fun, try it on your own resident student. My students were born, on the
average, in 1957. Some of their answers were these. "A very beautiful
blonde woman I met in my dental office." "Jackie Robinson—female or
male, related possibly to Mrs. Robinson in the movie 'The Graduate' &
in the song 'Mrs. Robinson' by Simon & Garfunkel. Or is it a baseball
player? A musician? I'm guessing."

Yes, baseball player, getting warm. Who was Jackie Robinson? "I 3
thought of a boxer," one student wrote. Another: "He might be a baseball player or a numbers runner." My one black student wrote: "Jackie
Robinson is a baseball player. This is a real person, in fact, he played on
a baseball team. Not sure what the team was."

The most nearly correct answer was this: "All I know (think) is he's 4
the first black man to play major-league baseball—broke the color
barrier." . . .

In ancient 1947, Robinson, male, a baseball player, a real person, became 5
the first black man to play big-league baseball, and a lonesome figure he
was. In 1947 we had sixteen major-league baseball teams, and every player
on every team was white and *that was that.* Except for Robinson, who
played first base for the (then) Brooklyn Dodgers of the National League.

If some people had had their way he would have been not only the first 6
but the last. The fact that those people did not have their way is due in
large part to Robinson's interior fortitude. But he could also hit and run
and field with superior skill at several positions. He had played in four
sports at UCLA. He soon became not only an outstanding player but the
spiritual leader of his own group (the Dodgers) and a dreaded opponent
of all the other groups (the other teams of the National League), whose
spirits he often destroyed with his daring and his surprises.

Robinson had been specially selected by Branch Rickey for the pio- 7
neer work he did. Rickey, the Dodgers' president, was one of baseball's
shrewdest innovators. He had invented the minor-league "farm system"
by which big-league organizations developed and nurtured talented
young players. Now he was to embark upon a second major innovation:
the introduction of black players into organized baseball. The first black
player would need to be an extraordinary human being. He would suffer anguish and abuse throughout the cities of the league. The shock of
Robinson's presence would not be cushioned in a day.

In 1946, when Robinson was signed to a contract by the Brooklyn orga- 8
nization, a sportswriter in St. Louis assured me that neither Robinson
nor any other Negro (that was the proper word then) would ever play
ball against the Cardinals. But after an extremely productive season
in Montreal, which was (then) in the International League, Robinson
did play baseball—for the Dodgers, against the Cardinals, who at first
refused to take the field. When at length the St. Louis players obeyed the
order of (then) National League president Ford Flick to play or be punished, baseball and America had arrived at a new moment.

In his first game for Montreal, Robinson hit one home run and three 9
singles, stole two bases, scored four runs. It was only the beginning. He
was to be remembered finally, however, not for statistics alone but for
incalculable moments when he won baseball games in ways that never
enter the box score. He played several positions afield, and he was several persons at the bat; he could hit long balls and he could bunt. He
could hit to left or right. He could run very fast and stop very short. He
could feint, and he could feint feinting.

He took long, careless leads off base, forcing opposition pitchers into 10 foolish errors. Since he was not only powerful but frequently enraged, he often inflicted injury upon other players in skirmishes along the base paths. His power was sustained by a mission not only personal but historic. Every game, every event, was in the interest of Robinson, of the Dodgers, and of Robinson's equalitarian interpretation of the United States Constitution. During warm-up for an exhibition game in New Orleans he once took time to condemn the black fans when they cheered because a new section of grandstand was opened to them: in Robinson's view, their expanded location was not a gift but a *right*. . . .

What if the Robinson experiment had failed? Nobody will ever know 11 whether the thing that succeeded was good old-fashioned liberal tradition in its most happy manifestation, or whether the thing that succeeded was old-fashioned dollar pragmatism. Robinson was a winner, and Brooklyn loved a winner, even if he was black. One winner drew a second, and so forth, and their names were Campanella, Black, Newcombe, Gilliam, and they were black, and they all played for Brooklyn during the decade 1947–1956, when the Dodgers won six pennants.

In the American League the Cleveland Indians with a black outfielder 12 named Larry Doby won the pennant in 1948. Doby was the first black *American* League player at a time when I could count on my fingers all the black players. As time passed, my fingers were unable to keep up.

It began with Robinson, Brooklyn, 1947—and radio. In those days—my 13 diary always tells it this way—I "listened to the ball game." In 1950 I more and more "watched the ball game," and anyone could see that the hitter's head or the pitcher's head was the size of the screen itself, and sometimes black. It was color television.

Thus the generation of my students, born in 1957 and propped at an 14 early age in front of the tube for the Game of the Day or Night or Year, must have believed from infancy that baseball players had always come in two colors. One never imagined that any such person existed who could be described as "the first black player" any more than anyone could name the first white player. . . .

The appearance of Robinson and the consciousness he raised among 15 athletes quickened thinking and hastened expectations upon many topics apart from race. He broke more than the color barrier. Robinson meant not only to play the game equally with all Americans but to sleep equally in hotels, and he rallied other black players, often to their discomfort, for they sometimes said to him, "Jackie, we like it here, don't rock the boat." But he had already rocked it climbing in, and the spirit of reform was contagious. White players joined black players to demand unprecedented rights through union organization and other forms of professional representation.

Their ultimate achievement was freedom from the "reserve clause" in 16 players' contracts. In the past, this clause gave the baseball organization or "club" exclusive rights to the players' services. Simply stated, a player was deprived of the opportunity to seek another employer, and therefore he was effectively denied the opportunity to bargain for his own wage. Players now won the right to be "free agents," to own themselves. The odd resemblance of the "reserve clause" to features of black slavery was remote in quality but similar in outline. . . .

A good deal of my own perception of Robinson's character and historic uniqueness I gleaned from Roger Kahn's wonderful book, *The Boys of Summer*. When Robinson died, October 24, 1972, Kahn was quoted in the papers. Someone asked him what Jackie Robinson had done for his race. Kahn, a white man, beautifully replied, "His race was humanity, and he did a great deal for us." 17

Questions about the Reading

1. What is the most important reason for Jackie Robinson's fame?
2. Who was responsible for giving Jackie Robinson his start in baseball? Did this person pick Robinson for his skill in baseball or for another reason? If so, what was the reason?
3. What happened when Robinson played baseball for the Dodgers against the Cardinals?
4. Explain why Robinson condemned black baseball fans in New Orleans.

Questions about the Writer's Strategies

1. What is the *point of view*—in regard to *time*—at the beginning of the essay? What words does the writer use to indicate a change in time? (See *point of view* and *time* in Glossary.)
2. What is the dominant *mode* that the writer uses in the essay? What other modes does he use? (See *mode of development* in Glossary.)
3. In paragraphs 13 and 14, how does the writer indicate the time of events? What is the purpose of the two paragraphs?
4. Does the writer develop the essay by using primarily one extended example or by using several examples?

Writing Assignments

1. Write a paper in which you tell about a person who changed the attitudes of another person or group. What did the person do to achieve the change?
2. Write a paper in which you use two or more examples of individuals who have made a particular contribution to one of the following: sports, art, music, literature, science, or business. What contribution did they make? How did they do it?

Between Two Wars, 1913–1945

Kathryn VanSpanckeren

The writer details the changes that took place in the United States between World War I and World War II and provides examples of writers and novels in which the changes are depicted.

Words to Know

edifice   large, imposing building

Freudian psychology   psychoanalysis; treatment of mental disorders, based on the method developed by Sigmund Freud, an Austrian physician and psychiatrist

proliferated   grew by multiplying

prophetically   forecast the future

Getting Started

What changes have taken place in your life since September 11, 2001? What changes do you think will take place in the United States following the end of the war on terrorism?

Many historians have characterized the period between the two world wars as the United States' traumatic "coming of age," despite the fact that U.S. direct involvement was relatively brief (1917–1918) and its casualties many fewer than those of its European allies and foes. John Dos Passos expressed America's postwar disillusionment in the novel *Three Soldiers* (1921), when he noted that civilization was a "vast edifice of sham, and the war, instead of its crumbling, was its fullest and most ultimate expression." Shocked and permanently changed, Americans returned to their homeland but could never regain their innocence.

Nor could soldiers from rural America easily return to their roots. After experiencing the world, many now yearned for a modern, urban life. New farm machines such as planters, harvesters, and binders had drastically reduced the demand for farm jobs; yet despite their increased productivity, farmers were poor. Crop prices, like urban workers' wages, depended on unrestrained market forces heavily influenced by business interests: Government subsidies for farmers and effective workers' unions had not yet become established. "The chief business of the American people is business," President Calvin Coolidge proclaimed in 1925, and most agreed.

In the postwar "Big Boom," business flourished, and the successful pros-   3
pered beyond their wildest dreams. For the first time, many Americans
enrolled in higher education—in the 1920s college enrollment doubled.
The middle-class prospered; Americans began to enjoy the world's highest
national average income in this era, and many people purchased the
ultimate status symbol—an automobile. The typical urban American
home glowed with electric lights and boasted a radio that connected
the house with the outside world, and perhaps a telephone, a camera,
a typewriter, or a sewing machine. Like the businessman protagonist
of Sinclair Lewis's novel *Babbitt* (1922), the average American approved
of these machines because they were modern and because most were
American inventions and American-made.

Americans of the "Roaring Twenties" fell in love with other mod-   4
ern entertainments. Most people went to the movies once a week.
Although Prohibition—a nationwide ban on the production, transport,
and sale of alcohol instituted through the 18th Amendment to the U.S.
Constitution—began in 1919, underground "speakeasies" and nightclubs proliferated, featuring jazz music, cocktails, and daring modes of
dress and dance. Dancing, moviegoing, automobile touring, and radio
were national crazes. American women, in particular, felt liberated.
Many had left farms and villages for homefront duty in American cities during World War I, and had become resolutely modern. They cut
their hair short ("bobbed"), wore short "flapper" dresses, and gloried
in the right to vote assured by the 19th Amendment to the Constitution,
passed in 1920. They boldly spoke their mind and took public roles
in society.

Western youths were rebelling, angry and disillusioned with the   5
savage war, the older generation they held responsible, and difficult
postwar economic conditions that, ironically, allowed Americans with
dollars—like writers F. Scott Fitzgerald, Ernest Hemingway, Gertrude
Stein, and Ezra Pound—to live abroad handsomely on very little
money. Intellectual currents, particularly Freudian psychology and to a
lesser extent Marxism (like the earlier Darwinian theory of evolution),
implied a "godless" world view and contributed to the breakdown
of traditional values. Americans abroad absorbed these views and
brought them back to the United States where they took root, firing the
imagination of young writers and artists. William Faulkner, for example, a 20th-century American novelist, employed Freudian elements in
all his works, as did virtually all serious American fiction writers after
World War I.

Despite outward gaiety, modernity, and unparalleled material pros-   6
perity, young Americans of the 1920s were "the lost generation"—so
named by literary portraitist Gertrude Stein. Without a stable, traditional

structure of values, the individual lost a sense of identity. The secure, supportive family life; the familiar, settled community; the natural and eternal rhythms of nature that guide the planting and harvesting on a farm; the sustaining sense of patriotism; moral values inculcated by religious beliefs and observations—all seemed undermined by World War I and its aftermath.

Numerous novels, notably Hemingway's *The Sun Also Rises* (1926) and Fitzgerald's *This Side of Paradise* (1920), evoke the extravagance and disillusionment of the lost generation. In T. S. Eliot's influential long poem *The Waste Land* (1922), Western civilization is symbolized by a bleak desert in desperate need of rain (spiritual renewal). 7

The world depression of the 1930s affected most of the population of the United States. Workers lost their jobs, and factories shut down; businesses and banks failed; farmers, unable to harvest, transport, or sell their crops, could not pay their debts and lost their farms. Midwestern droughts turned the "breadbasket" of America into a dust bowl. Many farmers left the Midwest for California in search of jobs, as vividly described in John Steinbeck's *The Grapes of Wrath* (1939). At the peak of the Depression, one-third of all Americans were out of work. Soup kitchens, shanty towns, and armies of hobos—unemployed men illegally riding freight trains—became part of national life. Many saw the Depression as a punishment for sins of excessive materialism and loose living. The dust storms that blackened the midwestern sky, they believed, constituted an Old Testament judgment: the "whirlwind by day and the darkness at noon." 8

The Depression turned the world upside down. The United States had preached a gospel of business in the 1920s; now, many Americans supported a more active role for government in the New Deal programs of President Franklin D. Roosevelt. Federal money created jobs in public works, conservation, and rural electrification. Artists and intellectuals were paid to create murals and state handbooks. These remedies helped, but only the industrial build-up of World War II renewed prosperity. After Japan attacked the United States at Pearl Harbor on December 7, 1941, disused shipyards and factories came to bustling life mass-producing ships, airplanes, jeeps, and supplies. War production and experimentation led to new technologies, including the nuclear bomb. Witnessing the first experimental nuclear blast, Robert Oppenheimer, leader of an international team of nuclear scientists, prophetically quoted a Hindu poem: "I am become Death, the shatterer of worlds." 9

Questions about the Reading

1. What does the writer mean by "civilization was a 'vast edifice of sham, and the war, instead of its crumbling, was its fullest and most ultimate expression'"?
2. What was the effect on colleges and American families of the post-war boom in business?
3. What is the 19th Amendment to the Constitution, when was it passed, and whom did it benefit? What is the 18th Amendment to the Constitution, and what was its effect?
4. What changed in people's attitudes toward business and government after the 1930s? What caused the change in attitudes?

Questions about the Writer's Strategies

1. What is the thesis of the essay? State it in your own words.
2. What is the main idea of each paragraph? Is it stated or implied? If stated, in which sentence or sentences? If implied, state it in your own words.
3. Could any of the paragraphs be combined? If so, which ones? Why?

Writing Assignments

1. Write an essay using examples to explain the major changes that have taken place in the United States since the end of World War II.

2. Use the Internet to find out more about the Lost Generation. Do some research on Hemingway, Stein, and Fitzgerald, and give examples of their experiences in Paris during the post–World War I years.
3. Write an essay using examples to explain the significant changes that have taken place in the United States since the September 11, 2001, terror attack.
4. Write an essay using examples to explain how September 11, 2001, affected your life or a relative's or friend's life.

My Mother Never Worked

Bonnie Smith-Yackel

Bonnie Smith-Yackel's family survived on a farm during the Great Depression, a time when both the weather and the economy made the hardships of farm life nearly overwhelming. In this personal essay, Smith-Yackel uses the example of her mother's life to illustrate the unfairness in American attitudes toward women and the work they do to keep their families intact.

Words to Know

cholera   a contagious, often fatal disease, usually restricted to farm animals in this country

reciprocated   returned

sustenance   nourishment, support for life

widow's pension   the Social Security payments made to a widow, based on her deceased husband's eligibility

Getting Started

What do you think about our government's policy that homemakers are not legally workers?

"**S**ocial Security Office." (The voice answering the telephone sounds   1
very self-assured.)

"I'm calling about . . . I . . . my mother just died . . . I was told to call   2
you and see about a . . . death-benefit check, I think they call it . . ."

"I see. Was your mother on Social Security? How old was she?"   3

"Yes . . . she was seventy-eight . . ."   4

"Do you know her number?"   5

"No . . . I, ah . . . don't you have a record?"   6

"Certainly. I'll look it up. Her name?"   7

"Smith. Martha Smith. Or maybe she used Martha Ruth Smith . . .   8
Sometimes she used her maiden name . . . Martha Jerabek Smith."

"If you'd care to hold on, I'll check our records—it'll be a few   9
minutes."

"Yes . . ."   10

Her love letters—to and from Daddy—were in an old box, tied with   11
ribbons and stiff, rigid-with-age leather thongs: 1918 through 1920; hers
written on stationery from the general store she had worked in full-time
and managed, single-handed, after her graduation from high school in

1913; and his, at first, on YMCA or Soldiers and Sailors Club stationery dispensed to the fighting men of World War I. He wooed her thoroughly and persistently by mail, and though she reciprocated all his feelings for her, she dreaded marriage . . .

"It's so hard for me to decide when to have my wedding day—that's 12 all I've thought about these last two days. I have told you dozens of times that I won't be afraid of married life, but when it comes down to setting the date and then picturing myself a married woman with half a dozen or more kids to look after, it just makes me sick . . . I am weeping right now—I hope that some day I can look back and say how foolish I was to dread it all."

They married in February, 1921, and began farming. Their first baby, 13 a daughter, was born in January, 1922, when my mother was 26 years old. The second baby, a son, was born in March, 1923. They were renting farms; my father, besides working his own fields, also was a hired man for two other farmers. They had no capital initially, and had to gain it slowly, working from dawn until midnight every day. My town-bred mother learned to set hens and raise chickens, feed pigs, milk cows, plant and harvest a garden, and can every fruit and vegetable she could scrounge. She carried water nearly a quarter of a mile from the well to fill her wash boilers in order to do her laundry on a scrub board. She learned to shuck grain, feed threshers, shuck and husk corn, feed corn pickers. In September, 1925, the third baby came, and in June, 1927, the fourth child—both daughters. In 1930, my parents had enough money to buy their own farm, and that March they moved all their livestock and belongings themselves, 55 miles over rutted, muddy roads.

In the summer of 1930 my mother and her two eldest children 14 reclaimed a 40-acre field from Canadian thistles, by chopping them all out with a hoe. In the other fields, when the oats and flax began to head out, the green and blue of the crops were hidden by the bright yellow of wild mustard. My mother walked the fields day after day, pulling each mustard plant. She raised a new flock of baby chicks—500—and she spaded up, planted, hoed, and harvested a half-acre garden.

During the next spring their hogs caught cholera and died. No cash 15 that fall.

And in the next year the drought hit. My mother and father trudged 16 from the well to the chickens, the well to the calf pasture, the well to the barn, and from the well to the garden. The sun came out hot and bright, endlessly, day after day. The crops shriveled and died. They harvested half the corn, and ground the other half, stalks and all, and fed it to the cattle as fodder. With the price at four cents a bushel for the harvested crop, they couldn't afford to haul it into town. They burned it in the furnace for fuel that winter.

In 1934, in February, when the dust was still so thick in the Min- 17 nesota air that my parents couldn't always see from the house to the barn, their fifth child—a fourth daughter—was born. My father hunted rabbits daily, and my mother stewed them, fried them, canned them, and wished out loud that she could taste hamburger once more. In the fall the shotgun brought prairie chickens, ducks, pheasant, and grouse. My mother plucked each bird, carefully reserving the breast feathers for pillows.

In the winter she sewed night after night, endlessly, begging cast-off 18 clothing from relatives, ripping apart coats, dresses, blouses, and trousers to remake them to fit her four daughters and son. Every morning and every evening she milked cows, fed pigs and calves, cared for chickens, picked eggs, cooked meals, washed dishes, scrubbed floors, and tended and loved her children. In the spring she planted a garden once more, dragging pails of water to nourish and sustain the vegetables for the family. In 1936 she lost a baby in her sixth month.

In 1937 her fifth daughter was born. She was 42 years old. In 1939 a 19 second son, and in 1941 her eighth child—and third son.

But the war had come, and prosperity of a sort. The herd of cattle had 20 grown to 30 head; she still milked morning and evening. Her garden was more than a half acre—the rains had come, and by now the Rural Electricity Administration and indoor plumbing. Still she sewed—dresses and jackets for the children, house dresses and aprons for herself, weekly patching of jeans, overalls, and denim shirts. Still she made pillows, using the feathers she had plucked, and quilts every year—intricate patterns as well as patchwork, stitched as well as tied—all necessary bedding for her family. Every scrap of cloth too small to be used in quilts was carefully saved and painstakingly sewed together in strips to make rugs. She still went out in the fields to help with the haying whenever there was a threat of rain.

In 1959 my mother's last child graduated from high school. A year 21 later the cows were sold. She still raised chickens and ducks, plucked feathers, made pillows, baked her own bread, and every year made a new quilt—now for a married child or for a grandchild. And her garden, that huge, undying symbol of sustenance, was as large and cared for as in all the years before. The canning, and now freezing, continued.

In 1969, on a June afternoon, mother and father started out for town 22 so that she could buy sugar to make rhubarb jam for a daughter who lived in Texas. The car crashed into a ditch. She was paralyzed from the waist down.

In 1970 her husband, my father, died. My mother struggled to regain 23 some competence and dignity and order in her life. At the rehabilitation institute, where they gave her physical therapy and trained her to live usefully in a wheelchair, the therapist told me: "She did fifteen pushups today—fifteen! She's almost seventy-five years old! I've never known a woman so strong!"

From her wheelchair she canned pickles, baked bread, ironed clothes, 24 wrote dozens of letters weekly to her friends and her "half dozen or more kids," and made three patchwork housecoats and one quilt. She made balls and balls of carpet rags—enough for five rugs. And kept all her love letters.

"I think I've found your mother's records—Martha Ruth Smith; mar- 25 ried to Ben F. Smith?"

"Yes, that's right."   26

"Well, I see that she was getting a widow's pension . . ."   27

"Yes, that's right."   28

"Well, your mother isn't entitled to our $255 death benefit."   29

"Not entitled! But why?"   30

The voice on the telephone explains patiently: 31

"Well, you see—your mother never worked."   32

Questions about the Reading

1. Why didn't the writer's mother want to get married?
2. How old was the writer's mother when she had her eighth child? How old was she when she was paralyzed?
3. In her later years, how do you think Mrs. Smith's attitude had changed from the one she expressed in the letter quoted in paragraph 12? What had become of her fears of marriage?
4. Why did Mrs. Smith do the pushups, and why did she continue to work in her final years, when she really didn't have to?
5. Speculate about why Mrs. Smith kept her love letters. Why do you think the writer mentions the fact in paragraph 24?

Questions about the Writer's Strategies

1. What is the thesis in this essay? Where is it expressed?
2. How well do the writer's examples support her thesis?
3. Aside from the extended example of her mother's life, what other mode of development does the writer use in the essay?
4. Describe the writer's point of view in the essay. How does she use time? Does her tone change during the essay?
5. Why does the writer provide so few details about her father and the family's children?

Writing Assignments

1. Write an essay giving examples of the obstacles women have to over-come in today's society.
2. Think of an extraordinary person you know, and write an essay using examples to show what makes that person extraordinary and why he or she is important to others.
3. Write an essay using examples, or one extended example, to show what the word *sacrifice* means.

5

Classification and Division

Suppose you are looking over the clothing in your closet, trying to sort out the confusion. You decide to classify your clothing into several categories: good clothes for looking your best on the job; older clothes for weekends and informal occasions; and very old clothes that have some stains and holes (but that you can still use when you wash the car or the dog). You have now classified all your clothes into three orderly categories, according to their various uses. You may even want to expand your classification by adding a fourth category: clothes that are no longer useful and should be thrown away. You may have washed the dog in them once too often.

The purpose of **classification** is to take many of the same type of thing—for example, clothing, school papers, presidents, recipes, or music—and organize this large, unsorted group into categories. You may decide to classify your group of similar things, such as music, into the categories of classical, jazz, and rock and roll. Or you might classify recipes into main dishes, salads, and desserts.

You should determine your categories by a quality or characteristic that the items have in common. In each case, you will have to search for the categories that will help you classify an unsorted group of items.

In the following example, the writer classifies mothers of handicapped children in three categories of attitudes.

Topic sentence	Researchers note three frequent attitudes among mothers of handicapped children. The first attitude is reflected by those mothers who reject their child or are unable to accept the child as a handicapped person. Complex love-hate and acceptance-rejection relationships are found within this group. Rejected children not only have problems in adjusting to themselves and their disabilities, but they also have to contend with disturbed family relationships and emotional insecurity. Unfortunately, such children receive even less	1
Category 1: rejection		

encouragement than the normal child and have to absorb more criticism of their behavior.

Category 2: over compensation

A second relationship involves mothers who overcompensate in their reactions to their child and the disorder. They tend to be unrealistic, rigid, and overprotective. Often, such parents try to compensate by being overzealous and giving continuous instruction and training in the hope of establishing superior ability.   2

Category 3: acceptance

The third group consists of mothers who accept their children along with their disorders. These mothers have gained the ability to provide for the special needs of their handicapped children while continuing to live a normal life and tending to family and home as well as civic and social obligations. The child's chances are best with parents who have accepted both their child and the defects.   3

Janet W. Lerner,
Learning Disabilities, Fifth Edition

A **division** paper requires taking one thing—a man's suit, for example—and dividing it into its component parts or characteristics: jacket, pants, and vest (maybe).

Classification and division are often used together. For example, you might want to *divide* your neighborhood into sections (north, south, east, and west). You might then *classify* the sections by how much noise and traffic are present in each—noisy, relatively quiet, and quiet. The purpose of classification and division is to categorize a complex whole into simple, useful categories or subdivisions.

In the following example, the writer classifies three police officer positions and then divides each position by the duties required.

Classification

The presidential crime commission offered a partial solution to overworked police forces: Split up the policeman's job

Division 1

three different ways. Under this plan, a "community service officer," often a youth from the ghetto, would perform minor investigative chores, rescue cats, and keep in touch with com-

Division 2

bustible young people. A police officer, one step higher, would control traffic, hold back crowds at parades, and investigate

Division 3

more serious crimes. A police agent, the best-trained, best-educated man on the ladder, would patrol high-crime areas, respond to delicate racial situations, and take care of tense confrontations.

"The Police Need Help," *Time* (October 4, 1968), p. 27

Whether using classification or division, you should be sure that the categories are logical and appropriate, with as little overlap between categories as possible. If you are classifying chocolate desserts, you should not add vanilla custard to your list. You should also make your categories reasonably complete. You would not want to leave out chocolate cake in your classification of chocolate desserts.

If you are groping for a method of classification, you may want to try *several* ways of categorizing the same information. If you are classifying your clothes based on how attractive they look in your closet, you might sort them by color. But if you want to make the best use of the space in your closet, you might sort your clothes by type of garment—jackets, pants, shirts, and so forth. In short, you should choose your method of classifying any group of items based on the idea or point you want to support.

In the following paragraph, the writer uses classification to recommend ways to categorize book owners.

Topic sentence: classification Category 1: nonreaders	There are three kinds of book owners. The first has all the standard sets and best-sellers—unread, untouched. (This deluded individual owns woodpulp and ink, not books.) The second has a great many books—a few of them read through, most
Category 2: occasional readers	of them dipped into, but all of them as clean and shiny as the day they were bought. (This person would probably like to make books his own, but is restrained by a false respect for their physical appearance.) The third has a few books
Category 3: devoted readers	or many—every one of them dog-eared and dilapidated, shaken and loosened by continual use, marked and scribbled in from front to back. (This man owns books.)

Mortimer J. Adler, "How to Mark a Book"

Notice, too, that the transitional words *first, second,* and *third* are used to identify the book owner according to how much each owner reads books. The words *first, second,* and *third* also help move the reader from one point to another. Some other transitional words and phrases that often are used in classification and division are *one, two, three;* and *for one thing, for another thing, finally.* As you write and revise your paragraphs and essays, you will want to think about using transitions to help maintain the **unity** and logical flow, or **coherence,** of your writing.

Like Adler, author of the paragraph on book owners, writers often use topic sentences such as "A safe city street must have three main qualities" (see chapter 1, page 6) or "The treatment prescribed for the disease was aspirin, bed rest, and fluids" to indicate the categories that will follow in the body of a paragraph or essay. Following "A safe city street must have three main qualities," the writer would explain the three specific qualities that make a city street safe. Following "The treatment prescribed for the disease was aspirin, bed rest, and fluids," the writer would probably explain the reasons for prescribing aspirin, bed rest, and fluids.

Usually, too, writers will *follow the same order* in discussing the divisions (or categories) that they used in first introducing them. For instance, suppose the topic is "Four methods can be used to cook fish: broiling, baking, poaching, and frying." Ordinarily the writer would explain (1) broiling, then (2) baking, (3) poaching, and (4) frying. Listing the categories and explaining them in order can make the composition easier for the reader to follow. In the revised student essay that follows, the three students who collaborated in writing it initially classified students as "unconcerned," "ambitious," and "inconsistent." Although they did not follow this order in their first draft, in **revising** the essay, the students changed the order to unconcerned, inconsistent, and ambitious. This order—which followed an undesirable-to-desirable pattern—was then used as the basis for the order of the paragraphs.

Thesis statement: classification	Students come in all ages, races, and genders. You can find the unconcerned, inconsistent, and ambitious in any group of students.	1
Category 1: unconcerned students	First, Ralph, a student in my English class, is an example of a student who has an unconcerned attitude. He has a negative outlook on life, and at times his attitude is downright hostile. He enters the classroom late and disrupts the class by slamming the door or by talking to other students while the teacher is giving a lecture. He does not care at all about the importance of an education. Ralph is more interested in watching sports, enjoying some form of entertainment, or going to parties.	2
Category 2: inconsistent students	Second, an inconsistent student can be described as a person whose attitude toward education changes or varies. For example, a first grader's grades have gone up and down. She has been in school for only two semesters, but she has shown a big change in her grades. The first semester she received an E (Excellent) in reading and an S (Satisfactory) in math. The second semester she received an N (Not satisfactory) in reading and an E in math. When asked why her reading grade dropped, she said because she no longer liked reading. After her teacher taught her how to have fun doing her math, she no longer concentrated on reading. As a result, she would only take her math homework out of her book bag when it came time to do her homework.	3
Category 3: ambitious students	Last, there are many ambitious students who are eager to do well in their studies and to achieve degrees. Their priorities have been set, and they have made plans for reaching their goals. Their sole ambition is to excel and succeed. Many students can be classified as ambitious. Valerie, who is pursuing a degree in nursing, is a classic example. She attends class eagerly and regularly, even though she has two children and a home to care for. Recently, she had an illness that caused her to be absent for two weeks and to fall behind in her assignments. She returned and, with her usual ambition, soon caught up with her overdue assignments and achieved Bs or better grades in her courses.	4
Conclusion: restatement of thesis	In conclusion, the attitudes exemplified above can be found in students of any age, race, or gender. Whether they are attending grade school, high school, or college, students can be found who are unconcerned, inconsistent, or ambitious.	5

As with any piece of writing, a useful practice is to jot down many ideas and make rough lists as part of your **brainstorming** and prewriting. Do not skimp on your planning, and do expect to revise—perhaps several times—to produce a clear, understandable, and effective paragraph or essay.

Chili

Charles Kuralt

There are as many chili recipes as there are chili cooks. Charles Kuralt could have chosen to organize his classification by ingredients or by degree of spiciness, but he instead chooses a classification system that reveals his amused attitude about the subject of chili.

Word to Know

affectation   pretension

Getting Started

How would you classify your favorite desserts?

Some people really like chili, apparently, but nobody can agree how the stuff should be made. C. V. Wood, twice winner at Terlingua, uses flank steak, pork chops, chicken, and green chilis. My friend Hughes Rudd of CBS News, who imported five hundred pounds of chili powder into Russia as a condition of accepting employment as Moscow correspondent, favors coarse-ground beef. Isadore Bleckman, the cameraman I must live with on the road, insists upon one-inch cubes of stew beef and puts garlic in his chili, an Illinois affectation. An Indian of my acquaintance, Mr. Fulton Batisse, who eats chili for breakfast when he can, uses buffalo meat and plays an Indian drum while it's cooking. I ask you.

Questions about the Reading

1. What is the main idea (topic) of the paragraph? Is it directly stated? If so, in which sentences?
2. How does the writer let you know where his cameraman comes from?
3. How does Kuralt feel about the way the Indian cooks chili? Which sentence tells you that?

Questions about the Writer's Strategies

1. Although the writer classifies chili, he does so by combining classification with another **mode.** What is that mode?

2. What is the ingredient that is used consistently by the writer to classify chili?

3. What **order** does the writer use in discussing the different categories of chili?

Writing Assignments

1. Write a paper in which you *classify* one of the following: people you admire, neighbors, friends, dogs, or cats. Be sure to use a consistent characteristic as the basis for establishing the categories of the classification.

2. Write a paper in which you *divide* and then describe a house according to the functions of its rooms.

3. Think of a food that many people prepare, such as fried chicken, hot dogs, or hamburgers. *Classify* the food according to the different ways in which cooks prepare it.

March of Science

James K. Page Jr.

In the paragraph that follows, an unusual subject is classified—the noise of foods when they are eaten.

Words to Know

alluring enticing

extol praise

spectrum range

vibrations rapid back-and-forth movements, sounds from that movement

Getting Started

How would you classify the sound of women's shoes on a sidewalk?

You will be relieved to learn that . . . science has now examined yet another habit which Americans indulge to excess: eating—specifically, the delights of eating crunchy, crispy things. . . . Our delight has to do with noise, reports *Chemistry* (Vol. 50, No. 6) a bit breathlessly. Through . . . analysis of the sounds of green peppers, cookies, potato chips and so forth, three categories on the upper end of the noisy-crispy/quiet-not-crispy range can be specified.

- Wet-crisp, as when the living cells of celery or green peppers—filled with fluid and pressure—explode under the force of a tooth. The more pressure, the louder the crunch.
- Dry-crisp, as when the air-filled brittle cells of crackers bend and break, then snap back to position. The vibrations build up into a sound pressure wave.
- Chip-crisp, as when a potato chip is broken by the teeth. Potato chips, only a few cells thick, are noisier (crispier) than you'd expect. Why? Being curved, they are repeatedly broken, which causes many crisp and noisy sounds.

Questions about the Reading

1. Are the words used to describe the noise of foods precise? Support your answer with a statement from the reading.

2. What are the categories of noise that are described by the writer?
3. Why are potato chips noisier than you might expect?

Questions about the Writer's Strategies

1. What is the **point of view** in the paragraph?
2. What is the **tone** of the paragraph? Support your answer with words or statements from the reading.
3. Does the writer use **examples** to illustrate statements or points made in the paragraph? If so, identify the examples.

Writing Assignments

1. Write a paper in which you classify the sounds people make when they laugh.
2. Write a paper in which you classify noises in your neighborhood or vocal sounds of various singers.
3. Select a group of fruits and write a paper in which you classify them according to how juicy they are.

Fans

Paul Gallico

Paul Gallico is known for his sports writing and for his books, including Mrs. 'Arris Goes to New York *and* The Snow Goose. *In the following paragraph he classifies sports fans.*

Words to Know

aristocratic   upper class
commiseration   sympathy
incandescents   very bright, shining lights
lurks   lies in wait

Getting Started

How would you classify the people who attend a rock concert, a musical play, a symphony, and an opera performance?

The fight crowd is a beast that lurks in the darkness behind the fringe of white light shed over the first six rows by the incandescents atop the ring, and is not to be trusted with pop bottles or other hardware. The tennis crowd is always preening and shushing itself. The golf crowd is the most unwieldy and most sympathetic, and is the only horde given to mass production of that absurd noise written generally as "tsk tsk tsk tsk," and made between tongue and teeth with head-waggings to denote extreme commiseration. The baseball crowd is the most hysterical, the football crowd the best-natured and the polo crowd the most aristocratic. Racing crowds are the most restless, wrestling crowds the most tolerant, and soccer crowds the most easily incitable to riot and disorder. Every sports crowd takes on the characteristics of the individuals who compose it. Each has its particular note of hysteria, its own little cruelties, mannerisms, and bad mannerisms, its own code of sportsmanship and its own method of expressing its emotions.

Questions about the Reading

1. What are the classifications of sports fans that the writer discusses?
2. Which crowd is the most likely to be disorderly?
3. What determines the characteristics of each sports crowd?

4. What do you think happens to make a golf crowd go "tsk tsk tsk tsk" to show "extreme commiseration"?
5. Which crowd is the most hysterical?

Questions about the Writer's Strategies

1. What is the main idea (topic) of the paragraph?
2. Which sentence(s) state the topic of the paragraph?
3. Where are the topic sentence(s) located in the paragraph?
4. What is the metaphor the writer uses for the fight crowd?
5. What appears to determine the order in which the writer discusses the different crowds? If you were writing the paragraph, would you use a different order? If so, explain how you might change the order.

Writing Assignments

1. Write a paragraph in which you classify the crowds at three different musical events.
2. Write a paragraph in which you classify the cars in a parking lot.

Brain Power

Lester C. Thurow

The writer identifies the inventions that led to our first and second industrial revolutions but maintains that the third, the "information revolution," is not based on information.

Words to Know

biotechnology   application of technology to biology
denominator   controlling or common term
misnomer   incorrect name or term

Getting Started

How would you classify the changes that have taken place in your life as a result of the invention of the computer?

Future economic historians looking back will probably see the end of the 20th century as the third industrial revolution. In the first industrial revolution, at the beginning of the 19th century, the steam engine brought 8,000 years of agricultural dominance to an end and created the modern industrial era. At the end of the 19th century, electrification caused the second industrial revolution. Electrical power generation and distribution quickly became a big industry. The telephone could be invented. Electric lights made work or leisure into nighttime as well as daytime activities. People slept less. The third industrial revolution is sometimes called an information revolution, but that is a misnomer since many of the industries involved in the revolution, such as biotechnology and new designer-made materials, are not information industries. Its key distinguishing characteristic and common denominator is not information, but rather a world in which skills and knowledge are the dominant sources of wealth. Bill Gates, now the world's richest man, is the best symbol of this shift.

Questions about the Reading

1. What was the first industrial revolution, and what did it replace as our dominant industry?
2. What inventions led to the first and second industrial revolutions?

3. What is the third revolution called? Why does Thurow say the term is a misnomer?
4. What does Thurow say is the third revolution's characteristic? Why? Who is the best symbol of this revolution?

Questions about the Writer's Strategies

1. What is the main idea of the paragraph? State it in your own words.
2. What order does the writer use?
3. In addition to classification, what other modes of development does the writer use?
4. If you wanted to divide the paragraph into more than one paragraph, where would you divide it? What would be the main idea and topic sentence of each paragraph?

Writing Assignments

1. Write a paragraph in which you classify the ways in which the computer has changed or influenced your life.
2. Write a paragraph in which you classify the inventions you use for doing your household tasks and explain how they have changed your way from the way your parents or grandparents did these tasks.

"Ever Et Raw Meat?"

Stephen King

Stephen King, best known for such horror novels and movies as Carrie *and* Misery, *classifies readers according to the questions they ask him.*

Words to Know

blasphemous   irreverent, profane
E. E. Cummings   American poet known for experimenting with form, punctuation, spelling, and syntax in his poetry
enumerate   name one by one
flagellate   beat, whip
kleptomaniac   a person who has an impulse or compulsion to steal
laconic   concise expression; expressed in few words
modicum   small amount
self-abnegation   self-denial, giving up of one's rights
Zen   Buddhist sect

Getting Started

What questions would you like to ask Stephen King?

It seems to me that, in the minds of readers, writers actually exist to 1
serve two purposes, and the more important may not be the writing of
books and stories. The primary function of writers, it seems, is to answer
readers' questions. These fall into three categories. The third is the one
that fascinates me most, but I'll identify the other two first.

The One-of-a-Kind Question

Each day's mail brings a few of these. Often they reflect the writer's field 2
of interest—history, horror, romance, the American West, outer space,
big business. The only thing they have in common is their uniqueness.
Novelists are frequently asked where they get their ideas (see category
No. 2), but writers must wonder where this relentless curiosity, these
really strange questions, come from.

There was, for instance, the young woman who wrote to me from a 3
penal institution in Minnesota. She informed me she was a kleptomaniac.
She further informed me that I was her favorite writer, and she had stolen

every one of my books she could get her hands on. "But after I stole *Different Seasons* from the library and read it, I felt moved to send it back," she wrote. "Do you think this means you wrote this one the best?" After due consideration, I decided that reform on the part of the reader has nothing to do with artistic merit. I came close to writing back to find out if she had stolen *Misery* yet but decided I ought to just keep my mouth shut.

From Bill V. in North Carolina: "I see you have a beard. Are you morbid of razors?"   4

From Carol K. in Hawaii: "Will you soon write of pimples or some other facial blemish?"   5

From Don G., no address (and a blurry postmark): "Why do you keep up this disgusting mother worship when anyone with any sense knows a MAN has no use to his mother once he is weaned?"   6

From Raymond R. in Mississippi: "Ever et raw meat?" (It's the laconic ones like this that really get me.)   7

I have been asked if I beat my children and/or my wife. I have been asked to parties in places I have never been and hope never to go. I was once asked to give away the bride at a wedding, and one young woman sent me an ounce of pot, with the attached question: "This is where I get my inspiration—where do you get yours?" Actually, mine usually comes in envelopes—the kind through which you can view your name and address printed by a computer—that arrive at the end of every month.   8

My favorite question of this type, from Anchorage, asked simply: "How could you write such a why?" Unsigned. If E. E. Cummings were still alive, I'd try to find out if he'd moved to the Big North.   9

The Old Standards

These are the questions writers dream of answering when they are collecting rejection slips, and the ones they tire of quickest once they start to publish. In other words, they are the questions that come up without fail in every dull interview the writer has ever given or will ever give. I'll enumerate a few of them: 10

Where do you get your ideas? (I get mine in Utica.)   11

How do you get an agent? (Sell your soul to the Devil.)   12

Do you have to know somebody to get published? (Yes; in fact, it helps to grovel, toady, and be willing to perform twisted acts of sexual depravity at a moment's notice, and in public if necessary.)   13

How do you start a novel? (I usually start by writing the number 1 in the upper right-hand corner of a clean sheet of paper.)   14

How do you write best sellers? (Same way you get an agent.)   15

How do you sell your book to the movies? (Tell them they don't want it.) 16

What time of day do you write? (It doesn't matter; if I don't keep busy enough, the time inevitably comes.)   17

Do you ever run out of ideas? (Does a bear defecate in the woods?)   18

Who is your favorite writer? (Anyone who writes stories I would have 19
written had I thought of them first.)

There are others, but they're pretty boring, so let us march on.   20

The Real Weirdies

Here I am, bopping down the street, on my morning walk, when some guy 21
pulls over in his pickup truck or just happens to walk by and says, "Hi, Steve!
Writing any good books lately?" I have an answer for this; I've developed it
over the years out of pure necessity. I say, "I'm taking some time off." I say
that even if I'm working like mad, thundering down homestretch on a book.
The reason why I say this is because no other answer seems to fit. Believe me,
I know. In the course of the trial and error that has finally resulted in "I'm
taking some time off," I have discarded about 500 other answers.

Having an answer for "You writing any good books lately?" is a good 22
thing, but I'd be lying if I said it solves the problem of *what the question
means.* It is this inability on my part to make sense of this odd query,
which reminds me of that Zen riddle—"Why is a mouse when it runs?"—
that leaves me feeling mentally shaken and impotent. You see, it isn't just
one question; it is a *bundle* of questions, cunningly wrapped up in one
package. It's like that old favorite, "Are you still beating your wife?"

If I answer in the affirmative, it means I may have written—how many 23
books? two? four?—(all of them good) in the last—how long? Well, how
long is "lately"? It could mean I wrote maybe three good books just last
week, or maybe two *on this very walk up to Bangor International Airport and
back!* On the other hand, if I say no, what does *that* mean? I wrote three or
four *bad* books in the last "lately" (surely "lately" can be no longer than
a month, six weeks at the outside)?

Or here I am, signing books at the Betts' Bookstore or B. Dalton's in the 24
local consumer factory (nicknamed "the mall"). This is something I do
twice a year, and it serves much the same purpose as those little bundles
of twigs religious people in the Middle Ages used to braid into whips
and flagellate themselves with. During the course of this exercise in mad-
ness and self-abnegation, at least a dozen people will approach the little
coffee table where I sit behind a barrier of books and ask brightly, "Don't
you wish you had a rubber stamp?"

I have an answer to this one, too, an answer that has been developed 25
over the years in a trial-and-error method similar to "I'm taking some time
off." The answer to the rubber-stamp questions is: "No, I don't mind."

Never mind if I really do or don't (this time it's my own motivations I 26
want to skip over, you'll notice); the question is, Why does such an illogical
query occur to so many people? My signature is actually stamped on the
covers of several of my books, but people seem just as eager to get these

signed as those that aren't so stamped. Would these questioners stand in line for the privilege of watching me slam a rubber stamp down on the title page of *The Shining* or *Pet Sematary?* I don't think they would.

If you still don't sense something peculiar in these questions, this one 27 might help convince you. I'm sitting in the cafe around the corner from my house, grabbing a little lunch by myself and reading a book (reading at the table is one of the few bad habits acquired in my youth that I have nobly resisted giving up) until a customer or maybe even a waitress sidles up and asks, "How come you're not reading one of your own books?"

This hasn't happened just once, or even occasionally; it happens *a lot.* 28 The computer-generated answer to this question usually gains a chuckle, although it is nothing but the pure, logical and apparent truth. "I know how they all come out," I say. End of exchange. Back to lunch, with only a pause to wonder why people assume you want to read what you wrote, rewrote, read again following the obligatory editorial conference and yet again during the process of correcting the mistakes that a good copy editor always prods, screaming, from their hiding places (I once heard a crime writer suggest that God could have used a copy editor, and while I find the notion slightly blasphemous, I tend to agree).

And then people sometimes ask in that chatty, let's-strike-up-a- 29 conversation way people have, "How long does it take you to write a book?" Perfectly reasonable question—at least until you try to answer it and discover there is no answer. This time the computer-generated answer is a total falsehood, but it at least serves the purpose of advancing the conversation to some more discussable topic. "Usually about nine months," I say, "the same length of time it takes to make a baby." This satisfies everyone but me. I know that nine months is just an average, and probably a completely fictional one at that. It ignores *The Running Man* (published under the name Richard Bachman), which was written in four days during a snowy February vacation when I was teaching high school. It also ignores *It* and my latest, *The Tommyknockers. It* is over 1,000 pages long and took four years to write. *The Tommyknockers* is 400 pages shorter but took five years to write.

Do I mind these questions? Yes . . . and no. Anyone minds questions 30 that have no real answers and thus expose the fellow being questioned to be not a real doctor but a sort of witch doctor. But no one—at least no one with a modicum of simple human kindness—resents questions from people who honestly want answers. And now and then someone will ask a really interesting question, like, Do you write in the nude? The answer—not generated by computer—is: I don't think I ever have, but if it works, I'm willing to try it.

Questions about the Reading

1. According to King, what seems to be the primary function of writers?
2. What do the one-of-a-kind questions have in common?
3. What does the writer mean when he says he gets his inspiration from what "comes in envelopes—the kind through which you can view your name and address printed by computer—that arrive at the end of every month"?
4. What are the writer's definitions of "old standards" and "real weirdies"?
5. What are the four "real weirdies" the writer has been asked?

Questions about the Writer's Strategies

1. What are the different modes of development that the writer uses in the essay?
2. What is the point of view in person and time? Are they consistent throughout the essay?
3. What is the tone of the essay? Is it consistent throughout?
4. What organizational pattern and modes of development does the writer use in describing "one-of-a-kind questions" and "old standards"?
5. What organizational pattern does the writer use in describing "real weirdies"?

Writing Assignments

1. Choose three or more of the following famous writers represented in this text: John Updike, Russell Baker, John Grogan, Barbara Kingsolver, Charles Kuralt, Paul Gallico, Stephen King, Anna Quindlen, Thomas L. Friedman, Jack London, or Isaac Asimov. Using the Internet or your library, choose a book or essay written by each writer and then write an essay about the questions you would like to ask each writer about his or her book or essay.
2. *Working Together* Join with some classmates to write an essay about the questions you would like to ask Babe Ruth, Michael Jordan, and Martina Navratilova.

Eggs, Twinkies, and Ethnic Stereotypes

Jeanne Park

> *Jeanne Park, an Asian American, found herself labeled as intelligent while in elementary school. In high school, she learned that her intelligence did not set her apart in the classroom but that outside the classroom her ethnic background did.*

Words to Know

condescending   patronizing
metamorphose   change in nature

Getting Started

At lunchtime, do the students at your school segregate themselves according to their racial or ethnic background?

Who am I?   1

For Asian-American students, the answer is a diligent, hardwork- 2
ing and intelligent young person. But living up to this reputation has
secretly haunted me.

The labeling starts in elementary school. It's not uncommon for a teacher 3
to remark, "You're Asian, you're supposed to do well in math." The under-
lying message is, "You're Asian and you're supposed to be smarter."

Not to say being labeled intelligent isn't flattering, because it is, or not 4
to deny that basking in the limelight of being top of my class isn't ego-
boosting, because frankly it is. But at a certain point, the pressure became
crushing. I felt as if doing poorly on my next spelling quiz would stain
the exalted reputation of all Asian students forever.

So I continued to be an academic overachiever, as were my friends. 5
By junior high school I started to believe I was indeed smarter. I became
condescending toward non-Asians. I was a bigot; all my friends were
Asians. The thought of intermingling occurred rarely if ever.

My elitist opinion of Asian students changed, however, in high school. 6
As a student at what is considered one of the nation's most competitive science and math schools, I found that being on top is no longer an easy feat.

I quickly learned that Asian students were not smarter. How could I 7
ever have believed such a thing? All around me are intelligent, ambitious
people who are not only Asian but white, black and Hispanic.

Superiority complexes aside, the problem of social segregation still 8
exists in the schools. With a few exceptions, each race socializes only

with its "own kind." Students see one another in the classroom, but outside the classroom there remains distinct segregation.

Racist lingo abounds. An Asian student who socializes only with other 9 Asians is believed to be an Asian Supremacist or, at the very least, arrogant and closed off. Yet an Asian student who socializes only with whites is called a "twinkie," one who is yellow on the outside but white on the inside.

A white teenager who socializes only with whites is thought of as 10 prejudiced, yet one who socializes with Asians is considered an "egg," white on the outside and yellow on the inside.

These culinary classifications go on endlessly, needless to say, leaving 11 many confused, and leaving many more fearful than ever of social experimentation. Because the stereotypes are accepted almost unanimously, they are rarely challenged. Many develop harmful stereotypes of entire races. We label people before we even know them.

Labels learned at a young age later metamorphose into more visible 12 acts of racism. For example, my parents once accused and ultimately fired a Puerto Rican cashier, believing she had stolen $200 from the register at their grocery store. They later learned it was a mistake. An Asian shopkeeper nearby once beat a young Hispanic youth who worked there with a baseball bat because he believed the boy to be lazy and dishonest.

We all hold misleading stereotypes of people that limit us as indi- 13 viduals in that we cheat ourselves out of the benefits different cultures can contribute. We can grow and learn from each culture whether it be Chinese, Korean or African American.

Just recently some Asian boys in my neighborhood were attacked by a 14 group of young white boys who have christened themselves the Master Race. Rather than being angered by this act, I feel pity for this generation that lives in a state of bigotry.

It may be too late for our parents' generation to accept that each per- 15 son can only be judged for the characteristics that set him or her apart as an individual. We, however, can do better.

Questions about the Reading

1. How did it affect the writer to be labeled as *intelligent?*
2. What did the writer learn about other students when she went to the competitive high school?
3. What is an Asian Supremacist? A "twinkie"? An "egg"?
4. According to the writer, how do the culinary classifications influence people's behavior?
5. According to the writer, how should we judge people?

Questions about the Writer's Strategies

1. Is the essay developed using classification or using division?
2. What mode of development does the writer use in paragraph 4?
3. What is the topic of paragraph 12? What mode of development does the writer use in the paragraph?
4. What are some transitional words the writer uses?
5. What is the thesis of the essay? Is it stated or implied?
6. Is the essay objective, subjective, or both?

Writing Assignments

1. Write an essay in which you classify the people in your neighborhood according to the cars they drive.
2. Write an essay in which you classify the students in your school according to what they eat for lunch.
3. Write an essay in which you divide a house, a car, or an item of clothing into its parts.

A Brief, Yet Helpful, Guide to Civil Disobedience

Woody Allen

Woody Allen's comic style is familiar to readers of his books, fans of his comedy albums, and viewers of his movies. In this essay, he shows us the silliness we can get into when we try to impose too neat a scheme of classification on what is, after all, a rather untidy world. More important, though, he makes us see some truths—and he makes us laugh.

Words to Know

concessions agreements, allowances
faction side, group
forfeited given up
insidious stealthy, wily, sneaky
insurrection uprising
mime mimic

Getting Started

What current school, city, state, or federal policy would you like to join a protest against?

In perpetrating a revolution, there are two requirements: someone or 1 something to revolt against and someone to actually show up and do the revolting. Dress is usually casual and both parties may be flexible about time and place, but if either faction fails to attend, the whole enterprise is likely to come off badly. In the Chinese Revolution of 1650 neither party showed up and the deposit on the hall was forfeited.

The people or parties revolted against are called the "oppressors" and 2 are easily recognized as they seem to be the ones having all the fun. The "oppressors" generally get to wear suits, own land, and play their radios late at night without being yelled at. Their job is to maintain the "status quo," a condition where everything remains the same although they may be willing to paint every two years.

When the "oppressors" become too strict, we have what is known as a 3 police state wherein all dissent is forbidden as is chuckling, showing up in a bow tie, or referring to the mayor as "Fats." Civil liberties are greatly curtailed in a police state and freedom of speech is unheard of although one is allowed to mime to a record. Opinions critical of the government are not tolerated, particularly about their dancing. Freedom of the press is also curtailed and the ruling party "manages" the news, permitting the citizens to hear only acceptable political ideas and ball scores that will not cause unrest.

The groups who revolt are called the "oppressed" and can generally   4
be seen milling about and grumbling or claiming to have headaches. (It should be noted that the oppressors never revolt and attempt to become the oppressed as that would entail a change of underwear.) . . .

It should be noted that after a revolution is over, the "oppressed"   5
frequently take over and begin acting like the "oppressors." Of course by then it is very hard to get them on the phone and money lent for ciga-rettes and gum during the fighting may as well be forgotten about.

Methods of civil disobedience: 6

Hunger Strike. Here the oppressed goes without food until his demands   7
are met. Insidious politicians will often leave biscuits within easy reach or perhaps some cheddar cheese, but they must be resisted. If the party in power can get the striker to eat, they usually have little trouble putting down the insurrection. If they can get him to eat and also lift the cheek, they have won for sure. In Pakistan, a hunger strike was broken when the Gov-ernment produced an exceptionally fine veal cordon bleu which the masses found was too appealing to turn down, but such gourmet dishes are rare.

The problem with the hunger strike is that after several days one can get   8
quite hungry, particularly since sound-trucks are paid to go through the street saying, "Um . . . what nice chicken—umm . . . some peas . . . umm . . ."

A modified form of the Hunger Strike for those whose political con-   9
victions are not quite so radical is giving up chives. This small gesture, when used properly, can greatly influence a government, and it is well known that Mahatma Gandhi's insistence on eating his salads untossed shamed the British Government into many concessions. Other things besides food one can give up are: whist, smiling, and standing on one foot and imitating a crane.

Sit-down Strike. Proceed to a designated spot and then sit down, but   10
sit all the way down. Otherwise you are squatting, a position that makes no political point unless the government is also squatting. (This is rare, although a government will occasionally crouch in cold weather.) The trick is to remain seated until concessions are made, but as in the Hunger Strike, the government will try subtle means of making the striker rise. They may say, "Okay, everybody up, we're closing." Or, "Can you get up for a minute, we'd just like to see how tall you are?"

Demonstration and Marches. The key point about a demonstration is   11
that it must be seen. Hence the term, "demonstration." If a person dem-onstrates privately in his own home, this is not technically a demonstra-tion but merely "acting silly," or "behaving like an ass."

A fine example of a demonstration was The Boston Tea Party, where   12
outraged Americans disguised as Indians dumped British tea into the har-bor. Later, Indians disguised as outraged Americans dumped actual British

into the harbor. Following that, the British disguised as tea, dumped each other into the harbor. Finally, German mercenaries clad only in costumes from "The Trojan Women" leapt into the harbor for no apparent reason.

When demonstrating, it is good to carry a placard stating one's position. Some suggested positions are: (1) lower taxes, (2) raise taxes, and (3) stop grinning at Persians.   13

Miscellaneous methods of civil disobedience: 14

Standing in front of City Hall and chanting the word "pudding" until one's demands are met.   15

Tying up traffic by leading a flock of sheep into the shopping area.   16

Phoning members of "the establishment" and singing "Bess, You Is My Woman, Now" into the phone.   17

Dressing as a policeman and then skipping.   18

Pretending to be an artichoke but punching people as they pass.   19

Questions about the Reading

1. What does Allen say are the requirements for carrying on a revolution?
2. At the end of paragraph 4, Allen says, "It should be noted that the oppressors never revolt and attempt to become the oppressed as that would entail a change of underwear." What does Allen actually mean by "a change of underwear"?
3. What does Allen tell us in paragraph 5 about the cycle of revolutions?

Questions about the Writer's Strategies

1. What is the dominant *mode of development* in the essay? (See Glossary for *mode of development*.)
2. Allen discusses revolution in paragraphs 1 through 5, then turns to methods of civil disobedience. What relation is there between revolution and civil disobedience? Does Allen identify the relation? Is his handling of the shift from revolution to civil disobedience a characteristic of his writing style?
3. What is the *tone* of the essay? Support your answer by identifying words and statements in the reading. (See Glossary for *tone*.)

Writing Assignments

1. Identify and explain at least three kinds of behavior that a young child might exhibit on the first day of school.
2. Identify and explain at least three acceptable ways you might protest against a government policy with which you disagree.
3. Identify and explain at least three current situations that you feel people should have demonstrations *for* rather than against.

Secrets of Man's Unspoken Language

Desmond Morris

A distinguished scientist offers a classification of the gestures that we experience in our lives and tells us what they mean.

Words to Know

aborigines   natives, earliest known inhabitants of a region
doffed   removed, took off
effigies   likeness or replica of, usually, a person
maligned   disliked, spoke negatively of
relic   souvenir
repertoire   stock, group, or knowledge of
salutation   greeting, acknowledgment

Getting Started

What gestures do you and your friends use to greet or say goodbye to each other?

If a Norwegian, a Korean and a Masai were suddenly marooned 1 together on a desert island, communication would still be possible: they could easily convey their basic moods and intentions to one another without words, because all humanity shares a large repertoire of common visual signals. The true origin of many of these gestures is no longer known. But students of human behavior can trace certain actions that we take for granted today. Most are centuries old and steeped in history.

The nod. The vertical head nod, always a yes sign, occurs almost every- 2 where in the world. Remote tribes, from the Australian aborigines to the natives of Tierra del Fuego, were found to be nodding for yes when first encountered by white men. It has even been recorded in people born deaf and blind. This strongly suggests that affirmative nodding may be an inborn action for the human species—a pattern programmed by our genes. Essentially, it is the beginning of a bow—a way of lowering the body to show submission.

The head shake. This, too, is virtually global in range and is always 3 a negative sign. Like many important gestures, it is thought to be a relic from our personal past—from our early infancy when we were nursed at the breast or the bottle. The baby who is not hungry rejects the breast by turning the head sharply to the side. From this beginning, it is argued, has come our adult sign for negation. When a parent warns a child not to do something by wagging a forefinger, he is using the finger in imitation of the shaken head—often adding speed and vigor to the signal.

Crossing the fingers. When we say, "Keep your fingers crossed," 4 we are, historically speaking, requesting an act of Christian worship. Crossing oneself—making the sign of the cross by moving the arm downward and then sideways in front of the body—is an ancient protective device of the Christian Church. In earlier times, crossing the second finger tightly over the first was the secret version of this, and was done with the hand carefully hidden from view. But lacking any obvious religious character, the action easily slid into everyday use, even by non-Christians, as a casual wish for good fortune. Although still done secretly to protect oneself from the consequences of lying, as a "good luck" sign it has now come out into the open.

Thumbing the nose. The origin of this gesture—one of the most com- 5 mon and widespread insults in the world—is uncertain. It is usually thought to represent the hostile, erect comb of a fighting cock. (Animal signs are a favorite form of insult; the mocking, hands-to-ears flapping action popular among children, for example, mimics the long ears of the much-maligned donkey.) But the "cockscomb" sign has also been explained as a deformed salute, an imitation of grotesque, long-nosed effigies, or the mock firing of a catapult.

The OK sign. When an American wants to signal that something is 6 OK, fine, perfect, he raises his hand and makes a circle with his thumb and forefinger. This sign derives from a gesture people all over the world make unconsciously when speaking about some fine point. To say that something is precise or exact, we go through the motions of holding something very small between the tips of our thumb and forefinger, which then automatically form a ring. In America this unconscious movement became a deliberate signal meaning "perfect." But be careful with this one: in other countries the circle sign can mean something quite different. In Japan, it means money (because coins are circular); in France it means "nothing" or "worthless" (the circle meaning zero); in Malta, Sardinia and Greece it is an obscene insult.

Clasped hands raised above the head. This traditional posture 7 adopted by boxers and wrestlers after winning a fight is one of the many "triumph displays" that grow out of the surge of feeling following a victory. In nearly all triumphant moments, the victor expresses his sudden increase in status by raising his height in some way. Young children are likely to jump up and down excitedly. Among adults, the display differs from context to context, but there is often a raising of the arms high above the head.

Triumphant arm-raising may be amplified by raising the victorious 8
individual on the shoulders of his supporters, or parading him on top of
some kind of vehicle. Without realizing it, the modern sports or political
hero who parades through the streets of his hometown in an open car is
recreating the ancient Roman Triumph, in which a conquering general
entered Rome at the head of his army in a four-horse chariot decorated
with laurel, a golden crown held above his head by a slave, and his face
reddened with vermilion to simulate the blood of sacrificial victims.

The salute began as an act of token submission: removing the hat as 9
part of a formal bow. In earlier centuries the bow was so deep that the
doffed hat almost touched the floor. This was abbreviated into the modern military salute in which the hand is brought smartly up to touch the
temple. The same gesture survives as a friendly greeting: casually touching the brim of the hat, or the temple, with the fingers.

Thumbs up, thumbs down. When a Roman gladiator was defeated in 10
combat in the arena, he might be spared, or killed on the spot by his victor;
the spectators could influence the decision by the position of their thumbs.
The gesture for death was thrusting the thumb downward—apparently an
imitation of thrusting the sword into the victim. It is popularly believed
that the life sign was thumbs up, but this appears to be a misinterpreta-
tion. The phrase used in ancient writings, *pollice compresso*, literally means
"thumbs compressed"; the spectators held out their hands with the thumbs
hidden inside their closed fingers, meaning do *not* make the sword thrust.

The modern thumbs-up sign meaning "OK, fine, good," like the 11
V-for-Victory sign made famous by Sir Winston Churchill, was spread
across much of the world by the British during World War II. Many Ital-
ians refer to it as the "English OK" signal. So a popular gesture which
started out as a mistranslation from the literature of ancient Rome is now
"returning" to the city from which it never really came.

Tapping the temple. Many people understand this as a sign for stu- 12
pidity. To make the meaning more precise, you might instead twist your
forefinger against your temple, indicating "a screw loose," or rotate your
forefinger close to your temple, signaling that the brain is going round
and round, but even these actions would be confusing to some people.
In Saudi Arabia, for example, stupidity can be signaled by touching the
lower eyelid with the tip of the forefinger. Other local stupidity gestures
include tapping the elbow of the raised forearm, flapping the hand up
and down in front of half-closed eyes, rotating a raised hand or laying
one forefinger flat across the forehead.

The salutation. People seem almost incapable of beginning or ending 13
any kind of encounter without some type of salutation. Man appears to
have needed such "salutation displays" for many thousands of years.
Early man established a major division of labor, with the male hunters

leaving the group at specific times, then returning to home base with the kill. The importance of success or failure on the hunt meant that these were vital moments in the life of the primeval tribe, so elaborate rituals of greeting and farewell were developed.

The main moment of greeting was—and is—when actual body con- 14 tact is made; at full intensity this consists of a total embrace, with much hugging, patting, squeezing, kissing, laughing and even weeping. But before this, comes the moment when friends recognize each other from a distance. Apparently some form of arm action at the moment of first sighting is global for mankind. Clearly, the vertical, up-and-down wave of the hand is a way of patting the friend's body at a distance in anticipation of the embrace to come.

The handshake, too, is a salutation display. Different cultures have 15 formalized, in different ways, the body contact which comes at the key moment of greeting.

Some emphasize head-to-head contact as in nose-rubbing or stylized 16 mutual cheek-kissing. Westerners use a whole range of body contacts of decreasing strength, right down to the formal handshake. But they are all variations on a basic theme—the body embrace. This is the fundamental human-contact action, the one we all know as babies, infants and growing children, and to which we return whenever the rules permit and we wish to demonstrate feelings of attachment for another individual.

Questions about the Reading

1. How can people who speak different languages communicate with one another?
2. What are the global signals for "yes" and "no"?
3. What is the historical meaning of crossed fingers?
4. What does the crossed fingers signal usually mean now?
5. Why should you be careful about using the OK sign in other countries?

Questions about the Writer's Strategies

1. What is the thesis of the essay? State it in your own words.
2. Besides classification, what other modes of development does the writer use?
3. What are the divisions of salutations the writer provides in paragraphs 13 through 16?
4. How would you change paragraphs 13 through 16 to clarify the salutation divisions?

Writing Assignments

1. *Working Together* Join with some classmates to write an essay in which you classify any special or unique gestures each person uses.
2. Write an essay in which you classify the gestures that are used by the police before and after a large sports event.

3. Research nonverbal communication on the Internet. Classify some examples of gestures from various countries and describe how they differ from your own interpretation of the same gestures.

Start Spreading the News: Seven Things You Should Know Before Moving to New York City

Courtney Reimer

If you think you might want to live in New York, Courtney Reimer tells you what you need to know about that city before moving there.

Words to Know

accoutrements   equipment, trappings
ostensibly   apparently, evidently
permeates   fills, penetrates
perspective   view
plethora   abundance
proximity   closeness
quixotic   impractical, idealistic
unequivocally   without question, definitely

Getting Started

What are the characteristics of the town you live in?

Like many stereotypes, New York City's are grounded for the most 1
part in truth: it is dirty, smelly, loud, expensive, a hassle. And those are
just the top five. Plus, thanks to a mayor who says he desires to clear our
environment of secondhand smoke, loud nightclubs, and ringing cell
phones (but immediately upon entering office slashed a finally opera-
tional recycling program), it's only getting worse. Yet the city is crowded
with eight million people who, at least ostensibly, want to live here. It's
the most populous city in the union and, to judge by the steady stream
of fresh-faced wannabe New Yorkers arriving here every day at least,
it's only going to get more crowded. Optimists choose to look the other
way and follow the advice of all the Pollyannas who've made this place
some kind of promised land. Thanks to them, New York City has become
known as the place to make it.

Then again, who am I to talk? I too made a run for the Big City, a 2
head full of quixotic dreams fueling my flight. Abetted by Hollywood
and countless pop songs (yes, Sinatra), I jumped the oh-so-secure ship of
Seattle, shedding the accoutrements of early adulthood (a fuel-efficient

sedan; a residence with a parking space; a job with a private office bigger than most New York apartments) and headed East.

Now, with a few years' perspective on the whole thing, I can finally 3 admit it: New York is definitely dirty, smelly, loud, expensive, and a huge hassle. Had I known a few other things prior to moving here, though, I might have been able to duck the blows New York has since dealt me. At least I might have been ready to punch back.

1. **The little things are much bigger in New York.** And I'm not just 4 talking laundry, with which I had a bit of an unfair advantage in Seattle. (Mom was just a fifteen-minute drive away, a drive I took weekly.) But yes, clean garments can be a challenge here. I have rarely found a New York City apartment building that contains a laundry room, and owning an in-apartment washer and dryer is a pipe dream you'd best disabuse yourself of before coming to town.

Then there's getting from your home to your place of work and back 5 again each day. Sure, once you find your groove, the New York commute can be accomplished in your sleep. But take one look at the snake-like snarl of subway lines on any New York map and tell me you're not a little bit daunted. And don't even think about making a phone call en route, since you will be doing most of your commuting on the subway. (Trust me—six million people daily can't be wrong.) Until they find a way to get a cellular signal underground, subways will remain chatter free—which is nice if you want to read, daydream, or nap. But if you've been owing your mom a phone call for two weeks, it can be more than a little frustrating.

And finally: shoes. Your feet are going to hurt here. You may never 6 have considered yourself a "sensible shoe" type, but pain can be a strong motivator. Before you know it, you will be trotting around Manhattan in a pair of Rockports. Trust me on this, too.

2. **Feeding yourself is all too easy here, yet all too difficult.** Whereas 7 in your old hometown eating out was a luxury, a special occasion, in Gotham the opposite becomes true—and all as the result of a lack of acceptable grocery options. Not only are the corner stores known as bodegas tiny, dirty, and poorly stocked; these sorry substitutes for supermarkets keep wildly inconsistent hours. Really, they should amend "The City That Never Sleeps" with the asterisk disclaimer: "except grocery stores." As a result, it's next to impossible to obtain the ingredients needed for a supposedly simple home-cooked meal.

So. Before you pack your things for a move to the Big Apple (ironic 8 that the city should be nicknamed for produce, but I digress), take a long, last look at that clean, well-lighted, stocked-to-the-ceiling-with-multiple-selections-of-whatever-your-tummy-desires, open 24-7 grocery store. You're going to miss it more than you know.

3. **"Love the One You're With" could be a New Yorker's theme song.** 9 Considering the sheer number of people who live here, New York is probably one of the harder places on the planet to make and maintain fulfilling relationships, both platonic and otherwise. In New York, the plethora of options—and the many neighborhoods one could feasibly lay one's head at the end of the night—actually limits the number of acquaintanceships available. In short, it's the old rule of being paralyzed by too many choices. Because of the excessive planning, commuting, and plain old waiting that a New York social life requires, you have to really, really want to hang out with someone here in order to do it.

On the other hand, that same vastness can foster all kinds of unsa- 10 vory one-night-stand behavior. That new, ahem, friend you drunkenly brought home last night? The one whose name you can't for the life of you remember? Not to worry. The chances of running into him or her again are slim to zero.

4. **Chicago is the Windy City, Seattle is rainy, Alaska is downright** 11 **cold. So what?** It's nothing compared to the meteorological beating we New Yorkers take on a regular basis. It's dumbfounding to me that eight million people continue to subject themselves to months on end of subfreezing temperatures, followed by endless weeks of heat and humidity so extreme that it actually feels like you're living in a giant bowl of soup. At least in most other cities you can hop into your personal climate-controlled vehicle and protect yourself from the elements—even propel yourself away from them, should you so desire. In New York, the subway stations are neither heated nor air-conditioned. I seriously wouldn't be surprised to learn that people routinely freeze to death while waiting for the N or R train in the winter or expire from the heat on the A train platform in the summer. Sure, you could hail a cab—assuming there's one around when you need it—but that would tap your drink budget. Speaking of which . . .

5. **I'm not as think as you drunk I am.** The food, the theater, the jobs, the 12 music. While all of that's up for debate, one thing that unequivocally is not better in New York, at least for us imbibers, is the drinks. In a word, they are weak. Maybe bartenders in other cities have spoiled me with their generosity, but unless you specifically order a double here, don't expect the person behind the bar to pour liberally. A near and dear Seattle friend nearly socked the bartender the first time she ordered a Jack Daniels and Coke that was, well, heavier on the "and Coke" than she was

used to. I'm guessing the pervading logic among New York bartenders is that if they pour a less-strong drink, they'll make more tips from the more drinks bought to compensate for their miserly ways. Sorry Charlie. At six dollars a pop (on the low end) and twelve dollars a pop (at the high end), we want to be able at least to taste the alcohol in our drinks. Otherwise, why not just stay home and drink your own damn liquor? It's probably not such a good idea to be drunkenly stumbling around the big, bad city of New York, anyway.

6. **New Yorkers aren't the masters of wit and wisdom you may have** 13 **thought.** Perhaps I've seen one too many Woody Allen movies, but one of the many stereotypes about Manhattan I brought with me from Seattle is that people are smarter here. Perhaps you too had the impression that every New Yorker is an OED-toting, Ivy League-educated, world-traveled smarty-pants with ten bulging bookshelves. Clearly I had not accounted for the proximity of New Jersey.

Holy moly, are there a lot of idiots in this joint. Or is it just the num- 14 ber of people who sound dumb when they talk? (No, I'm not going to "cawl.") No wonder longtime New York residents such as Madonna have adopted British accents—years of immersion in the local way of speaking would make anyone run for the nearest diction consultant. For that matter, my nonscientific survey shows that for every nine subway riders reading the Rupert Murdoch–owned tabloid, just one is reading *The New York Times.* Oh wait, I forgot, it is more important to know what hotel heiress was spotted with Jimmy Fallon than how many bodies are piling up in the Middle East and why.

7. **It's actually not rude, it's efficient. Really!** New Yorkers are much 15 easier to be around than a lot of my former neighbors in Seattle. Face it: the person behind the counter at the deli where you buy your coffee doesn't care how your day is, and you don't care how hers is. Sound rude? No, what's rude is wasting a person's time with chitchat. Believe me, the people in line behind you right now are nodding in agreement.

Surprisingly, the people here are much more approachable than the 16 residents of most cities. A sort of "we're in this together" mentality per-meates New York, and thus it's not deemed brash to strike up a casual conversation with the person next to you on the subway platform about, I don't know . . . what the hell is taking the train so goddamn long. Were you to do the same thing in many other cities, you'd be met with silence and an attitude. And not simply because there's no subway in most of those cities.

Having said all this—and I've only scratched the surface—New 17 York is the best thing that ever happened to me. All of the above notwithstanding, the city has been good to me. Like a very loving but strict parent, New York builds character. It's also a perfect de facto finishing school for those of us who've been spoiled by the everybody's-a-star circumstances many years in one's hometown can breed.

The other day, sitting in a pizza place, I looked up and saw a poster, 18 dated 1977, with a quote that resonates particularly well with what I've been trying to convey over the past several pages:

"You have to be crazy to live in New York, but you'd be nuts to live 19 anywhere else."

Questions about the Reading

1. What are the seven things the writer thinks you should know before moving to New York City?
2. Where did the writer live before she moved to New York?
3. How does the writer describe the weather in New York?
4. Why is it "next to impossible" in New York to get the ingredients to cook a meal at home?

Questions about the Writer's Strategies

1. What is the thesis of the essay? State it in your own words.
2. What is the point of view (person, time, tone) of the essay?
3. What is the simile the writer uses to describe the map of the New York subway lines?

Writing Assignments

1. Write a classification/division essay in which you classify the advantages and disadvantages of your hometown.
2. *Working Together* Join with some classmates to write a classification/division essay about your college.

6

Comparison and Contrast

→←$^{diff.}$
↓

To COMPARE IS to show how items are alike. To **contrast** is to show how items are different. Thus, comparison and contrast involve pointing out the similarities or differences between two (or more) items. Birdwatchers, for instance, may compare bird A with bird B according to their common color but contrast them according to their difference in size.

In the preceding chapter, you learned about the **modes of development** called **classification** and **division**. The comparison and contrast modes are related to those modes. In deciding what to compare or contrast, you will want to make sure that the items share points in common. Thus, the items are usually the same kind or **class** of thing, and in comparing or contrasting them, you essentially establish at least two categories, showing the differences or similarities between them. For instance, you can compare two passenger cars—a Ford and a Chevrolet—with more precision than you can a Ford and a helicopter. Fords are compared with Chevrolets because they have many features in common—features that you can pinpoint. Similarly, you can usually compare two paintings more precisely than you can a novel and a painting.

Once you have selected the closely related items, you will want to explain as clearly as possible the ways in which the items are alike or different. In any one piece of writing, you may want to use comparison only—or contrast only. Or you may decide to use both in the same essay. These three possibilities are illustrated in the following paragraphs. Notice, in each case, how the writer compares or contrasts *specific* points.

Comparison

A Buick and a Cadillac, both built by General Motors, are alike in many ways. A Buick, which measures over 200 inches in length and weighs

141

over 3,000 pounds, is large and holds the road well. A Cadillac is similar in length and weight. Like a Buick, a Cadillac gets relatively low gas mileage compared with smaller economy cars made by the same manufacturer. The Buick provides an unusually comfortable ride, especially on cross-country trips on the highway, as does a Cadillac. And both cars enjoy a certain status as a luxury automobile.

Contrast

The twins are as different as two people can be. Sally, who is always hoping someone will have a party, has black hair, brown eyes, and an outgoing personality. She wants to be an actress or a popular singer. Susan, more serious and studious, has blonde hair, blue eyes, and a somewhat shy manner. Since she has done well in all her classes in graphic arts and math, she plans to become an architect or an engineer.

Mixed Comparison and Contrast

Most Americans would say it is not really possible to establish an ideal society. But time after time, a small dedicated group of people will drop out of the mainstream of American society to try, once more, to live according to the group's concept of an ideal society. Most of these groups have believed in holding their property in common. Most have used the word *family* to refer to all members of the group. Many of these groups, however, have differed widely in their attitudes toward sex and marriage.

Notice that all three of these paragraphs supply information but do not try to claim that one of the compared items is better or worse than the other. Notice, too, the **objective** tone of these paragraphs. However, writers also use comparison and contrast to support their opinions about subjects or to show how a certain thing or idea is superior to others in the same class. The writer of the paragraph about twins, for instance, could have used her information to support an opinion, as in the following revised paragraph.

The twins are as different as two people can be. Sally, who has black hair, brown eyes, and an outgoing, flighty personality, is always hoping someone will have a party. She fritters away her time and money shopping for the latest clothes, and she dreams of being an actress or a popular singer. But until she settles down and applies her energy to something useful, she will probably not be successful at anything. Susan, more serious and studious, has blonde hair, blue eyes, and a somewhat shy manner. Since she works hard and makes good use of her time, she has done well in all her classes in graphic arts and math. She plans to become an architect or an engineer and will no doubt be a good one.

Opinion

Opinion

As you plan a comparison-and-contrast composition, it is very useful to **brainstorm** for items of comparison. That is, as described in chapter 1, think about the subjects of your composition and briefly jot down

whatever comes to mind about them. You can then use your list in deciding on the content of your paragraph.

Organization

You should organize your comparison (or contrast) by whichever method
suits your material best. One simple method is to explain a characteristic
of item A, perhaps its cost, and then immediately compare it with the
same characteristic of item B—and then go on to compare the two items
point by point. For example, in contrasting two chocolate cakes, you may
first want to say cake A is more expensive to prepare than cake B. Second,
you may say that cake A, which requires more steps and ingredients,
takes more time to make than cake B. Third, cake A is richer—almost too
rich—and sweeter than cake B. You may conclude by saying that you
recommend cake B. In this manner, you move back and forth, mentioning
the specific differences between cake A and cake B in an orderly manner.

   When the writer compares (or contrasts) two objects item by item, it is
called the **alternating** or **point-by-point method**. The following diagram
shows how this method works in the paragraph comparing Buicks and
Cadillacs.

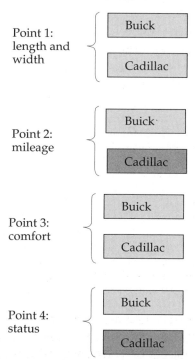

Alternating (or point-by-point) method
Topic sentence: "A Buick and a Cadillac . . . are alike in many ways."

Point 1:
length and
width
- Buick
- Cadillac

Point 2:
mileage
- Buick
- Cadillac

Point 3:
comfort
- Buick
- Cadillac

Point 4:
status
- Buick
- Cadillac

If the writer prefers a second type of organization, the **block method**, he or she explains all the characteristics of the first item together in a block and then explains all the characteristics of the second item in the same order in a corresponding block. The paragraphs contrasting the twins Sally and Susan (page 142) are organized in this block method.

Block method
Topic sentence: "The twins are as different as two people can be."

Block 1:

> Sally:
>
> point 1: appearance
> point 2: personality
> point 3: career

Block 2:

> Susan:
>
> point 1: appearance
> point 2: personality
> point 3: career

A third method, the **mixed method**, is useful when the writer wants to both compare and contrast in the same paragraph. All the similarities of the two items may first be explained and then all the differences. (Or, if the writer chooses, the differences may be explained first and then the similarities.) The following diagram shows this third method of organization, which was used in the paragraph on ideal societies (page 142).

Mixed comparison-and-contrast method
Topic sentence: "people . . . drop out of the mainstream of American society . . . to live according to the group's concept of an ideal society."

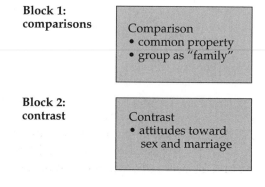

Block 1: comparisons

> Comparison
> • common property
> • group as "family"

Block 2: contrast

> Contrast
> • attitudes toward
>   sex and marriage

You will want to use these same three methods—alternating, block, and mixed—in writing longer essays. In the following essay, the writer uses the alternating method of organization to contrast types of people.

There are only two types of people in the world, Type A and Type Z. It isn't hard to tell which type you are. How long before the plane leaves do you arrive at the airport?

Point 1: catching a plane

Early plane-catchers, Type A, pack their bags at least a day in advance, and they pack neatly. If they're booked on a flight that leaves at four in the afternoon, they get up at 5:30 that morning. If they haven't left the house by noon, they're worried about missing the plane.

Late plane-catchers, Type Z, pack hastily at the last minute and arrive at the airport too late to buy a newspaper.

Point 2: reading a book

What do you do with a new book? Type A reads more carefully and finishes every book, even though it isn't any good.

Type Z skims through a lot of books and is more apt to write in the margins with a pencil.

Point 3: eating breakfast

Type A eats a good breakfast; Type Z grabs a cup of coffee.

Point 4: turning off lights

Type As turn off the lights when leaving a room and lock the doors when leaving a house. They go back to make sure they've locked it, and they worry later about whether they left the iron on or not. They didn't.

Type Zs leave the lights burning and if they lock the door at all when they leave the house, they're apt to have forgotten their keys.

Point 5: seeing the dentist

Type A sees the dentist twice a year, has an annual physical checkup and thinks he may have something.

Type Z has been meaning to see a doctor.

Point 6: using toothpaste

Type A squeezes a tube of toothpaste from the bottom, rolls it very carefully as he uses it and puts the top back on every time.

Type Z squeezes the tube from the middle, and he's lost the cap under the radiator.

Point 7: other characteristics

Type Zs are more apt to have some Type A characteristics than Type As are apt to have any Type Z characteristics.

Point 8: marriage

Type As always marry Type Zs.

Type Zs always marry Type As.

Andy Rooney,
"Types"

The comparison-and-contrast mode of development gives Rooney a framework for making use of **irony**. Irony is a device used by writers to imply something different or the opposite from what is actually stated. Here, Rooney uses irony for its humorous effect, with the ultimate irony being that Type As and Type Zs always marry their opposites.

Comparison and contrast, like classification and division, is a useful mode of development for writing on the academic subjects you will study in college courses. You will encounter it in textbooks, with comparison indicated by such transitional words as *similarly* and *by comparison* and contrast by *however, on the other hand,* and *on the contrary.* If you become comfortable with this mode, it will come in handy in your writing for other courses. Be alert, for example, to essay assignments and exam questions that begin "Compare and contrast . . ."

In the readings that follow, you will find the alternating, block, and mixed methods of comparison-and-contrast development. You will also see the variety of ideas that writers express through comparison and contrast.

Happy Returns

Sarah Bernard

Do you return gifts that you have received but don't like, or do you keep them for fear you will offend the giver? Here Sarah Bernard compares opinions about whether it is ethical to return a gift.

Words to Know

Chuck Schumer   United States senator from New York
faction   group of people with common interests or belief
faux-**fawning**   false flattery or attitude
ideological   idea, opinion
psychological   mental

Getting Started

What is the best gift that you ever received? What is the worst?

But is returning ethical? This is a question that splits giftees into ideological camps. One group holds that, no matter how awful the gift, you should never, ever take it back. You can tell my husband belongs to this faction just by looking at him: His shirts are wrinkled because he wedges them into a closet packed with years of accumulated gift disasters—some of which, I admit, I've given him. (Among my "favorites": a slopey-shouldered Sherlock Holmes–style overcoat and a professional-grade shoe-shine kit.) These people face twin psychological hurdles. They find the very act of approaching the counter, unwanted gift in hand, shameful. (Which is just what stores want, of course—even Chuck Schumer has found time to campaign against repeat-returner blacklists.) And they think that returning the gift is an insult. The other group (of which I am a member) believes in—even encourages—returns. It's our conviction that the point is to get something the recipient likes, so we make it clear adjustments won't offend. In fact, a *faux*-fawning response to gifts you secretly loathe makes a mockery of the giver. How does he learn your taste if you keep sending the wrong message?

Questions about the Reading

1. Why do some people believe a gift should never be taken back?
2. What does the writer's husband think about returning gifts?

3. What are the examples that the writer uses to illustrate her husband's opinion about returning gifts?
4. What is the writer's opinion about returning gifts? Do you think she would be offended if friends returned gifts she had given them?

Questions about the Writer's Strategies

1. What is the main idea of the paragraph? State it in your own words.
2. What is the tone of the paragraph?
3. Is the point of view (person) consistent throughout the paragraph? If not, are any changes justified?
4. What technique does the writer use in the final sentence of the paragraph?

Writing Assignments

1. What is the best or a very special birthday gift you have received? Write a paragraph is which you compare, contrast, or compare and contrast that gift with others and explain why you consider it the best or most special one.
2. Write a paragraph in which you compare, contrast, or compare and contrast the way your family members or friends have responded to gifts you have given them.

Good Girl, Bad Girl

Anna Quindlen

Understanding why two people become friends is sometimes difficult. In this paragraph, essayist Anna Quindlen provides a candid assessment of an unbalanced friendship from her days at a boarding school for girls.

Words to Know

dialectical   having to do with two opposite or contradictory forces
naïve   innocent
refectory   cafeteria, dining hall

Getting Started

What is it that attracts two friends to each other?

She was my best friend, and hard as it may have been to figure by the looks of us, she was the good girl, I the bad. I suppose everyone has at least one friendship like this in their lives. We were dialectical, she the thesis, I the antithesis. She was direct, trustworthy, kind, and naïve; I was manipulative, selfish, and clever. She laughed at all my jokes, took part in all my schemes, told everyone that I was the smartest and the funniest and the best. Like a B movie of boarding school life, we stole peanut butter from the refectory, short-sheeted beds, called drugstores and asked them if they had Prince Albert in a can. Whenever I hear a mother say, "If so-and-so told you to jump off the Brooklyn Bridge, would you do it?" I think of her. On my order, she would have jumped.

Questions about the Reading

1. How do you imagine the author and her friend looked? Reread the first sentence before you describe the two girls.
2. What does the writer mean when she says that her exploits were "like a B movie of boarding school life"?
3. Does the writer believe she and her friend had a healthy relationship? Why or why not?

Questions about the Writer's Strategies

1. Is the writer's mode of development comparison, contrast, or a combination of the two?

2. What other mode of development does the writer use?
3. What words does the writer use to describe herself? What words does she use to describe how her friend thought of her?
4. What simile does the author use to describe the friendship?

Writing Assignments

1. Write a narrative paragraph that compares your personality with that of one of your closest friends.
2. Write a paragraph in which you compare and contrast a childhood friendship with a current friendship.
3. In a paragraph, compare and contrast a relationship between friends with one between brothers and sisters. Use examples from your own experience to illustrate similarities and differences.

Dogs and Cats

Konrad Lorenz

> *Konrad Lorenz tells us what our dogs and cats have in common and how they differ.*

Words to Know

carnivores   meat-eating animals
domesticated   tamed
servitude   in service or bondage to another person
sphere   range
uncompromising   firm, unchanging

Getting Started

What pets do you have or have you had in the past?

Only two animals have entered the human household otherwise than as prisoners and become domesticated by other means than those of enforced servitude: the dog and the cat. Two things they have in common, namely, that both belong to the order of carnivores and both serve man in their capacity of hunters. In all other characteristics, above all in the manner of their association with man, they are as different as the night from the day. There is no domestic animal that has so radically altered its whole way of living, indeed its whole sphere of interests, that has become domestic in so true a sense as the dog; and there is no animal that, in the course of its centuries-old association with man, has altered so little as the cat. There is some truth in the assertion that the cat, with the exception of a few luxury breeds, such as Angoras, Persians and Siamese, is no domestic animal but a completely wild being. Maintaining its full independence it has taken up its abode in the houses and outhouses of man, for the simple reason that there are more mice there than elsewhere. The whole charm of the dog lies in the depth of the friendship and the strength of the spiritual ties with which he has bound himself to man, but the appeal of the cat lies in the very fact that she has formed no close bond with him, that she has the uncompromising independence of a tiger or a leopard while she is hunting in his stables and barns, that she still remains mysterious and remote when she is rubbing herself gently against the legs of her mistress or purring contentedly in front of the fire.

Questions about the Reading

1. What do a dog and a cat have in common?
2. How do a dog and a cat differ?
3. Why does a cat want to live in houses and outhouses?
4. How do a dog and a cat differ in their association with their owners?

Questions about the Writer's Strategies

1. What method of comparison and contrast does the writer use?
2. Could the paragraph be made into more than one paragraph? If so, how?
3. What is the main idea of the paragraph? Is it stated or implied? If stated, identify the sentences. If implied, state it in your own words.

Writing Assignments

1. Write a paragraph in which you compare and contrast the behavior of your pets or those of your friends. Identify the method or methods you used.

2. Visit a zoo and watch two different animals. Write a paragraph in which you explain the behaviors they have in common and those in which they differ. Identify the method or methods you used.
3. Explore animal diversity on the Internet. Choose some examples and compare and contrast two of your favorites.

Yin and Yang

Mary Paumier Jones

The yin-yang symbol comes from ancient Chinese cosmology. It represents both the dark and the light, or shaded and sunlit, sides of a mountain. The "yin" represents the female or shaded aspects of the symbol such as the earth, darkness, and passivity. The "yang" represents the male aspects of the symbol, such as light, sun, and activity. In this paragraph from her essay "The Opposite of Saffron," Mary Paumier Jones explains that the yin and yang movements in T'ai Chi, a Chinese form of exercise, form a perfect balance. (Adapted from **http://www2.cybernex.net/~jefkirsh/symbol.html.***)*

Words to Know

inscrutably   obscurely, mysteriously
intercourse   communication
simultaneous   at the same time

Getting Started

How are walking and running alike? How are they different?

In T'ai Chi class Dr. Young talked about yin and yang. In the beginning square form, each movement is followed by a pause: the movement is yin, the pause yang. To my Western ears this smacks of sexism; the masculine principle acting, the feminine doing nothing. But I eventually begin to learn the pause is not nothing. Given its proper weight, gravity, and time, the pause does its work, its stretch, its subtle modification of the quality of the move before and the one to come. Later in the round form, the movement is continuous. Yin and yang, though still opposite, are inscrutably simultaneous, engaged in an ancient abstract intercourse.

Questions about the Reading

1. What is yin and what is yang in the beginning square form of T'ai Chi?
2. Why does the writer think that the notion of yin and yang "smacks of sexism"?

3. What is the purpose of the pause?
4. How does the round form of T'ai Chi differ from the square?

Questions about the Writer's Strategies

1. What is the main idea of the paragraph? Is it stated or implied?
2. What is the point of view (person, time, tone) of the paragraph?
3. Is the point of view consistent throughout the paragraph? If not, where and in what way does it change?
4. If the point of view in the paragraph changes, is the change acceptable? Why or why not?

Writing Assignments

1. Write an essay about two sports you have played, explaining how the sports are alike and how they are different.
2. Write an essay about two subjects you have studied in school and explain how they are alike and how they are different.

Neat People vs. Sloppy People

Suzanne Britt

In this essay from her book Show and Tell, Suzanne Britt explains the differences between neat and sloppy people, claiming—surprisingly—that neat people are lazier and meaner than sloppy people.

Words to Know

cavalier easygoing, offhand
meticulously excessively
métier occupation
rectitude character, principles

Getting Started

How would you characterize neat people and sloppy people?

I've finally figured out the difference between neat people and sloppy   1
people. The distinction is, as always, moral. Neat people are lazier and
meaner than sloppy people.

Sloppy people, you see, are not really sloppy. Their sloppiness is merely   2
the unfortunate consequence of their extreme moral rectitude. Sloppy
people carry in their mind's eye a heavenly vision, a precise plan, that is so
stupendous, so perfect, it can't be achieved in this world or the next.

Sloppy people live in Never-Never Land. Someday is their métier.   3
Someday they are planning to alphabetize all their books and set up
home catalogs. Someday they will go through their wardrobes and
mark certain items for tentative mending and certain items for passing
on to relatives of similar shape and size. Someday sloppy people will
make family scrapbooks into which they will put newspaper clippings,
postcards, locks of hair, and the dried corsage from their senior prom.
Someday they will file everything on the surface on their desk, including
the cash receipts from coffee purchases at the snack shop. Someday they
will sit down and read all the back issues of *The New Yorker*.

For all these noble reasons and more, sloppy people never get neat.   4
They aim too high and wide. They save everything, planning someday
to file, order, and straighten out the world. But while these ambitious
plans take clearer and clearer shape in their heads, the books spill from
the shelves onto the floor, the clothes pile up in the hamper and closet,
the family mementos accumulate in every drawer, the surface of the desk

is buried under mounds of paper, and the unread magazines threaten to reach the ceiling.

Sloppy people can't bear to part with anything. They give loving atten- 5 tion to every detail. When sloppy people say they're going to tackle the surface of the desk, they really mean it. Not a paper will go unturned; not a rubber band will go unboxed. Four hours or two weeks into the excava- tion, the desk looks exactly the same, primarily because the sloppy per- son is meticulously creating new piles of papers with new headings and scrupulously stopping to read all the old book catalogs before he throws them away. A neat person would just bulldoze the desk.

Neat people are bums and clods at heart. They have cavalier attitudes 6 toward possessions, including family heirlooms. Everything is just another dust-catcher to them. If anything collects dust, it's got to go and that's that. Neat people will toy with the idea of throwing the children out of the house just to cut down on the clutter.

Neat people don't care about process. They like results. What they 7 want to do is get the whole thing over with so they can sit down and watch the rasslin' on TV. Neat people operate on two unvarying prin- ciples: Never handle any item twice, and throw everything away.

The only thing messy in a neat person's house is the trash can. The 8 minute something comes to a neat person's hand, he will look at it, try to decide if it has immediate use and, finding none, throw it in the trash.

Neat people are especially vicious with mail. They never go through 9 their mail unless they are standing directly over a trash can. If the trash can is beside the mailbox, even better. All ads, catalogs, pleas for charita- ble contributions, church bulletins and money-saving coupons go straight into the trash can without being opened. All letters from home, postcards from Europe, bills and paychecks are opened, immediately responded to, then dropped in the trash can. Neat people keep their receipts only for tax purposes. That's it. No sentimental salvaging of birthday cards or the last letter a dying relative ever wrote. Into the trash it goes.

Neat people place neatness above everything, even economics. They 10 are incredibly wasteful. Neat people throw away several toys every time they walk through the den. I knew a neat person once who threw away a perfectly good dish drainer because it had mold on it. The drainer was too much trouble to wash. And neat people sell their furniture when they move. They will sell a La-Z-Boy recliner while you are reclining in it.

Neat people are no good to borrow from. Neat people buy everything 11 in expensive little single portions. They get their flour and sugar in two- pound bags. They wouldn't consider clipping a coupon, saving a leftover, reusing plastic non-dairy whipped cream containers or rinsing off tin foil and draping it over the unmoldy dish drainer. You can never borrow a neat person's newspaper to see what's playing at the movies. Neat people have the paper all wadded up and in the trash by 7:05 A.M.

Neat people cut a clean swath through the organic as well as the 12 inorganic world. People, animals, and things are all one to them. They are so insensitive. After they've finished with the pantry, the medicine cabinet, and the attic, they will throw out the red geranium (too many leaves), sell the dog (too many fleas), and send the children off to boarding school (too many scuff marks on the hardwood floors).

Questions about the Reading

1. What is the reason, according to the writer, that people are sloppy?
2. What do sloppy people intend to do with everything they keep?
3. Why do sloppy people never get neat?
4. Why are people neat?
5. How do neat people handle their mail?

Questions about the Writer's Strategies

1. What is the comparison/contrast method used by the writer?
2. What is the topic of each paragraph, beginning with the second?
3. Is each topic stated in a sentence? If so, what are the topic sentences?
4. What is the tone of the essay? Is it consistent throughout?

Writing Assignments

1. Write an essay in which you compare, contrast, or compare and contrast shopping in different grocery stores.
2. *Working Together* Join with some classmates to compare, contrast, or compare and contrast how people in different neighborhoods keep their yards.

Conversational Ballgames

Nancy Masterson Sakamoto

The difference between Western and Japanese conversation styles is like the difference between tennis or volleyball and bowling, according to Nancy Sakamoto, in this essay from her book Polite Fictions. *She is an American married to a Japanese man and is a professor of American Studies at a Japanese university.*

Words to Know

elaboration   further information, additional details
indispensable   necessary, essential
unconsciously   unknowingly

Getting Started

Is there a difference between the way you talk to a friend and the way you talk to a teacher, a stranger, or an older person?

After I was married and had lived in Japan for a while, my Japanese 1 gradually improved to the point where I could take part in simple conversations with my husband and his friends and family. And I began to notice that often, when I joined in, the others would look startled, and the conversational topic would come to a halt. After this happened several times, it became clear to me that I was doing something wrong. But for a long time, I didn't know what it was.

Finally, after listening carefully to many Japanese conversations, I dis- 2 covered what my problem was. Even though I was speaking Japanese, I was handling the conversation in a western way.

Japanese-style conversations develop quite differently from western- 3 style conversations. And the difference isn't only in the languages. I realized that just as I kept trying to hold western-style conversations even when I was speaking Japanese, so my English students kept trying to hold Japanese-style conversations even when they were speaking English. We were unconsciously playing entirely different conversational ballgames.

A western-style conversation between two people is like a game of 4 tennis. If I introduce a topic, a conversational ball, I expect you to hit it back. If you agree with me, I don't expect you simply to agree and do nothing more. I expect you to add something—a reason for agreeing, another example, or an elaboration to carry the idea further. But I don't expect you always to agree. I am just as happy if you question me, or

158

challenge me, or completely disagree with me. Whether you agree or disagree, your response will return the ball to me.

And then it is my turn again. I don't serve a new ball from my original 5 starting line. I hit your ball back again from where it has bounced. I carry your idea further, or answer your questions or objections, or challenge or question you. And so the ball goes back and forth, with each of us doing our best to give it a new twist, an original spin, or a powerful smash.

And the more vigorous the action, the more interesting and exciting 6 the game. Of course, if one of us gets angry, it spoils the conversation, just as it spoils a tennis game. But getting excited is not at all the same as getting angry. After all, we are not trying to hit each other. We are trying to hit the ball. So long as we attack only each other's opinions, and do not attack each other personally, we don't expect anyone to get hurt. A good conversation is supposed to be interesting and exciting.

If there are more than two people in the conversation, then it is like 7 doubles in tennis, or like volleyball. There's no waiting in line. Whoever is nearest and quickest hits the ball, and if you step back, someone else will hit it. No one stops the game to give you a turn. You're responsible for taking your own turn.

But whether it's two players or a group, everyone does his best to keep 8 the ball going, and no one person has the ball for very long.

A Japanese-style conversation, however, is not at all like tennis or vol- 9 leyball. It's like bowling. You wait for your turn. And you always know your place in line. It depends on such things as whether you are older or younger, a close friend or a relative stranger to the previous speaker, in a senior or junior position, and so on.

When your turn comes, you step up to the starting line with your 10 bowling ball, and carefully bowl it. Everyone else stands back and watches politely, murmuring encouragement. Everyone waits until the ball has reached the end of the alley, and watches to see if it knocks down all the pins, or only some of them, or none of them. There is a pause, while everyone registers your score.

Then, after everyone is sure that you have completely finished your 11 turn, the next person in line steps up to the same starting line, with a different ball. He doesn't return your ball, and he does not begin from where your ball stopped. There is no back and forth at all. All the balls run parallel. And there is always a suitable pause between turns. There is no rush, no excitement, no scramble for the ball.

No wonder everyone looked startled when I took part in Japanese 12 conversations. I paid no attention to whose turn it was, and kept snatching the ball halfway down the alley and throwing it back at the bowler. Of course the conversation died. I was playing the wrong game.

This explains why it is almost impossible to get a western-style con- 13
versation or discussion going with English students in Japan. I used to
think that the problem was their lack of English language ability. But I
finally came to realize that the biggest problem is that they, too, are playing the wrong game.

Whenever I serve a volleyball, everyone just stands back and watches 14
it fall, with occasional murmurs of encouragement. No one hits it back.
Everyone waits until I call on someone to take a turn. And when that
person speaks, he doesn't hit my ball back. He serves a new ball. Again,
everyone just watches it fall.

So I call on someone else. This person does not refer to what the previ- 15
ous speaker has said. He also serves a new ball. Nobody seems to have
paid any attention to what anyone else has said. Everyone begins again
from the same starting line, and all the balls run parallel. There is never
any back and forth. Everyone is trying to bowl with a volleyball.

And if I try a simpler conversation, with only two of us, then the other 16
person tries to bowl with my tennis ball. No wonder foreign English
teachers in Japan get discouraged.

Now that you know about the difference in the conversational ball- 17
games, you may think that all your troubles are over. But if you have
been trained all your life to play one game, it is no simple matter to
switch to another, even if you know the rules. Knowing the rules is not
at all the same thing as playing the game.

Even now, during a conversation in Japanese I will notice a startled 18
reaction, and belatedly realize that once again I have rudely interrupted
by instinctively trying to hit back the other person's bowling ball. It is
no easier for me to "just listen" during a conversation, than it is for my
Japanese students to "just relax" when speaking with foreigners. Now I
can truly sympathize with how hard they must find it to try to carry on
a western-style conversation.

If I have not yet learned to do conversational bowling in Japanese, at 19
least I have figured out one thing that puzzled me for a long time. After
his first trip to America, my husband complained that Americans asked
him so many questions and made him talk so much at the dinner table
that he never had a chance to eat. When I asked him why he couldn't talk
and eat at the same time, he said that Japanese do not customarily think
that dinner, especially on fairly formal occasions, is a suitable time for
extended conversation.

Since westerners think that conversation is an indispensable part of 20
dining, and indeed would consider it impolite not to converse with one's
dinner partner, I found this Japanese custom rather strange. Still, I could
accept it as a cultural difference even though I didn't really understand
it. But when my husband added, in explanation, that Japanese consider

it extremely rude to talk with one's mouth full, I got confused. Talking with one's mouth full is certainly not an American custom. We think it very rude, too. Yet we still manage to talk a lot and eat at the same time. How do we do it?

For a long time, I couldn't explain it, and it bothered me. But after I 21 discovered the conversational ballgames, I finally found the answer. Of course! In a western-style conversation, you hit the ball, and while someone else is hitting it back, you take a bite, chew, and swallow. Then you hit the ball again, and then eat some more. The more people there are in the conversation, the more chances you have to eat. But even with only two of you talking, you still have plenty of chances to eat.

Maybe that's why polite conversation at the dinner table has never 22 been a traditional part of Japanese etiquette. Your turn to talk would last so long without interruption that you'd never get a chance to eat.

Questions about the Reading
1. How did the writer's Japanese husband, family, and friends react to her participation in conversations?
2. What does the writer say was wrong with how she was handling the conversations?
3. How does the writer characterize Western-style conversation? To what does she compare Western-style conversation?
4. How does the writer characterize Japanese-style conversation? To what does she compare Japanese-style conversation?
5. What did the writer's Japanese husband complain about after his first trip to America?

Questions about the Writer's Strategies
1. What is the thesis of the essay?
2. What method of comparison-and-contrast organization does the writer use?
3. What is the simile the writer uses for a Western-style conversation between two people? What simile does she use for a conversation among several people?
4. What simile does the writer use for a Japanese-style conversation?
5. How do Westerners manage to carry on a conversation while they are eating and not talk with their mouths full?
6. Does the writer use any mode of development in addition to contrast? If so, what is it and in which paragraphs is it found?

Writing Assignments

1. Write an essay in which you contrast the way you talk to your best friends with the way you talk to neighborhood or school friends. Use dialogue to illustrate the differences.
2. Go to a shopping mall and listen to the people who are walking around or working in the stores. Classify the different people you see and write an essay in which you compare and/or contrast their conversations.

Indy 500

Chris Hanley (student)

We are often told that young drivers are reckless and have a high accident rate. In his essay, Chris Hanley tells us a different story.

Words to Know

ER   Emergency Room
neurotic   nervous disorder
paranoid   delusional
senility   old age infirmity

Getting Started

What are some things—like driving, washing dishes, or cleaning house—that you feel you do better or more efficiently than other members of your family?

Having lived in St. Louis all my life, I have encountered many a strange 1 driver. I have seen the speedy driver, the crazy driver, and the overly cautious driver, but none of these drivers compares to my mother. My mother is a neurotic, paranoid racecar driver stuck behind the wheel of a four-wheel deathtrap. She scares me to death as I am often forced to ride as a passenger in her car when we run family errands here and there around town. It is during these rides that my life flashes before me, usually more than once, that I realize why I am so confident in my abilities to drive, and why I quickly offer to drive wherever we go. To say that our driving styles are opposites would be like hitting the bull's-eye at the local county fair.

My mother is only fifty-two years old, and I am quite sure that senility 2 has not yet set in, but yet someone would assume something is not right. This lady I admire just hasn't a clue; she seems to have no control over her body when she sits behind the wheel of her car. Sometimes it seems as if she just doesn't care who she runs over or scares the heck out of as she bounces down the road, heading to work or off on some odd errand she must run for the family. Let me try to describe for you the typical scenario that would play out on a short trip to the store. As we pull out into traffic from the four-way stop by our house, she swerves at a car two lanes over and rants that he should not be so close; then she proceeds to drive ten miles over the posted speed limit. Coming to a halt at a stoplight involves a process that an Indy pit crew could only appreciate; screeching brakes and feeling suspended from the seatbelts truly give one the almost-there feeling. No need to attempt to peel myself off the front windshield because John Force in the driver's seat has burnt rubber leaving the light to try and cut off the guy in a Yugo trying to merge into traffic two lights up from us. From the look on the face of the Yugo driver, somehow he doesn't believe the fact my mom has her blinker on and is fully intending on making a turn that only Paul Tracy would attempt on a good day. Sliding sideways into the parking lot of the local Shop 'N Save, nearly taking out the cart attendant and a little old lady with a walker, she races to the front of the first available lane, gunning for the first open parking spot. Screech go the tires once more as we come to a sliding, grinding halt, finally parked at our destination that is only concluded with my thanking God that I am still alive but praying that I may be allowed to drive home.

My mother's driving skills in no way show in the way I drive; my   3 driving ability makes my mother look like a monkey trying to ride a tricycle. My skills are much more refined and smooth; I pride myself on being a very good driver, an above-average driver in my eyes. As I beg and plead with my mother to allow me to drive home, I use my trump card and inform her that I have an English paper due and wouldn't be able to finish if I ended up in the ER. Unwillingly, my mother finally gives up the keys and lets me drive, though watching her buckle up as though she were being launched into orbit via the space shuttle isn't very reassuring, to say the least. I shrug off this little bit of a visual crack my mother has made about my driving because I know that I am the better driver without any thought. Cautiously, as I place the car in reverse and proceed to check all lines of sight and attempt to back out of the parking space, "LOOK OUT" is all I hear, as if I had run over somebody. "What seems to be the problem?" My mom looks at me and says, "You almost hit that car." Urgently looking to see this mysterious car I almost hit, thus almost blemishing my perfect driving record, I look around, and the closest car to us is a hundred feet away at the beginning of the aisle we were in. I look at my mother and almost fall out of my seat. "What?" I ask. "You could have hit that car pulling out of the parking spot that fast," she comments. "Are you serious?" I say. "Yes," she replies. Reversing out of the parking space with no further issues or near heart attacks, I proceed to exit the parking lot and merge into traffic easily and effortlessly; it's amazing what common sense and blinkers can do for someone. As I drive down the road doing the posted speed limit, my mother constantly asks, "Why are you driving so slow?" "Because it's the speed limit," I reply. She looks at me as if I were wearing a clown suit and telling jokes; she's almost laughing at me because I am obeying the law. Driving carefully and confidently made for an uneventful and much safer trip home than the one to the store. To say that I was a lot calmer when we got home than when we arrived at the store is an understatement of monumental proportions.

My mother tends to think that I drive too cautiously and that I could   4
learn a thing or two from her style of driving. On the other hand, I tend
to think that driving cautiously and safely would be an example my
mother would be trying to set for her son, but it seems as if I am way off
target. Agreeing to disagree about our driving styles is something that is
quite obvious when we bicker about each other's driving types. What is
apparent is that although we both drive the same roads, we do them as
differently as we can get, but as long as we both continue to arrive at our
locations in one piece, I can't really complain.

Questions about the Reading

1. What are the different kinds of drivers the writer has seen in St. Louis?
2. Who, according to the writer, would appreciate the way his mother comes to a halt at a stoplight?
3. What is the "visual crack" the writer's mother makes about his driving when she agrees to let him drive home?
4. Who are John Force and Paul Tracy? How are they related to the title of the essay? Use the Internet to find out about them.

Questions about the Writer's Strategies

1. What is the tone of the essay?
2. What order does the writer use in contrasting his driving with that of his mother?
3. What modes of development does the writer use in addition to compare or contrast?
4. What is the simile the writer uses in the third paragraph?

Writing Assignments

1. *Working Together* Join with some classmates to write an essay in which you compare or contrast your school schedules, registration experiences, or study habits.
2. Write an essay in which you compare, contrast, or compare and contrast your driving, lawn mowing, dishwashing, or performance of another household chore with that of a family member, friend, or neighbor.

Shopping in Pajamas
Francine Mercier (student)

Francine Mercier is originally from French Canada and now lives in San Francisco. She is a part-time student at the City College of San Francisco and a volunteer docent for a Victorian house-museum. Her interests are history and architecture, and she hopes to combine those interests in her future occupation.

Word to Know

avatar   image, replica

Getting Started

What are the similarities and differences between doing research in a library and on a computer?

Have you ever had a dream in which you are at the supermarket or at 1
the mall shopping in your pajamas? When you wake up, you realize that you are still in bed and that if you want to go shopping, you have to get dressed. What a disappointment. But wait! If you decide to shop online instead of going to the store, you can stay in your pajamas, sit in front of your computer with a steaming cup of coffee, and shop from the comfort of your home. Online shopping is far more convenient than in-store shopping, and it has the additional benefit of allowing substantial savings.

I had many unpleasant experiences while shopping in-store, but it 2
was this one particular experience that really convinced me of how much more convenient online shopping can be. One sunny Saturday afternoon, I decided to go shopping downtown. Unfortunately, I was not the only one who thought it was the ideal moment for this activity, and as such, the streets were heavily congested. It took me a long time to get to the parking lot, and when I finally got there, it was full. After going around an additional hour in a sea of vehicles, I was able to park. Reaching my destination was only the beginning of my problems. On that day, the stores, like the roads, were crowded. Everywhere I went, swarms of shoppers surrounded me, which limited my ability to look at the merchandise and created long waiting lines at the cashier. I went shopping planning to have a good time, but instead I came back home with a pair of socks, a book, and a lot of tension created by this whole experience. I could have escaped this nightmare by shopping online. Although I would not have been able to enjoy my pair of socks and my book right away, I could have avoided the traffic, the time spent to find a parking space, the crowd, and the long wait at the cashier. When shopping online, you can shop on your own terms. You can shop when you want,

compare items from different stores, and purchase what you need in a fraction of the time you would spend if you were shopping in a store. For additional convenience, your merchandise is delivered at your doorstep, which eliminates all the traffic and parking-related problems.

Besides offering convenience, online shopping provides more opportunities to save money on your purchases than in-store shopping. Comparing prices between stores is one of the golden rules for saving money, and shopping online provides a quick and easy way to do it. Web sites like Nextag.com and Bizrate.com compare the prices of one item from several stores at once. You can then choose the best deal. It would be extremely time-consuming, even impossible, to do this type of comparison if you were shopping in-store. To save even more, online shopping makes many purchasing options available. You can buy new or used items or even auction for what you want on eBay. For example, when I compared the price of books at my neighborhood bookstore and online at Amazon.com, I was surprised to find the same item for 15 to 20 percent less. Not only was the price lower for a new item, but I also had the option to purchase a used item, which was even cheaper. Although it is true that sometimes shipping fees can increase the product's price, overall, the ability to compare prices quickly between different stores and the variety of ways to purchase an item frequently result in lower prices. 3

In the end, having experienced both shopping in-store and online, I definitely prefer the additional convenience and the lower prices offered by online shopping. The convenience and lower prices compensate for the one thing online shopping does not yet offer, which is direct contact with the product. I have to concede that for some items—for example, shoes or clothing—nothing can replace trying an item on to see how it fits. However, this inconvenience might soon become a thing of the past since online stores like Levi Strauss have started to experiment with the use of technology that can scan your body and create a three-dimensional avatar that provides the online store with your dimensions. With this information, the store is then able to point out which item will fit your body and will even enhance your best features. 4

Questions about the Reading

1. What is the writer's opinion of shopping online?
2. What were the problems the writer experienced when she went shopping downtown on a Saturday afternoon?
3. What are the specific conveniences the writer finds in shopping online?

4. What is the experimental technology that may eliminate needing to go to the stores to shop for shoes or clothing?

Questions about the Writer's Strategies

1. What is the organizational method the writer uses?
2. What is the thesis of the essay? Is it stated or implied? State it in your own words.
3. What is the point of view (person, time, tone) of the essay?
4. What modes of development does the writer use in addition to compare and contrast?

Writing Assignments

1. Write an essay in which you compare and contrast researching a subject in your school library and on your computer.

2. *Working Together* Join with some classmates to go on a shopping trip for a specific item. Then use the Internet and shop for the same item. Write an essay in which you compare and contrast the experiences you had in the different stores and the prices you found for the item in stores and on the Internet.

7

Process

If you want to hook up your new computer, you will probably follow the directions, or a **process**, provided by the manufacturer. A process is a method of doing a task or a job, usually in orderly steps, to achieve a desired result. For example, directions and recipes are both detailed explanations of processes. So are all articles and essays that tell how to prepare for a job interview, assemble a stereo system, dress for success, or operate a personal computer. So, too, are essays that describe how someone else used a process to accomplish something or complete a task.

In an essay explaining how to carry out a process, the writer needs to give clear and accurate guidance or directions, making the steps as simple as possible for the reader to follow. To do this, the writer must decide exactly what the reader already knows and what he or she needs to be told. The burden is on the writer to provide complete information to enable the reader to perform the task. If the writer forgets to mention how long the cookies should bake, the cook may be left with burned chocolate-chip cookies and disappointed friends.

The written explanation of such a process must be organized with particular care. Each step or part of the directions should be discussed in the same order as it occurs in the process. The following sample paragraph is a recipe for shrimp—one you might want to try. Notice that the writer begins with the purchase of the shrimp and then proceeds, step by step, through preparing, cooking, and serving the shrimp.

Topic sentence

Step 1: choose size

Step 2: choose quantity

When fresh shrimp can be had, have it. What size? Medium for reasons of economy and common sense. Huge shrimps are magnificently expensive while small ones come in such numbers per pound that shelling them becomes slave labor. Buy two pounds of fresh shrimp and shell them.

Step 3: shell shrimp

> First, with a thumbnail pinch the tail shell hard crosswise (so the tail segments will come out intact), then handle the headless animals like so many pea pods; split them lengthwise, save the contents, and throw the husks away.

Step 4: cooking directions

> Sauté the shrimp with three crushed garlic cloves in two-thirds of a stick of butter. When the shrimp turn pink, add a 12-ounce can of Italian tomatoes (which taste better than the fresh supermarket kind), two bay leaves, a teaspoon of dried oregano, a half-cup of dry white wine, and the juice of a lemon. Simmer for ten minutes, sprinkle with chopped parsley and serve with rice.

Philip Kopper, "Delicacies de la Mer"

Because this paragraph is telling the reader what to do, the **point of view** is **second person** (you), and it is in the present tense (*come, buy, save, throw,* and so forth). But the word *you* is unstated, which makes the paragraph seem to address the reader even more directly. This **tone** is commonly used in process writing that instructs the reader.

Not all process essays are such clear-cut models of process writing as the previous example. In some cases, a paragraph or essay describing a process may serve a purpose similar to that of a **narrative** or a **description**. That is, whereas strictly process writing is intended primarily to **instruct**, process writing also can be adapted to situations in which the writer mainly wants to **inform** or **describe**. In such cases, a process is often combined with narration and description, as in the following example. Notice that in describing the process—the way the woman packs her suitcases and leaves the house—the writer describes her character. You also know, by the contrast between her habits and those of her husband, that her basic character differs sharply from his. By detailing the process of packing and combining it with other narrative details, the writer tells you indirectly what has previously happened in the woman's life.

Introduction— narrative

> He slammed the door angrily behind him, and she heard the squeal of the tires as he raced off in the car. For a moment, she felt her usual fear. She knew he shouldn't drive after he'd been drinking heavily.   1

Step 1: preparation

> But then she turned, went to the linen closet, and took out a clean towel. She spread the towel out on her neatly made bed.   2

Step 2: finding suitcases

> Next, she got her overnight bag and a larger suitcase from the closet and put them carefully on the towel on her bed.   3

> Methodically, she took neatly folded underwear, stockings, and nightgowns from her drawers and packed them in neat rows in the two bags. One set in the overnight bag, and five in the larger suitcase. She laid aside a nightgown with a matching robe to pack last.

Step 3: packing suitcases

> Next, she lifted dresses and suits, carefully hung on the hangers and buttoned up so they wouldn't wrinkle, from her   4

closet and folded them into the larger suitcase. Two extra blouses and a dress went into the overnight bag. She'd wear the suit she had on.

She brought plastic bags from the kitchen and put her   5
shoes into them. One pair went into the overnight bag; two pairs, one for the dresses and one for the suits, went into the larger bag. Then she put her bedroom slippers and the night-gown with the matching robe on top of the other clothes in the overnight bag. She would take only the overnight bag into her parents' house, at least at first. No need for them to know right away that this time was for more than one night. They'd always said that she wasn't going to change him and that the marriage wouldn't last.

She sighed again, closed the suitcases, carried them out   6
to her car, and then went back into the house for one last look around. Almost ready, she took her coat from the hall closet, folded it carefully over her arm, and took a last look

**Step 4: final check
and look around**

at his shoes and socks left beside his chair and the newspa-per flung across the couch where it would leave newsprint on the upholstery. She left the shoes and socks but couldn't resist folding the newspaper and putting it on a table. Finally, she went out, closed the door silently behind her, got into her car, and drove quietly and slowly away.

As you started reading this essay, you probably realized right away that it would be more narrative and descriptive than instructive of a pro-cess. Two signals that alerted you are that the point of view is **third person** (*she*) and past tense (*took, packed, lifted, laid*, and so on). Think, for a minute, about writing a clear process explanation using that person and tense. Experienced writers may use varying **points of view** in process writing, but for clear point-by-point process explanations, the **second person** (*you*), the present tense (*take, pour, measure*), and a straightfor-ward tone are the most common.

Although a process approach can sometimes be useful in writing narratives and descriptions that deal with significant activities or accom-plishments, you usually will use process for giving directions, describing how a mechanical gadget works, or reporting on science experiments. In these situations you may combine process with other modes like **defini-tion** (chapter 9), **examples** (chapter 4), and **cause and effect** (chapter 8). Always remember that three factors are essential to an effective process essay. First, be sure that the steps or procedures are carefully organized, step by step—usually in the same order as they should be carried out—so that the reader can understand and follow your explanation. Second, be sure that you include any information that the reader needs about any special materials or preliminary steps. And, third, include *all* the specific steps in the process.

The Supply Chain

Thomas L. Friedman

In this paragraph from his best-selling book The World Is Flat, *Tom Friedman,* New York Times *prize-winning columnist, explains the computerized supply chain used by Wal-Mart to keep merchandise flowing seamlessly from thousands of suppliers—whether they are in China or Maine—to four thousand Wal-Mart stores worldwide.*

Words to Know

conveyor belt   mechanized device for moving an item from one
  place to another
finale   ending, conclusion

Getting Started

What advantages are there to you, as a consumer, from the efficiency of Wal-Mart's supply-chain system?

I had never seen what a supply chain looked like in action until I visited Wal-Mart headquarters in Bentonville, Arkansas. My Wal-Mart hosts took me over to the 1.2-million-square-foot distribution center, where we climbed up to a viewing perch and watched the show. On one side of the building, scores of white Wal-Mart trailer trucks were dropping off boxes of merchandise from thousands of different suppliers. Boxes large and small were fed up a conveyor belt at each loading dock. These little conveyor belts fed into a bigger belt, like streams feeding into a powerful river. Twenty-four hours a day, seven days a week, the suppliers' trucks feed the twelve miles of conveyor streams, and the conveyor streams feed into a huge Wal-Mart river of boxed products. But that is just half the show. As the Wal-Mart river flows along, an electric eye reads the bar codes on each box on its way to the other side of the building. There, the river parts again into a hundred streams. Electric arms from each stream reach out and guide the boxes—ordered by particular Wal-Mart stores—off the main river and down its stream, where another conveyor belt sweeps them into a waiting Wal-Mart truck, which will rush these particular products onto the shelves of a particular Wal-Mart store somewhere in the country. There, a consumer will lift one of these products off the shelf, and the cashier will scan it in, and the moment that happens, a signal will be generated. That signal will go out across the Wal-Mart network to the supplier of that product—whether that supplier's factory is in coastal China or coastal Maine. That signal will pop up on the supplier's computer screen and prompt him to make another of that item and ship it via the Wal-Mart supply chain, and the whole cycle will start anew. So no sooner does your arm lift a product off the local Wal-Mart's shelf and onto the checkout counter than another mechanical arm starts making another one somewhere in the world. Call it "the Wal-Mart Symphony" in multiple movements—with no finale. It just plays over and over 24/7/365: delivery, sorting, packing, distribution, buying, manufacturing, reordering, delivery, sorting, packing....

Questions about the Reading

1. What is the size of Wal-Mart's distribution center?
2. What are the stages or steps in the supply-chain process?
3. When does the supply chain operate? What makes it start over again?
4. What makes the supply chain an example of the world's being flat?

Questions about the Writer's Strategies

1. What is the main idea of the paragraph?
2. What is the metaphor the writer uses for the supply chain?
3. What is the simile the writer uses for the little conveyor belts?
4. What is the metaphor the writer uses for the continuous nature of the supply chain?

Writing Assignments

1. Write a paragraph in which you explain the process you follow in getting ready for and getting to school.
2. Visit your local Wal-Mart, supermarket, or clothing store and ask the manager to let you observe the process followed from the receiving to the selling of its merchandise. Then write an extended paragraph explaining the process.

How to Bathe a Cat

The Dog

Don't take this process seriously, but if you've ever owned a cat, would you want to try it?

Word to Know

soothe   calm

Getting Started

As they say in television ads showing dangerous stunts, "Don't try this at home."

---

1. Thoroughly clean the toilet. 2. Add the required amount of shampoo to the toilet water and have both lids up. 3. Find the cat and soothe him while you carry him towards the bathroom. 4. In one smooth movement, put the cat in the toilet and close both lids. (You may need to stand on the lid so that he cannot escape.) The cat will self-agitate and make ample suds. Never mind the noises that come from your toilet; the cat is actually enjoying this. CAUTION: Do not get any part of your body too close to the edge, as his paws will be reaching out for anything they can find. 5. Flush the toilet three or four times. This provides a "Power Wash" and "Rinse," which I have found to be quite effective. 6. Have someone open the door to the outside and ensure that there are no people between the toilet and the outside door. 7. Stand behind the toilet as far as you can and quickly lift both lids. 8. The now clean cat will rocket out of the toilet and run outside where he will dry himself.

Sincerely,
The Dog

Questions about the Reading

1. Why should you stand on the lid of the toilet when bathing the cat?
2. What is the purpose of flushing the toilet several times?

Questions about the Writer's Strategies

1. What is the main idea of the paragraph?
2. What is the point of view of the paragraph?

Writing Assignments

1. Write a humorous paragraph in which you explain the process of washing dishes, mowing the lawn, getting to school, or studying for an exam.
2. Write a paragraph in which you explain the process you would follow in washing a dog.

Brewing Beer

Grace Lichtenstein

It's a lengthy and exacting process to produce a bottle of Coors beer.

Words to Know
amber   brownish gold color
fermentation   breakdown of molecules in a compound

Getting Started
What is your favorite dessert? What is the process in making that dessert?

Like other beers, Coors [beer] is produced from barley. Most of the big Midwestern brewers use barley grown in North Dakota and Minnesota. Coors is the single American brewer to use a Moravian strain, grown under company supervision, on farms in Colorado, Idaho, Wyoming and Montana. At the brewery, the barley is turned into malt by being soaked in water—which must be biologically pure and of a known mineral content—for several days, causing it to sprout and producing a chemical change—breaking down starch into sugar. The malt is toasted, a process that halts the sprouting and determines the color and sweetness (the more the roasting, the darker, more bitter the beer). It is ground into flour and brewed, with more pure water, in huge copper-domed kettles until it is the consistency of oatmeal. Rice and refined starch are added to make mash; solids are strained out, leaving an amber liquid malt extract, which is boiled with hops—the dried cones from the hop vine which add to the bitterness, or tang. The hops are strained, yeast is added, turning the sugar to alcohol, and the beer is aged in huge red vats at near-freezing temperatures for almost two months, during which the second fermentation takes place and the liquid becomes carbonated, or bubbly. (Many breweries chemically age their beer to speed up production; Coors people say only naturally aged brew can be called a true "lager.") Next, the beer is filtered through cellulose filters to remove bacteria, and finally is pumped into cans, bottles or kegs for shipping.

Questions about the Reading

1. What makes the grain used by Coors different from that used by other brewers?
2. What are the products used in making beer?
3. What is special about the water used in producing beer?
4. What are the steps followed in making beer?
5. What makes beer carbonated or bubbly? What is necessary to make a beer called "lager"?

Questions about the Writer's Strategies

1. What is the writer's purpose in explaining the beer-making process?
2. What is the point of view in the paragraph? Is it consistent?
3. In addition to process, what other modes of development are used by the writer?

Writing Assignments

1. Write a paragraph in which you explain the process of making your favorite dessert.
2. Write a paragraph in which you explain, in detail, the process of registering for classes in person.
3. Write a paragraph in which you explain, in detail, the process of registering for classes on the Internet.

The Right Way to Eat an Ice-Cream Cone

L. Rust Hills

Rust Hills was fiction editor of Esquire *and the* Saturday Evening Post *and is now a free lance writer. In this paragraph, taken from his book* How To Do Things Right, *he explains his technique, which was perfected through years of taking his children to ice-cream cone stands. Having told us the preliminary pitfalls—melted ice cream on car upholstery, choosing a flavor, holding more than one cone—he delivers the ultimate instructions on eating the cone.*

Words to Know

forgoing   deciding against
jostling   bumping together
molecules   very small particles
stance   way of standing

1

Getting Started

What is the best or right way to eat spaghetti?

Grasp the cone with the right hand firmly but gently between thumb and at least one but not more than three fingers, two-thirds of the way up the cone. Then dart swiftly away to an open area, away from the jostling crowd at the stand. Now take up the classic ice-cream-cone-eating stance: feet from one to two feet apart, body bent forward from the waist at a twenty-five-degree angle, right elbow well up, right forearm horizontal, at a level with your collarbone and about twelve inches from it. But don't start eating yet! Check first to see what emergency repairs may be necessary. Sometimes a sugar cone will be so crushed or broken or cracked that all one can do is gulp at the thing like a savage, getting what he can of it and letting the rest drop to the ground, and then evacuating the area of catastrophe as quickly as possible. Checking the cone for possible trouble can be done in a second or two, if one knows where to look and does it systematically. A trouble spot some people overlook is the bottom tip of the cone. This may have been broken off. Or the flap of the cone material at the bottom, usually wrapped over itself in that funny spiral construction, may be folded in a way that is imperfect and leaves an opening. No need to say that through this opening—in a matter of perhaps thirty or, at most, ninety seconds—will begin to pour hundreds of thousands of sticky molecules of melted ice cream. You know in this case that you must instantly get the paper napkin in your left hand under and around the bottom of the cone to stem the forthcoming flow, or else be doomed to eat the cone far too rapidly. It is a grim moment. No one wants to eat a cone under that kind of pressure, but neither does anyone want to end up with the bottom of the cone stuck to a messy napkin. There's one other alternative—one that takes both skill and courage: Forgoing any cradling action, grasp the cone more firmly between thumb and forefinger and extend the other fingers so that they are out of the way of the dripping from the bottom, then increase the waist-bend angle from twenty-five to thirty-five degrees, and then eat the cone, *allowing* it to drip out of the bottom onto the ground in front of you! Experienced and thoughtful cone-eaters enjoy facing up to this kind of sudden challenge.

Questions about the Reading

1. How many ways are there to eat an ice-cream cone?
2. Despite all of the problems with ice-cream cones, does the writer like to eat them?

Questions about the Writer's Strategies

1. When faced with having to write a clear and easy-to-understand description of a complicated process (how to prepare income-tax returns, do minor home repairs, or operate a computer), writers must use very precise language. Which words or phrases in this paragraph have a technical precision that makes this process clear to the reader?
2. The writer describes a number of problems associated with ice-cream cones. Which words or phrases does he use to help the reader know when he is about to identify these problems?

Writing Assignments

1. Choose another popular yet sometimes hard-to-eat food, for example spaghetti and meatballs, and imagine that you have to write directions for eating this food for someone who is wearing a new white suit and has never eaten this before. Write a paragraph of directions.
2. Choose some simple, everyday activity such as making a peanut-butter sandwich or brushing your teeth and write a paragraph describing the *process* (steps, necessary equipment) involved. Imagine that your reader has never handled jars, sliced bread, or toothbrush and toothpaste.

The Cook

Barbara Lewis (student)

Barbara Lewis takes us through the process of preparing dinner at a busy restaurant. She juggles meat, potatoes, and a seemingly endless stream of sauces and other delectables in a two-hour race with the dinner bell. And she does all this after a day of classes at Cuyahoga Community College in Cleveland, Ohio.

Words to Know

au jus natural, unthickened juices or gravy
escargots snails
requisition a formal written order
sauté to fry food quickly in a little fat
scampi shrimp

Getting Started

At what times in your life have you felt like the busiest, most pressured person in the world? What factors contributed to your state of mind?

Preparing food for the sauté line at the restaurant where I work is a hectic two-hour job. I come to work at 3:00 P.M. knowing that everything must be done by 5:00 P.M. The first thing I do is to check the requisition for the day and order my food. Then I have to clean and season five or six prime rib roasts and place them in the slow-cooking oven. After this, I clean and season five trays of white potatoes for baking and put them in the fast oven. Now I have two things cooking, prime ribs and potatoes, at different times and temperatures, and they both have to be watched very closely. In the meantime, I must put three trays of bacon in the oven. The bacon needs very close watching, too, because it burns very easily. Now I have prime ribs, potatoes, and bacon all cooking at the same time—and all needing constant watching. Next, I make popovers, which are unseasoned rolls. These also go into an oven for baking. Now I have prime ribs, baking potatoes, bacon, and popovers cooking at the same time and all of them needing to be closely watched. With my work area set up, I must make clarified butter and garlic butter. The clarified butter is for cooking liver, veal, and fish. The garlic butter is for stuffing escargots. I have to make ground meat stuffing also. Half of the ground meat will be mixed with wild rice and will be used to stuff breasts of chicken. The other half of the ground meat mixture will be used to stuff mushrooms.

I have to prepare veal, cut and season scampi, and clean and sauté mushrooms and onions. In the meantime, I check the prime ribs and potatoes, take the bacon and the popovers out of the oven, and put the veal and chicken into the oven. Now I make au jus, which is served over the prime ribs, make the soup for the day, and cook the vegetables and rice. Then I heat the bordelaise sauce, make the special for the day, and last of all, cook food for the employees. This and sometimes more has to be done by five o'clock. Is it any wonder that I say preparing food for the sauté line at the restaurant where I work is a very hectic two-hour job!

Questions about the Reading

1. Run through the cook's list again. For about how many people do you think she is preparing food?
2. Classify the food the cook is responsible for.
3. Do you think the cook likes her job? Explain your answer.

Questions about the Writer's Strategies

1. Where is the topic sentence of the paragraph? Does the writer restate the topic sentence anywhere in the paragraph? If so, where? Does the sentence then serve a second purpose? What is that purpose?
2. Do you think *hectic* is an effective word for describing this job?
3. The cook states at the beginning that she has two things to watch carefully. The list of things she watches continues to grow during the paragraph. Identify the sentences where she reemphasizes this point. Does this help support her statement that the job is hectic?
4. What order does the writer use to organize her information in the paragraph?

Writing Assignments

1. We all have moments when we feel under pressure. Write a process paragraph illustrating one of your busy days.
2. Imagine that the restaurant has decided to hire you as a helper for the cook. Write a process paragraph explaining the steps you would take to assist the cook and how you would blend your activities with hers.

3. Use the Internet to find out how to prepare a favorite egg-based meal. Write about the process involved so that you will end up with a perfect meal.

A Guide to Proper Hand-Washing Technique

Jennifer Traig

It's true that you should wash your hands to help prevent disease, but how do you keep them clean when you still have to turn off the faucet, dry them, and get out the door? Jennifer Traig tells you how, but it isn't easy.

Words to Know

contemplate   think about

hepatitis   inflammation of the liver

Getting Started

What process—doing the laundry, mowing the lawn, or shopping—do you especially dislike? Why?

Did you know that your hands are loaded with bacteria and other con- 1
taminants? They're filthy! They spread disease! Oh, it's just awful. And it's not scientifically possible to sterilize your hands. You can, however, get them really, really clean. Here's how!

1. First, you need to get some water going. We want it hot, hot, hot! The 2
   hot-water tap is contaminated, but that's okay, because you're about to wash. Touch it again, just to show how brave you are. Touch it one more time. Three taps wards off bad things. Now we're ready to wash!

2. Next, choose your poison. What kind of soap is for you? Bar soap is 3
   out; other people have probably used it (a possibility too horrible to contemplate), and even if it's unopened, it's made from animal fats, which is revolting. The whole thing just seems so dirty. Liquid soap it is! Choose an antibacterial formula if you're worried about con-tamination from germs. If you're worried about contamination from death, choose dishwashing liquid. It's so death-free it's safe to use on plates and flatware! But only if it's BRAND-NEW. Even then, you never know. Okay, let's skip the soap altogether. Plain water will be fine.

3. Rub your hands together vigorously and scrub, scrub, scrub. The 4
   Centers for Disease Control recommend you wash your hands for ten seconds, but what do they know? If they're such geniuses, why do people still get hepatitis? A full minute, minimum. How about this: you keep your hands under that tap until you answer the philo-sophical question "Is water clean?"

4. I don't know if water is clean. What if water isn't clean? What if 5
   water just makes you dirtier?
5. You'll wash and wash and wash, but you'll never be safe.   6
6. Okay, try not to think about it. Let's just say water is clean and move on. 7
7. But what if it's not clean?   8
8. We're moving on. This next part is tricky. Your hands are clean—but 9
   they're wet. How to get them dry without getting them dirty again?
   The air-dry technique is best. Sure, it's slow, but it's safe. Simply
   hold your hands in the air until they're completely dry. Be sure not
   to touch anything! If you touch something, or if for some reason you
   think you maybe touched something, go back to Step 1. Yes, let's go
   back to Step 1 just to be safe.
9. Now we're in a hurry. You're going to have to dry your hands with 10
   paper napkins. That's fine. Just make sure it's a new package. Did
   you touch the part of the package that was sealed with glue? Is that
   glue? Glue is dirty. Wash again, just to be safe, then dry your hands
   on a napkin that absolutely for sure didn't touch the glue.
10. Use a napkin to turn off the tap and another napkin to open the 11
   door on the way out. Some people won't even touch the door with a
   napkin; they'll just wait until somebody comes to open the door for
   them. But they're crazy!

Questions about the Reading

1. Why does the writer say you need to get your hands "really, really clean"?
2. How many times does the writer start over in the process of washing
   her hands?
3. What is the writer's opinion of different soaps? What does she mean
   by saying dishwashing soap is "death-free"?

Questions about the Writer's Strategies

1. What is the tone of the essay?
2. Is the point of view (person) of the essay consistent? If it changes, is
   the change justified or necessary? Why or why not?
3. What is the irony in the essay?

Writing Assignments

1. Write an essay in which you explain making a peanut butter and jelly
   sandwich, changing the oil in a car, or opening a bank account.
2. Write an essay in which you explain the process of painting a room
   in your house.

The Beekeeper

Sue Hubbell

Preparing for a job as a beekeeper is a painstaking process that actually requires, as Sue Hubbell shows us, taking pain.

Words to Know

anaphylactic   severe reaction with possible collapse or death
supers   wooden boxes that contain the bees' honey

Getting Started

Do you follow a process in getting ready to do your homework?

The time to harvest honey is summer's end, when it is hot. The tem- 1
per of the bees requires that we wear protective clothing: a full set of
overalls, a zippered bee veil and leather gloves. Even a very strong
young man works up a sweat wrapped in a bee suit in the heat, hustling
60-pound supers while being harassed by angry bees. It is a hard job,
harder even than haying, but jobs are scarce here and I've always been
able to hire help.

This year David, the son of a friend of mine, is working for me. He is 2
big and strong and used to labor, but he was nervous about bees. After
we had made the job arrangement I set about desensitizing him to bee
stings. I put a piece of ice on his arm to numb it and then, holding a bee
carefully by its head, I put it on the numbed spot and let it sting him. A
bee stinger is barbed and stays in the flesh, pulling loose from the body
of the bee as it struggles to free itself. The bulbous poison sac at the top
of the stinger continues to pulsate after the bee has left, pumping the
venom and forcing the stinger deeper into the flesh.

That first day I wanted David to have only a partial dose of venom, 3
so after a minute I scraped the stinger out. A few people are seriously
sensitive to bee venom; each sting they receive can cause a more severe
reaction than the one before—reactions ranging from hives, breathing
difficulties, accelerated heart beat and choking to anaphylactic shock and
death. I didn't think David would be allergic in that way, but I wanted
to make sure.

We sat down and had a cup of coffee and I watched him. The spot 4
where the stinger went in grew red and began to swell. That was a normal reaction, and so was the itching that he felt later on.

The next day I coaxed a bee into stinging him again, repeating the 5 procedure, but I left the stinger in place for 10 minutes, until the venom sac was empty. Again the spot was red, swollen and itchy but had disappeared in 24 hours. By that time David was ready to catch a bee himself and administer his own sting. He also decided that the ice cube was a bother and gave it up. I told him to keep to one sting a day until he had no redness or swelling and then to increase to two stings. He was ready for them the next day. The greater amount of venom caused redness and swelling for a few days, but soon his body could tolerate it without reaction and he increased the number of stings once again.

Today he told me he was up to six stings. His arms look as though 6 they have track marks on them, but the fresh stings are having little effect. I'll keep him at it until he can tolerate 10 a day with no reaction and then I'll not worry about taking him out to the bee yard.

Questions about the Reading

1. When is the honey harvested? Why is the honey harvested then?
2. How much do the supers that hold the honey weigh?
3. Why is the beekeeper able to hire help in harvesting the honey?
4. How many stings per day does the beekeeper want her helper to tolerate before taking him to the bee yard?

Questions about the Writer's Strategies

1. Identify the steps in the desensitizing process.
2. Could the selection as a whole or the sentences within it be classified by any other modes of development? If so, which modes and which sentences?
3. What is the thesis of the selection? Is it stated? If so, identify it; if not, state the thesis in your own words.

Writing Assignments

1. Write an essay in which you explain the process you follow in getting ready for work, doing your laundry, or repairing your car or some household item.
2. Write an essay in which you explain the process you follow in preparing to buy groceries and then in buying them.

Koto

Edna Yano (student)

In her prize-winning essay, Edna Yano of Leeward Community College, located in Pearl City, Hawaii, helps us understand how difficult it is to learn to play the koto, a Japanese thirteen-string zither.

Word to Know

simultaneously   at the same time

Getting Started

Is there a musical instrument you would like to learn to play?

Who would have ever thought that learning how to play the koto for 1 six months would be of any help? I was in Japan a couple of years ago, and while I was there, I had a valuable opportunity to learn to play the koto (thirteen-string Japanese zither). I bought my very own set of ivory nails . . . it cost 5,000 ¥ (equivalent to about 50 U.S. dollars), and I also bought my Tengaku music book filled with various koto songs. When I first opened that book, my eyes were getting dizzy, as it was impossible to read. I tried not to panic.

The first day of instruction, we had a short prayer to help our hearts 2 to focus on learning. We all sat on the Japanese tatami mats, sitting *seiza* (Japanese-style sitting). My legs started to get numb. The koto lay in front of my knees. My wishes to pick these strings have finally started to unfold in front of my very eyes.

Our teacher, Akari Sensei, told us to put on our three ivory nails, one 3 on the thumb, the other on the index finger, and the third one on our middle finger. I was immediately told, "Yano-san, your nails are facing the wrong way." That was embarrassing. I twisted each one to face the right way, which is opposite of my actual nails.

Now we were learning how to read the notes, and believe me, it 4 wasn't the kind of notes you see in piano books. These koto notes were all squiggly Chinese characters with weird-looking symbols next to them. I was learning this thing from zero. Every so often I could sense that Akari Sensei was getting frustrated with trying to teach me. It was hard enough teaching native Japanese people. And here I was, just a Japanese-American from Hawaii trying to learn something already difficult.

186

I cried alone a couple of times, practicing this stringed instrument in the 5
music room at night. As much as I was frustrated, I felt like I was being a
nuisance to the other people who could do so well. But I wasn't going to
give up now. I spent fifty bucks on these nails. This was the chance that
I had always dreamt of. So every day after the evening prayer session, I
would go up to the gloomy music room to practice by myself for about
an hour. That room is very old, and sometimes these monster palm-sized
spiders would fall from the ceiling and scurry about on the tatami mat.
It scared me to death. But knowing that practice makes perfect, nothing
seemed to scare me after that. There are even legends that this room is
haunted, and you can hear someone playing the *ryuteki* (bamboo flute) in
the middle of the night. Ahh, let 'em come out. They would be so scared
of my awful playing that they wouldn't even show up.

Whenever I had time, I would go up to that room. I soon got used to 6
picking the strings. I was now able to play most of the songs without
even looking at my notes. Now the teacher started to focus attention on
how much improvement I had made over the course of a few weeks.

During the koto session, there were four separate days reserved for 7
actual service days, in which one of the koto students was assigned to be
the *oya* (the koto leader). This was an important task. She had to take the
rhythm of the entire orchestra, which included the gong, and the several
other instruments like the ryuteki, shichiriki, and the sho. That leader
was responsible for starting the song, and ending it on perfect note. I was
completely out of the question. There was no way the teacher would pick
me. I still lacked practice. I mean there were some veterans in this group;
what can I say?

The autumn service passed; then the winter; then came spring. I still 8
kept practicing in that room, even [though] our koto instruction [had]
ended a while ago. The summer ceremony was the final one, and the
grandest of them all. It was an honor if you were chosen to be oya for
this particular occasion. I knew I was out of the question, so I didn't
even want to know who was going to be chosen. As the service day
got close, the roles were posted on a thin sheet of paper on the bulletin
board. I scanned it quickly; then it caught my eye, Koto (oya): Yano-san. I
couldn't believe my eyes. I read it twice, just to make sure. Then a friend
passed by and said, "Hey, you're the next oya. Good luck." Yes, I needed
it. I was very excited, and nervous at the same time. This time, it's gotta
be perfect. I practiced even more since seeing my name posted up there.
Playing the koto was no problem; singing to the music was a challenge.

The day of the ceremony arrived. All musicians had to be dressed 9
in a white kimono, a black *haori* (Japanese coat) and a purple *hakama*
(Japanese skirt). The adrenaline was making me anxious. I wanted to
get over with it swiftly and safely. The *kachi* (wood clappers) clapped

once—signaling me to begin the koto and sing simultaneously. I've never felt so focused in my life. That was only part of my task; part two was ending the ceremony with the orchestra as well, and I had to lead everybody. It was a load of stress because I seriously didn't want to mess up on one note.

 The ending kachi clap went off, and I gave my koto a last pinch of 10 harmony on the two strings. It all ended perfectly. It was one of the proudest moments in my life. It may not mean much for other people, but for me—it was a blessed occasion. After the service was over, I gave my thanks to Akari Sensei for her patience; then she immediately recommended that I take this tradition back to Hawaii to teach the people the art of the koto and Tengaku music (ancient Japanese ceremony music). Believe me, if I was able to play that koto, anybody can.

Questions about the Reading

1. Why was it particularly difficult for the writer to read the music notes?
2. Why do you think the writer was determined to learn to play the koto? Does she tell you?
3. How long did the writer spend learning to play the koto?

Questions about the Writer's Strategies

1. What is the thesis of the essay? Is it stated or implied? State the thesis in your own words.
2. What is the point of view (person, tone) of the essay?
3. What is the order the writer uses in the essay?
4. What descriptive words and phrases does the writer use to describe the requirements for the oya ceremony?

Writing Assignments

1. Write an essay in which you explain the process you follow in writing an essay.
2. If you play a musical instrument, write an essay explaining the process of learning to play that instrument. If you do not play an instrument, interview a piano teacher and write an essay explaining the process you would need to follow to learn to play the piano.

8

Cause and Effect

IN YOUR LOCAL newspaper you notice a story about a car accident that took place late on a Saturday night. The driver missed a curve, slammed into a tree, and was badly injured. Police investigators reported that the young victim had been drinking heavily with friends and lost control of the car on the way home. This news article is a relatively clear example of a **cause,** heavy consumption of alcohol, and an **effect,** a serious accident.

Sometimes you can recognize immediately that cause and effect is part of a writer's **mode of development** because the writer uses words that signal a cause-and-effect relationship—transitional words like *because, therefore, as a result,* and *consequently.* However, writers will not necessarily indicate cause and effect so directly. Sometimes a cause-and-effect relationship will be clear only from the arrangement of ideas or the narrative sequence of events. Usually, though, the **topic sentence** or **thesis statement** will indicate that the writer is describing a cause-and-effect situation.

A cause-and-effect explanation tells *why* something turns out the way it does. In some cases, a single cause may contribute to one or more effects. In the following paragraph, the writer says that a single cause—the early release of prisoners—led to an increase in crimes.

Cause	To save money in the early 1980s, Illinois released 21,000 prisoners an average of three months early. James Austin of the National Council on Crime and Delinquency calculates
Effects	that the early releases produced 23 homicides, 32 rapes, 262 arsons, 681 robberies, 2,472 burglaries, 2,571 assaults and more than 8,000 other crimes. According to Harvard researchers David P. Cavanaugh and Mark A. R. Kleiman,
Effects	the $60 million the state saved cost Illinois crime victims $304 million, directly or indirectly.

Eugene H. Methvin,
"Pay Now—Or Pay Later" **189**

A writer may also say that several causes contributed to or resulted in a particular effect.

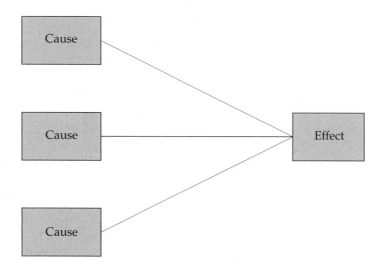

For example, in the following essay, the writer suggests three causes for the disappearance of moonshining—the secret manufacturing of whiskey—as a fine art.

The manufacture of illicit whiskey in the mountains is not dead. Far from it. As long as the operation of a still remains so financially rewarding, it will never die. There will always be men ready to take their chances against the law for such an attractive profit, and willing to take their punishment when they are caught.

Effect

Moonshining as a fine art, however, effectively disappeared some time ago. There were several reasons. One was

Cause 1: decline in use of home remedies containing corn whiskey

the age of aspirin and modern medicine. As home doctoring lost its stature, the demand for pure corn whiskey as an essential ingredient of many home remedies vanished along with those remedies. Increasing affluence was another reason.

Cause 2: young people finding easier ways to make money

Young people, rather than follow in their parents' footsteps, decided that there were easier ways to make money, and they were right.

Cause 3: greed causing producers to care more for quantity than quality

Third, and perhaps most influential of all, was the arrival, even in moonshining, of that peculiarly human disease known to most of us as greed. One fateful night, some force whispered in an unsuspecting moonshiner's ear, "Look. Add this gadget to your still and you'll double your production. Double your production, and you can double your profits."

Soon the small operators were being forced out of business, and moonshining, like most other manufacturing

1

2

3

4

enterprises, was quickly taken over by a breed of men bent on making money—and lots of it. Loss of pride in the product, and loss of time taken with the product increased in direct proportion to the desire for production; and thus moonshining as a fine art was buried in a quiet little ceremony attended only by those mourners who had once been the proud artists, known far and wide across the hills for the excellence of their product. Too old to continue making it themselves, and with no one following behind them, they were reduced to reminiscing about "the good old days when the whiskey that was made was *really* whiskey, and no questions asked."

Suddenly moonshining fell into the same category as   5
faith healing, planting by the signs, and all the other vanishing customs that were a part of a rugged, self-sufficient culture that is now disappearing.

Eliot Wigginton,
"Moonshining as a Fine Art"

In still other cases, one cause may have several effects.

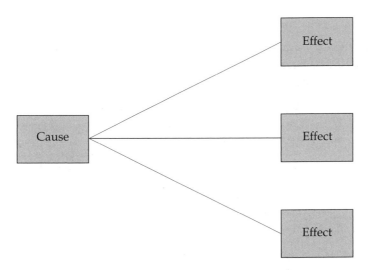

In the following paragraph, the writer explains that the explosion of a nuclear bomb (the cause) has five primary effects. Notice as you read that the writer combines **process** with the cause-and-effect explanation.

Topic

Cause

Whereas most conventional bombs produce only one destructive effect—the shock wave—nuclear weapons produce many destructive effects. At the moment of the explosion, when the temperature of the weapon material, instantly gasified, is at the superstellar level, the pressure is millions of times the normal atmospheric pressure. Immediately, radiation, consisting mainly of gamma rays, which are a very high-energy form of electromagnetic radiation, begins to stream outward into the environment. This is called the "initial nuclear radiation," and is the first of the destructive effects of a nuclear explosion. In an air burst of a one-megaton bomb—a bomb with the explosive yield of a million tons of TNT, which is a medium-sized weapon in present-day nuclear arsenals—the initial nuclear radiation can kill unprotected human beings in an area of some six square miles. Virtually simultaneously with the initial nuclear radiation, in a second destructive effect of the explosion, an electromagnetic pulse is generated by the intense gamma radiation acting on the air. In a high-altitude detonation, the pulse can knock out electrical equipment over a wide area by inducing a powerful surge of voltage through various conductors, such as antennas, overhead power lines, pipes, and railroad tracks.... When the fusion and fission reactions have blown themselves out, a fireball takes shape. As it expands, energy is absorbed in the form of X rays by the surrounding air, and then the air re-radiates a portion of that energy into the environment in the form of the thermal pulse—a wave of blinding light and intense heat—which is the third of the destructive effects of a nuclear explosion.... The thermal pulse of a one-megaton bomb lasts for about ten seconds and can cause second-degree burns in exposed human beings at a distance of nine and a half miles, or in an area of more than two hundred and eighty square miles.... As the fireball expands, it also sends out a blast wave in all directions, and this is the fourth destructive effect of the explosion. The blast wave of an air-burst one-megaton bomb can flatten or severely damage all but the strongest buildings within a radius of four and a half miles.... As the fireball burns, it rises, condensing water from the surrounding atmosphere to form the characteristic mushroom cloud. If the bomb has been set off on the ground or close enough to it so that the fireball touches the surface, a so-called ground burst, a crater will be formed, and tons of dust and debris will be fused with the intensely radioactive fission products and sucked up into the mushroom cloud. This mixture will return to earth as radioactive fallout, most of it in the form of fine ash, in the fifth destructive effect of the explosion. Depending upon the composition of the surface, from 40 to 70 percent of this fallout—often called the "early" or "local" fallout—descends to earth within about a day of the explosion, in the vicinity of the blast and downwind from it, exposing human beings to radiation disease, an illness that is fatal when exposure is intense.

Jonathan Schell,
The Fate of the Earth

Effect 1: initial nuclear radiation

Effect 2: electromagnetic pulse

Effect 3: thermal pulse

Effect 4: blast wave

Effect 5: radioactive fallout

You should notice still another characteristic in this sample paragraph: the writer describes both main causes and subordinate causes, and main effects and subordinate effects. One main cause, the explosion of the bomb, causes a series of five initial (main) effects. However, these effects become the causes for still other effects. The initial nuclear radiation (effect 1), for example, is also a cause that results in the death of unprotected human beings in a six-square-mile area (a subordinate effect). The electromagnetic pulse (effect 2) that is generated by the explosion is the cause, in turn, of the knocking out of electrical equipment (a subordinate effect). The thermal pulse (effect 3) causes second-degree burns (a subordinate effect) in exposed humans in a 280-square-mile area. The blast wave (effect 4) causes the destruction of buildings (a subordinate effect), and the radioactive fallout (effect 5) causes radiation disease (a subordinate effect) in humans. As the following chart shows, cause-and-effect relationships can be complicated.

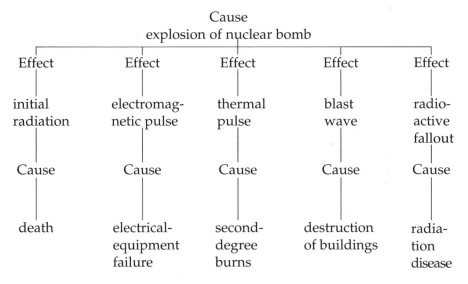

You should keep two factors in mind when you are writing and **revising** a cause-and-effect essay. First, be sure that you have actually thought through the causes and effects very carefully. You should not be satisfied with considering only obvious or simple causes. For example, we tend to oversimplify and cite one cause as the reason for a war—the attack on Pearl Harbor for the United States entering World War II, the firing on Fort Sumter for the start of the Civil War, and so on. For the most part, these tend to be the last of many contributing causes that led to the wars. A thoughtful discussion of such a topic in your writing would include an explanation of some of the contributing, less obvious but perhaps more important, causes.

Second, you should be careful that you do not mistake an event as a cause simply because it preceded a particular effect. For instance, if a child swallows a coin and then comes down with measles, it would be inaccurate and faulty reasoning, a **fallacy**—in this case, a *post hoc* (meaning "after this, therefore because of this") *fallacy*—to assume that swallowing the coin was a cause of the measles. Other common fallacies you should guard against in both your reading and your writing include the following.

- The *hasty generalization,* which is reasoning based on too few examples or insufficient evidence. "The cause of World War II was the Japanese bombing of Pearl Harbor."
- The *non sequitur,* which is claiming an effect that does not necessarily follow from the stated cause. "He believes in the supernatural because he has read the Harry Potter books."

Even though you need to guard against fallacies, you should also be aware that writers do not always state a cause-and-effect relationship directly. Sometimes they **imply** the relationship and leave it to the reader to **infer** the relationship. That is, the writer does not state the relationship, but arranges certain information in such a way that the reader will be able to conclude that the relationship exists, as in the following sentences.

> On the ground next to the parked Jeep, the compass glinted in the moonlight. Deep in the woods, shielded from the moon, the hungry teenager circled in the dark with little idea where he had been or how to get where he wanted to go.

Although the writer does not directly state what happened, it is not hard to infer that the teenager dropped his compass without realizing it, with the effect that he is now lost.

You will need to make inferences when you read cause-and-effect writing as well as other **modes of development.** When you make an inference, be sure that you can pinpoint the information and trace the logic on which your inference is based. When you are writing about cause and effect, be sure to give enough information, directly or indirectly, so that your reader can determine the cause-and-effect relationship.

You use cause-and-effect reasoning every day in solving problems and making decisions. Legislators create laws to address the causes of certain problems. In a similar way, scientists find cures for diseases when they are able to isolate the causes of those diseases. Understanding the relation between causes and effects is extremely important in both day-to-day living and long-range planning. Communicating your understanding in writing is significant evidence of your ability to reason clearly and accurately.

Giving In

Michelle Cottle

She didn't want to, but Michelle gives in and buys a minivan.

Words to Know

paraphernalia   collection of equipment
sociological   human, social meaning
unabashed   not ashamed, not embarrassed

Getting Started

Do you "label" people by the kind of car they drive, clothes they
wear, place where they live, or some other notion?

We did it. With less than two months to go until our second child is
scheduled to arrive, my husband and I swallowed our pride, plundered
our savings and joined the much ridiculed ranks of minivan owners. It
had to be done. Neither of our old vehicles had what it takes to handle
two car seats, two parents, the odd grandparent and the sheer tonnage
of baby paraphernalia required for even quick trips to the grocery. Still,
it took multiple visits to the dealership before I came to terms with the
sociological enormity of what we were about to do. In America, you are
what you drive. And as everyone knows, cruising around in a shiny new
minivan definitely announces to your fellow road warriors, "I am an
unabashed suburban breeder."

Questions about the Reading

1. What is it that the writer and her husband did?
2. What was the cause that made the writer and her husband take the
   action they did?
3. Why do you think the writer resisted doing what she and her husband eventually did?
4. What does the writer mean by "the sociological enormity" of what
   they did?

Questions about the Writer's Strategies

1. What is the point of view in person in the paragraph? Is it consistent? If it changes, is the change justified?
2. What is the symbol in the paragraph? What is it a symbol for, according to the writer?
3. What is the main idea of the paragraph? State it in your own words.

Writing Assignments

1. Write a paragraph in which you explain the cause or causes of your choice of the car you drive, the jeans you buy, or the school you attend.
2. Suppose that you are going out for dinner and a movie. Write a cause-and-effect paragraph in which you explain your choice of restaurant and movie.

3. Suppose that you need to buy a new (or used) car. Using the Internet, research the market and dealers in your town for the kind of car you want. Then write an extended paragraph in which you explain the cause or causes of your choice of car to buy and of dealer who sells the car. In addition to using cause and effect, include comparison and contrast and examples in your paragraph.

Why Eat Junk Food?

Judith Wurtman

*Each day, Americans eat 50 million pounds of sugar, 3 million gallons of
ice cream, and 5.8 million pounds of chocolate candy. Yet junk foods, as
they are commonly known, contain few if any of the nutrients needed to
maintain good health. Why, then, do people eat so much junk food? Judith
Wurtman suggests two reasons.*

Words to Know

confectionaries sweets, candies
depicted shown, represented
euphoria a feeling of well-being

Getting Started

What is your favorite junk food? Do you eat it very often?

We crunch and chew our way through vast quantities of snacks and
confectionaries and relieve our thirst with multicolored, flavored soft
drinks, with and without calories, for two basic reasons. The first is simple:
the food tastes good, and we enjoy the sensation of eating it. Second, we
associate these foods, often without being aware of it, with the highly plea-
surable experiences depicted in the advertisements used to promote their
sale. Current television advertisements demonstrate this point: people
turn from grumpiness to euphoria after crunching a corn chip. Others
water ski into the sunset with their loved ones while drinking a popular
soft drink. People entertain on the patio with friends, cook over campfires
without mosquitoes, or go to carnivals with granddad munching away at
the latest candy or snack food. The people portrayed in these scenarios are
all healthy, vigorous, and good looking; one wonders how popular the
food they convince us to eat would be if they would crunch or drink away
while complaining about low back pain or clogged sinuses.

Questions about the Reading

1. Why do people consume snacks and soft drinks?
2. How do television advertisements portray people eating snack foods?

3. What do you think would happen if television advertisements showed people complaining about poor health while eating snack foods?

Questions about the Writer's Strategies

1. Is the *topic* of this paragraph stated directly or implied? If it is stated directly, where is it located? If it is implied, state it in your own words.
2. What is the predominant *mode of development* of this paragraph? Are any other modes of development used?
3. Identify the cause-and-effect elements of this essay.

Writing Assignments

1. Go to the library or the Internet and research some of the long-term effects of eating a steady diet of junk food or food that isn't nutritious. Then write an essay explaining these effects.
2. Have you ever drunk too much coffee or soda that contains caffeine? Write a paragraph explaining the effects of consuming too much caffeine.
3. Aside from eating well, what other steps can you take to ensure good health? Write a paragraph that describes these steps and their effects on your health.

An Eyewitness Account

Jack London

> Jack London (1876–1916) is best known for such adventure novels as
> The Call of the Wild. In this paragraph from an essay published in May
> 1906 in Collier's Weekly, he describes the effects of the devastating San
> Francisco earthquake of April 16, 1906.

Words to Know

conflagration   destructive fire
imperial   magnificent, majestic
nabobs   rich men
wrought   caused

Getting Started

Have you ever experienced a fire, flood, or other natural disaster?

The earthquake shook down in San Francisco hundreds of thousands of dollars' worth of walls and chimneys. But the conflagration that followed burned up hundreds of millions of dollars' worth of property. There is no estimating within hundreds of millions the actual damage wrought. Not in history has a modern imperial city been so completely destroyed. San Francisco is gone! Nothing remains of it but memories and a fringe of dwelling houses on its outskirts. Its industrial section is wiped out. Its social and residential section is wiped out. The factories and warehouses, the great stores and newspaper buildings, the hotels and the palaces of the nabobs, are all gone. Remains only the fringe of dwelling houses on the outskirts of what was once San Francisco.

Questions about the Reading

1. According to the writer, how many dollars' worth of property were destroyed by the earthquake?
2. If the earthquake shook down walls and chimneys, what do you think caused the devastating fire that followed?
3. What happened to the San Francisco industrial section?
4. What were the only things that remained of San Francisco after the earthquake?

Questions about the Writer's Strategies

1. What is the tone of the paragraph?
2. Is the paragraph objective, subjective, or both?
3. Identify the cause-and-effect elements in the paragraph.
4. What modes of development does the writer use in addition to cause and effect?

Writing Assignments

1. Watch your local news report and write a paragraph in which you suggest the cause and effects of a reported fire, flood, robbery, or accident.
2. Write a paragraph in which you identify some of the effects of the closing of a business that employs many people in your city or town.
3. Write a paragraph in which you explain the possible effects on a business of its product being determined harmful.

A Momentous Arrest

Martin Luther King Jr.

> *Martin Luther King Jr. was catapulted into international fame when, working for the Southern Christian Leadership Conference, he organized blacks in Montgomery, Alabama, to boycott that city's segregated buses in 1955 and 1956. King, preaching nonviolent resistance to segregation, became the most important leader in the civil rights movement that changed American life so radically over the next decade. Here, in a simple, matter-of-fact tone, King tells of the incident that sparked the Montgomery bus boycott.*

Words to Know

accommodate   to make space for, oblige
complied   carried out willingly

Getting Started

Have you ever disobeyed a rule because you thought it was unfair?

On December 1, 1955, an attractive Negro seamstress, Mrs. Rosa Parks, boarded the Cleveland Avenue Bus in downtown Montgomery. She was returning home after her regular day's work in the Montgomery Fair—a leading department store. Tired from long hours on her feet, Mrs. Parks sat down in the first seat behind the section reserved for whites. Not long after she took her seat, the bus operator ordered her, along with three other Negro passengers, to move back in order to accommodate boarding white passengers. By this time every seat in the bus was taken. This meant that if Mrs. Parks followed the driver's command she would have to stand while a white male passenger, who had just boarded the bus, would sit. The other three Negro passengers immediately complied with the driver's request. But Mrs. Parks quietly refused. The result was her arrest.

Questions about the Reading

1. Was Mrs. Parks breaking any law or custom in sitting where she did?
2. Why didn't Mrs. Parks move when the bus driver asked her to? Do you think she would have moved if the white passenger had been a woman instead of a man?

3. Was Mrs. Parks thinking about the civil rights movement when she refused to move? Explain your answer.
4. What is it about Mrs. Parks's action that seems so symbolic of the early civil rights movement?

Questions about the Writer's Strategies

1. Which sentence states the cause in this paragraph? Which one states the effect? *FACTS   Emotions*
2. Do you think the writer presents the incident objectively or subjectively? Use words and phrases from the paragraph to support your answer.
3. Other than cause and effect, what mode of development dominates in this paragraph?
4. What is the order in which the incidents in the paragraph are arranged?
5. Do you sympathize with Mrs. Parks? Explain your answer, citing examples from the essay that influence your feelings.

Writing Assignments

1. Think of a situation that made you angry enough to defy authority and risk discipline or even arrest. Perhaps you protested an unfair grade, a school rule, an unjust traffic ticket, or something of more consequence, like contamination of your city's water supply. Using cause and effect as your mode of development, describe in a paragraph what happened. Try to write objectively.
2. The civil rights movement of the 1950s and 1960s brought about many positive changes in our country's attitude towards minorities. There are, however, still steps that can be taken. In a paragraph, suggest one possible change the country can make, and speculate on the effects it could have on the lives of minority citizens.

On Being Unemployed

Nelliejean Smith (student)

In the paragraph that follows, we learn of the many effects that unemployment can have on a person's life. The writer makes us see—and feel with her—that unemployment is a traumatic experience. Nelliejean Smith has proven, however, that she can cope with it, for she wrote this paragraph as a student at Cuyahoga Community College.

Words to Know

bureaucracy an administrative section of government that is often impersonal and inflexible, red tape

evoke to summon or call forth, to elicit

Getting Started

In what ways do the effects of unemployment reach deeper than an empty bank account?

Being unemployed creates many problems for my family and me. First of all, there are financial problems. We have cut back on the quality of groceries we purchase. We now buy two pounds of hamburger in place of two pounds of sirloin. This hamburger is also divided into quantities sufficient for three meals: one may be creole beef, one chili, and the other spaghetti. There is also less money for clothing. Dresses must be altered and made into blouses; pants make nice skirts after some alteration. I have two more very sticky problems. I've fallen behind in the rental payments for our apartment, and now I am experiencing difficulties trying to pay the back rent. The other sticky problem is my son's tuition payments. There does not seem to be any way that I can send a complete payment to his college. These are not the only problems I face. I also have psychological problems as a result of unemployment. Often I wonder why this has happened to me. Then depression and confusion take over, and I feel drained of all my abilities. The one question that fills my mind most often is the following: Why can't I get employment? This question evokes in me a lack of self-confidence and self-worth. I am haunted by an overall feeling of uselessness. My other problems center on trying to cope with the bureaucracy of the Employment Bureau. Once I get to the Employment Bureau, I stand in line to sign up. I then wait in another line to which I must report. Once I go through all of this, I am sent out for job interviews, only to find that the employer wants someone with more experience. To top everything off, I had to wait almost six months to receive my first unemployment check. As you can see, there is often a frustratingly long delay in receiving benefits. My family and I have suffered through many problems because of my unemployment.

Questions about the Reading

1. What do you think makes the inability to pay rent and her son's tuition particularly "sticky" problems for the writer?
2. What makes the writer feel "drained" of her abilities?
3. What psychological effects do you think the writer's unsuccessful job interviews have on her?

Questions about the Writer's Strategies

1. What is the main idea of this paragraph? Where is this idea first introduced? Where is it repeated?
2. Transitional words and phrases provide a bridge between points in this paragraph. Identify the writer's transitions.
3. The writer uses many examples to illustrate the effects of her unemployment. Identify two effects and two examples for each of these effects.
4. What order does the writer use in discussing the problems?

Writing Assignments

1. Is the employment bureau the writer describes doing a good job? In a paragraph, describe the effects of the bureau's procedures.
2. *Working Together* Join with some classmates to discuss the effects unemployment has on the American people as a whole. Do you think it has been affected by the outsourcing of jobs and/or global trade, or has the production of goods such as automobiles within our country offset outsourcing? Using the Internet and your library, read some articles on this topic. Then collaborate with your classmates to write a cause-and-effect essay in which you describe some of the social and economic effects of unemployment.

Wanted Children

Patrick Steptoe

When Louise Brown was born in England in 1978, the whole world knew about it. What was so significant about this baby? As a result of the long research and experiments of a doctor named Patrick Steptoe and a biologist named Robert Edwards, Louise was the first child ever conceived through a technique known as in vitro fertilization. *She was the first so-called test-tube baby. In the book* A Matter of Life, *Steptoe tells how an encounter early in his medical career with a woman who was unable to bear children started him on the lifelong quest that ended with the birth of Louise Brown.*

Words to Know

collaboration   a joint effort

digs   living quarters

feasible   capable of being accomplished or brought about

gynecologist   women's doctor

hypothetical   assumed to be true

irrevocable   not capable of being retracted or revoked

obstetrician   doctor who delivers babies

occluded   obstructed, shut off

perturbed   troubled

plight   a bad condition

repugnant   disagreeable

wont   custom

Getting Started

What is something you had to work hard to achieve?

$\mathbf{S}$he did not realize I was a medical student. Despite my youthful 1 appearance she called me, "Doctor," then briefly lost control. "What have I done wrong," she cried, "not to have a family of my own?" Perturbed I tried to comfort her and in a moment she managed to continue, "I would have liked to have a large family but I've been married seven years and . . ." Her voice trailed off.

I nodded. There were eight in my own family, eight brothers and 2 sisters in the happy Steptoe family. I was the fifth and youngest son. "I understand," I said.

Gently I asked her more questions and finally said, "Mr. Gwillim will 3 see you soon."

C. M. Gwillim was the consultant at St. George's Hospital in London.   4
He was a superb gynecologist and obstetrician and I was on his team.

Soon the notes I had made, her case history, lay on Mr. Gwillim's desk.   5
He read them out to the other medical students while I gazed beyond Mr.
Gwillim's head at the patient's tell-tale confirmatory X rays on the luminous
screens. It was evident that she, like millions of other women all over the
world, suffered from tubal occlusions, possibly as a result of some previous
infection, and consequently she would never be able to conceive and have
a baby. Her own ovum descending each month could not pass through her
blocked Fallopian tubes to be fertilized by any sperm ascending.

"In Britain alone," Mr. Gwillim told the students, "2 per cent of all   6
female adults have blocked tubes. To be sure, if these tubes could be
opened or reconstructed through surgery many women so afflicted
would no longer be infertile."

Surgery, even in those pre-war days when I was a medical student,   7
could help a small minority of women with occluded tubes. But the
vast majority were less fortunate and had their long-held hopes of having a family thwarted irrevocably. And so it remains to this day, despite
the advances in surgical techniques. Too often gynecologists like Mr.
Gwillim, before and since the war, have had to be truthful and tell the
dismayed patient, "I'm afraid you will never . . ." *Never.* That verdict of
"never," though softly spoken, leaves the woman shaking, empty, her
face too naked, her private grief too unconcealed. That word "never" is
one I have heard enunciated in gynecological Outpatients and wards too
often over the years. I have had to say it myself. Many times.

But now Mr. Gwillim was telling us, "I would remind you that when   8
a woman who has been married for a number of years, asks why it is she
cannot have a baby there are other causes besides tubal occlusion and
the fault, if fault it can be called, is not always to be found in the female
partner. In at least one-third of cases the male is solely responsible. In this
particular case though . . ." Mr. Gwillim hesitated and turned to a nurse.
"Ask the patient to step in, please."

I can't remember the name of that patient whose case history I had   9
recorded in St. George's Hospital and who soon appeared through the
door. But I recall how she had asked me earlier, "What have I done
wrong?" and how facing Mr. Gwillim intensely, quietly, she said, "I want
a baby, doctor, I want one of my own." I was a student and I felt for her
deeply. There have been so many other women since then expressing the
same longings, the same unnecessary guilt feelings, and I, older, a gynecologist myself, have felt the same rush of sympathy for them.

Mr. Gwillim spoke to her with great tact and delicacy but she looked 10
uncomprehendingly towards her own X rays on the lit screen, and the
students, I among them, shifted uneasily.

The consultant explained how her Fallopian tubes were severely 11 distorted and blocked as a result of some previous infection but it became evident that the patient did not understand what was meant by Fallopian tubes. So Mr. Gwillim began at the beginning, explaining everything gently.

"When a female egg-cell, an ovum, is released by a woman's ovary 12 it may proceed into those tubes that lead into and are attached to the womb—the Fallopian tubes. Then, after sexual intercourse, one of the many sperms swimming up from the opposite direction may meet that egg, may enter it and, as they say, fertilize it. That's the beginning of pregnancy, that's how the baby begins. For the fertilized egg soon divides into two cells, into four cells, and so on, becoming bigger and bigger and burrowing into the nourishing wall of the mother's womb. There it develops for nine months until the baby is ready to be born. . . . But if the egg can't descend down the Fallopian tubes because these are obstructed in the first place, none of that can happen."

The patient then asked an astonishing question. "Doctor, can't the Fal- 13 lopian tubes which you say are blocked be by-passed?"

"Oh no," Mr. Gwillim said, looking at the students. We shook our 14 heads.

We knew that if the Fallopian tubes could not be reopened or recon- 15 structed satisfactorily there was no way the sperm could reach the egg to fertilize it. The egg could not be taken from a woman's ovary, placed in a laboratory culture dish and her husband's sperm added to fertilize it. Nor could such a hypothetical fertilized egg be then placed into the same woman's womb to burrow into its wall, to be nourished there, to develop, to grow, to become, after nine months, a normal, much-desired and much-to-be-loved baby. No, we students did not think of such possibilities in those pre-war days.

So no hope was given to the patient that afternoon in the Outpatients 16 at St. George's. Mr. Gwillim had to say, "I'm so sorry." The patient had to leave the hospital defeated; later that evening I thought of her plight as I played the piano at my digs, played perhaps a Beethoven or Schubert sonata, as was my wont when I found myself in certain moods and is still my habit today. I did not know of course—in those days before the war—that one day the quest of by-passing the blocked Fallopian tubes would be one I would share with a Dr. Bob Edwards.

Round about the time that same patient had to leave St. George's 17 Hospital without hope, a Harvard scientist, Dr. John Rock, thought that he had actually managed to fertilize a human egg *in vitro*—that is, in the laboratory, outside the body (literally translated "in glass"). He reported that he had seen this fertilized egg divide into three cells. His claims were discounted. Dr. John Rock's observation of the three cells was considered by other scientists to be merely an example of parthenogenesis—that is to say, the egg had been stimulated to divide without being fertilized by a sperm. In subsequent years similar claims by others were also shown to be mistaken.

Thus when Bob Edwards and I eventually made our quest public, 18 scientists still did not truly believe that laboratory fertilization of the human egg was feasible. Many, if they considered the matter at all, thought such a procedure undesirable: the notion of initiating human life *in vitro* being repugnant to them, unacceptable in principle. Some were fearful of the physical consequences of fertilization *in vitro*. They asked, "Supposing the baby born is abnormal, a cyclops say, or some other monster?" One American Protestant theologian, Paul Ramsey of Princeton, even declared that he half-hoped that the first child born through such a method would be impaired and be publicly displayed!

Though our aspirations were only to help women like that patient 19 who years ago in Outpatients had whispered to me, a mere medical student, "What have I done wrong not to have a family of my own?" we certainly had to face opposition—sometimes from colleagues in the medical and scientific world on both sides of the Atlantic. So throughout our work, throughout our collaboration, we have had to be alive to the ethical considerations that are a natural accompaniment of the trend of scientific research and medical practice we undertook. We have had to confront objections raised and to resolve genuine doubts expressed. Most of the time though, our preoccupations have not been concerned with ethics; rather they have been dense with scientific speculations, technical problems. For on the way to our goal we experienced many setbacks, many disappointments, numerous difficulties.

The collaboration between Bob, a scientist trained in genetics, embry- 20 ology and immunology, and myself, a doctor specializing in gynecology, endures in confidence and friendship. Our collaboration began when we met each other in 1968. The quest began even before our meeting—more than a decade earlier when Bob observed fertilized mouse eggs while a very young scientist working in a laboratory in Edinburgh. The quest reached its culmination when both of us heard one Tuesday night in July 1978—we shall never forget it—the longed-for, normal cry of a baby, conceived out of the womb and now born in an operating theater in the Lancashire town of Oldham where for many years I have worked and near which I have long lived. The delighted mother of that baby was a young woman not too different, I dare say, from many other childless women I have seen over the years, desperate that they should remain irrevocably barren—indeed not utterly different from that patient who once attended Mr. Gwillim's Outpatients at St. George's Hospital and who walked out into the streets of pre-war London tearful and without hope.

Questions about the Reading

1. How did Dr. Steptoe become interested in helping women who could not have children through normal methods become pregnant?
2. When did this interest come about? How many years later did Dr. Steptoe become actively involved in scientific investigation to help women with blocked Fallopian tubes?
3. What is *in vitro* fertilization?
4. What did Dr. Steptoe and his colleague succeed in doing?

Questions about the Writer's Strategies

1. What *process* does Dr. Steptoe explain in this essay? Explain why his explanation of this process is an essential part of this cause-effect paper.
2. What *effect* did Dr. Steptoe's interest in women with blocked Fallopian tubes have on medical science?
3. Is more than one cause mentioned for Dr. Steptoe's interest in fertility? Do the causes seem a logical explanation for his willingness to work long years to cure infertility due to blocked Fallopian tubes?

Writing Assignments

1. Write a cause-effect paper in which you discuss the reasons why you are willing to put in long hours in your own work.
2. Write an essay in which you discuss the effects of your own hard work or that of someone you know well. Although your work did not change the world as Dr. Steptoe's did, perhaps it had an impact on the people around you or gave you a profound sense of self-satisfaction.

The Praise Method

Trent Jones and Carlton Stowers

What makes a child want to learn? It's a question every teacher and every parent must ask. Trent Jones, who teaches in the last one-room schoolhouse in Texas, here offers an answer that has worked for him. It appeared in the book Where the Rainbows Wait, which Jones wrote with Carlton Stowers.

Words to Know

allies   people united in formal or personal relationships
incredible   unbelievable

Getting Started

What do you think might cause a child to misbehave in school? What would you do to handle the situation?

When we moved to Terlingua one of the things I was most eager to try 1 was something I called the *praise method*. What I wanted to do was place a strong emphasis on the positive aspects of a student's accomplishments instead of constantly dealing with the things he did wrong.

One of the first real opportunities I had to put this method of teaching 2 to a strong test came about three years ago when a fourth-grader named Rodney, and his two older sisters, enrolled in the school. Their parents had moved to Terlingua Ranch and were selling real estate.

I can well remember my first impression of Rodney. He was a quiet 3 kid who never looked anyone directly in the eye, never spoke unless spoken to, and was constantly looking around as if to see who might be looking at him for whatever reason.

As I was signing the children up, it became immediately obvious 4 what Rodney's problem was. No sooner had I written their names on the registration forms than both of the sisters began telling me how poorly Rodney had done in the other schools they had attended and that the truth of the matter was that their little brother simply wasn't very smart. They told me that I shouldn't expect too much from Rodney. All this, mind you, while he was standing there, looking down at the floor with this embarrassed look on his face.

A few days later their mother stopped by the school and reempha- 5 sized what her daughters had told me. I listened to what she said, made

no comment myself, and privately made up my mind to prove to everyone in that family that Rodney wasn't as dumb as they thought. My first
chore, of course, would be to convince Rodney himself that he wasn't
an impossible case. I would have to make him believe in himself despite
what he was hearing at home. He had obviously not been allowed to
succeed at anything. To his family he was a failure. To himself he was a
failure. What I had to do was allow him to be a success.

So I very slowly began to work on him. At first he didn't want to   6
do anything. He didn't even want to try. But I kept after him, making
him do his work as best he could, and then I would pick something out
to praise. Sometimes I had to look pretty hard to find something but I
praised him constantly. Over and over. I would tell him his work was
wonderful and that I was very lucky to have him in my class.

It became apparent almost immediately that Rodney's greatest prob-   7
lem was reading. On the other hand, he did show some ability with numbers. So every day we would begin with his math lesson. He did it fairly
well and therefore started the day off with a feeling of accomplishment
and confidence. Having been successful with his math work and praised
for that success, he would then strive to succeed in his other subjects for
the remainder of the day.

Within a few months Rodney's personality began to undergo a com-   8
plete change. He began to smile occasionally. He even laughed now and
then. He began to do his work without so much prompting and was participating in class activities with the other students. Rodney was beginning to learn. And he was beginning to believe in himself.

Which is not to say the battle was over. He still had his sisters con-   9
stantly telling him that he wasn't on a level with the other kids in the
school. I tried to see to it that they didn't hound him about it at school,
but I knew for a fact that they stayed on him pretty good at home. And
the incredible thing about it all to me was the fact that evidently their
mother continued to agree with her daughters. At school I could offer
Rodney some measure of protection from the negative input. I tried to
work on his sisters, pointing out to them that if they cared about their
younger brother they could be a big help to him by not making him feel
like a failure. In that respect I failed miserably. They were so convinced
that their brother was dumb that they wouldn't even listen to me.

So what it boiled down to after a while was the fact that Rodney was   10
something of a success at school but still a miserable failure at home.

I decided, then, to really lay it on thick, to build Rodney's confidence   11
up to a point where he could stand on his own two feet regardless of
what others said to him. Not only did I flatter him privately, but did so

in front of the class whenever the opportunity arose. I wanted him to get to a point where he would tell his sisters, his parents, and the rest of the world that he was something.

With every passing day and every new word of praise, Rodney's 12 classroom performance improved. Before long he was boldly telling people that he was getting smarter and was "one of Mr. Jones's best students." I'd never seen such a complete change of attitude in a child and, quite honestly, was feeling pretty proud of myself.

Until I started getting flack from his parents. They simply were not 13 going to accept the fact that their son was doing so well. They challenged me about it, suggesting that the good grades he was bringing home were not really earned but, rather, just a gift from a pushover teacher who gave everyone good grades. They had made up their minds that Rodney was a dumb kid who had finally found a teacher who would simply give him good grades regardless. And sadly enough they let Rodney know how they felt about the matter.

I can only imagine the misery he must have gone through every after- 14 noon, having to go home to such a totally negative environment—and how excited he was each morning to return to school and get away from it.

Rodney's case is not really that unique. In my years of teaching I've 15 run across all too many cases like his. What it often boils down to is that the academic problems are not the fault of the student but the parents and sometimes even the teachers. Those people who are supposed to be a kid's strongest allies prove to be his biggest enemies.

A conversation I once had with another teacher perhaps best illus- 16 trates what I'm talking about. I was trying to explain my theory of praising a child to promote success and the teacher said to me, "What you're actually doing is lying to the kid. You're telling him that he's more than he really is. If a child is not as smart as the rest of the students, he simply has to learn to accept that fact and make the best of the situation."

That is what many of us in Terlingua would classify as garden variety 17 bullshit. What he was telling me, in effect, was that there are smart kids and dumb kids and that they had damn well better learn to accept their proper place in society. As tragic as it may seem, I'm afraid that this train of thought typifies the way many parents and teachers feel about their students and children. I personally think they are dead wrong. How can you be lying to a kid by telling him that he is somebody special, that he is capable of doing wonderful, self-satisfying things?

Questions about the Reading

1. What causes the writer to take such a strong interest in Rodney? Do you think that his reasons are justified? What *person* does the writer use in this essay? (See Glossary for *person*.)
2. What is the writer's first impression of Rodney?
3. How does Rodney change during the period of time covered by the essay?
4. What causes Rodney to change?
5. What effect does the writer's constant praise have on Rodney?
6. Is Rodney's family instrumental in helping him to change? Support your answer with details from the reading.
7. What does the writer's relationship with Rodney reveal about the possibilities of student/teacher relationships?

Questions about the Writer's Strategies

1. This essay follows the general model of a well-organized composition. What paragraph(s) make up the *introduction,* the *body,* and the *conclusion* of the essay? (See chapter 1.)
2. What *order* does the author use to organize his explanation of his method of helping Rodney? (See Glossary for *order*.)
3. What are the *effects*—the results—of the author's praise?
4. The author says, in paragraph 15, that "people who are supposed to be a kid's strongest allies prove to be his biggest enemies." What *mode of development* does the author use to support that point? (See Glossary for *mode of development*.)

Writing Assignments

1. Do you agree that a positive school or home environment may have a positive effect on students who have been labeled "slow learners"? Write an essay in which you discuss the effects of approaching people in a positive way. How does it affect you? How does it affect them?
2. What causes children to misbehave or fail in school? Write an essay in which you discuss the reasons.
3. You probably have had some positive influence on some person you know. Explain what actions you took (the causes) and the effect(s) of your actions.

Reading for Pure Pleasure

Eileen Simpson

Eileen Simpson suffers from dyslexia. This mysterious problem, only recently understood, is an inability to read words on a page. It does not seem to be connected with any other physical or mental deficiency. Not until she was a teenager did Simpson sit down and read an entire book from cover to cover. What made her do it then? Here she tells us what made her start, what made her keep going, and what she felt when she finished. The passage, from Reversals: A Personal Account of Victory over Dyslexia, *reads like an account of triumph in a great physical ordeal—and, for Simpson, it was.*

Words to Know

boisterous   noisy and unrestrained

evasive   intentionally vague

exhilarated   made joyous

incomprehensible   not understandable

interlude   time between events

malodorous   having a bad smell

motivation   stimulation or incentive to do an action

recourse   an appeal

relegated   assigned to a particular position or category

ruffian   a tough or rowdy fellow

tedious   boring

unaccustomed   not in the habit of

vexed   irritated, annoyed, bothered

Getting Started

What activities do you particularly dislike but must still do most days?

To read for pleasure never occurred to me—until Easter vacation 1
my sophomore year.

I remember the occasion clearly, as one does when one performs an 2
important and unaccustomed act. It was in the house of our Westchester
relatives. Uncle Charlie was down in his Maiden Lane office, Aunt Hilda
was out shopping, and Marie, my built-in companion, was upstairs in
bed with a cold. Heavy rain kept me indoors. I wandered from room to
room, ate a piece of fruit, picked out a tune on the piano, looked over the
window, flopped down in a wicker chair on the sun porch. Rain! For one
who lacked inner resources there was *nothing to do.*

On the glass-topped table next to the chair was a score pad for bridge. 3
In my new backhand, I made a list of my current crushes. Ray Tara led
the rest. I played a solitary game of tic-tac-toe. With little interest, I looked
at the book the pad had been resting on. *Years of Grace* it was called. At
one time there had been a lot of talk about it at the dinner table. A best-
seller, it had been read by everyone in the house—except, of course, me.
Afterward, it had been relegated to the bookcase on the sun porch. I was
about to put it back where it belonged. But then, remembering that I had
nothing else to do, I flipped through its pages. Chapters entitled "André"
and "Jimmy" reminded me of an earlier vacation and of an unanswered
question. During the Christmas holiday the year I was in eighth grade,
Marie and I were invited to Jimmy Doyle's house for the afternoon. We
had played with Jimmy's new chemistry set, making malodorous concoctions, and were having a boisterous game of round-robin Ping-Pong
when Mrs. Doyle called us to come to the dining room for a "little tea
party." There was an awkward moment when it became clear that the
French boy from up the street, who had been among those playing with
us, was not being invited to the table. Since I had been quite taken with
André's dark good looks and his silky accent, and much preferred him to
chubby and unexotic Jimmy, I was saddened and puzzled by his exclu-
sion. The expression on André's face as he turned away, pretending he
didn't care, came between me and the splendid refreshments.

A plate of sugar hearts, colored red for the season, was passed around 4
after the dainty sandwiches. At the end of the meal, I slipped one of the
hearts out of the dish and was wrapping it in my handkerchief when I felt
Mrs. Doyle's eyes on me. She gave me a long, questioning look and said,
"That's all right, dear. You may have it. Why don't you eat it now?"

It was not for me, I blurted out.   5

"For whom is it then?"   6

Embarrassed by what I was afraid she would take as a criticism of her 7
behavior, I fumbled and stuttered and tried to beg off answering. When
it was clear that she wouldn't let me join the others until I confessed, I
admitted it was for André.

"Well, then," she said coldly, taking the candy from my hand, "we'll 8
just put it back on the table, shall we?"

What was wrong with André? Aunt Hilda was evasive. She said per- 9
haps André was not the Doyles's "sort." Whatever did that mean? His
elegant manners made Jimmy and the other boys who had been at the
tea party seem like ruffians. I puzzled over this episode for some time
and then forgot about it. The startling coincidence of finding those two
names as chapter headings in *Years of Grace* aroused my curiosity again.

The "André" chapter, which opens the book, begins with dialogue. 10
Good. I like dialogue. It goes quickly. Jane and André, on whom she

has a crush, are in high school. So am I. Jane is fifteen. So am I. She daydreams about dances. So do I. André wears a beret. He is going to be an artist when he grows up. He'll live in Paris. He is so attractive (in an interesting way), and so gallant with Jane, that I am falling in love with him. The author leads me to believe that sooner or later he will kiss Jane—i.e., me. I hurry on, skipping descriptions, of which there are mercifully few, to the section where Jane and André go on an evening picnic. André's parents are with them. Now why did the author bring them along? Won't they be in the way? My impatience is growing. After a tedious interlude, during which André's father sings, "Au clair de la lune," Jane and André go for a walk. Alone. At last!

> "Jane—you *do* love me?" said André.
> Jane only wept the more.
> "Kiss me," said André.
> She raised her lips to his. The ground fell away from under her feet.
> The world was no more. Nothing existed but just—herself and—André.
> "My love," he said again.

The world was no more for me either. Torrid love scenes in movies 11 had not affected me so strongly. They were about gangsters' molls, spies, and sirens. This is about *me*. There is no question of stopping now.

When teachers had tried to interest me in reading by saying, "One 12 learns so much from books," I had thought they meant one learned so many facts, as in, "Your thinking is muddled. You've got to get the facts straight." Facts, except the facts of life, didn't interest me. What interested me was the way people behaved. And why. Why, for example, was Aunt Hilda's neighbor, Mrs. Bradbury, who had such an attractive and seemingly attentive husband, having an affair with another man? I had a feeling Margaret Ayer Barnes knew the answers, and would let me in on some of the secrets of life.

Spring rains and my sister's illness continued for most of the vaca- 13 tion. I read on and on. From time to time Aunt Hilda looked into the sun porch and put her hand to my forehead. Never having seen me read before, she suspected that I was coming down with the cold that had laid Marie low. The only reality for me now was between the covers of my book. The rest of life was a jarring interruption.

André promises Jane's mother, a narrow-minded woman who is dead 14 against him because he's a foreigner and a Catholic, that he won't write to Jane until she's twenty-one. He goes off to Paris. Jane goes to college, makes her debut, meets a nice American Protestant, whom her mother is crazy about, and, two chapters later, marries him. This unromantic match, as unsuitable as Jo's to Mr. Bhaer in *Little Women*, vexed me so much that I threw the book down. The next day, remembering that there was a chapter called "Jimmy," I picked it up again. While the original André had long since vanished from my life, Jimmy Doyle, considerably slimmed down, was very much in it.

The Jimmy in the novel is a composer, married to a college friend of 15 Jane's. When his concerto is played in Chicago, he visits Jane. They begin an affair. Aha! (I'd never heard the word "affair" used in this way until a few days earlier when Aunt Hilda was gossiping with a friend over tea and here it was again.) Jane's affair with Jimmy is rather confusing. What exactly is going on? Is it that the writing is becoming more difficult? Or is it that the strain, the fatigue of reading a whole book is beginning to tell? After ten pages or so I suddenly realize I haven't read a word. My mind has been a blank. Well, not really a blank, come to think of it. Haven't I been having a daydream about the real Jimmy? My daydream (which I am aware of perhaps for the first time) is much more interesting than what the author is saying at the moment. I'm not reading *and I know it*. I finish my daydream, skip the Jimmy section, and hurry to the end. Surely André will appear again and Jane will see what a mistake she made not to marry him.

André does indeed appear in the last chapter. When Jane goes to Paris 16 with her husband, she meets André, who is now a famous sculptor. He invites her to his studio. As she looks over his statues—all nudes!—she realizes that each one is a *different* woman. How right her mother was! Jane realizes that André is not her sort; she could never have been happy with him.

No, no, no! I protested, feeling cheated. Did a reader have no recourse 17 against an author? Before the end of the vacation I thought of a way to take revenge on Margaret Ayer Barnes, Jane's mother, and Mrs. Doyle. To cleanse the bad taste left in my mouth by the scene in the studio, I reread the opening chapter up to the ground-fell-away-from-Jane's-feet scene. When I closed the book, Jane and André were young again. And in love.

Slowly, very slowly, and without being aware of doing so, I had 18 picked up the skills, and equally important, the self-confidence that made it possible for me to read. What I had been lacking was the motivation. The rain, the separation from my sister and other companions, the unanswered questions about Mrs. Doyle's incomprehensible behavior, and a novel written in a straightforward, undemanding style, whose heroine I identified with, provided the necessary inducement.

Following this vacation, whenever my wildly extroverted life, which 19 was filled with activities infinitely more appealing, allowed, I read. I didn't by any means understand everything I read, I didn't develop the habit of reading, but I read. *Years of Grace* had done for me what a solo cross-country automobile trip does for the beginning driver. Having driven through the novel to the end, with no prodding by anyone, carried along by interest and excitement, I was tired but exhilarated. I had overcome my fear of books.

Questions about the Reading

1. What causes the author to begin reading during the Easter vacation of her sophomore year?
2. What activities does the author try before she begins reading?
3. Why does the author become so absorbed by the events in *Years of Grace* that she is willing to take the time to sit still and read the book?
4. What is the reaction of the author's aunt when she sees her reading? Why does she react in this manner?
5. This first experience in reading for pleasure has some effects on the author's life. What are they?

Questions about the Writer's Strategies

1. This essay reads like a *narrative* or story—but it is a true experience rather than a fictional one. What are some of the elements or characteristics present in the work that make it resemble a narrative. (See Chapter 2, "Narration," pages 13–17.)
2. In giving the sequence of steps that made her become interested in reading *Years of Grace*, the narrator also makes use of *process*. At what point in the essay does this happen? What process is involved in her growing fascination with reading? (See "Process," pp. 169–171.)
3. At one point in the essay, the author summarizes the effects of reading her first book for pleasure. Where does this summary occur? What information does it contain?
4. Identify the various *modes of development* found in this essay. Which do you think is the major mode? (See Glossary for *modes of development*.)

Writing Assignments

1. Recall a time when other people were constantly trying to get you to do some activity you didn't especially want to do—such as practicing a musical instrument. Did you ever begin doing this activity on your own? What caused you to do it? What happened as a result? Write an essay in which you explain.
2. Write an essay in which you discuss the long-term effects or benefits that reading for pleasure may have on your life.
3. Do you like or dislike reading? Write a paper in which you explain what you feel are the reasons for your liking or disliking reading.

The Thirsty Animal

Brian Manning

In this personal essay, Brian Manning recounts how he developed into a problem drinker and describes his life now as an alcoholic who has quit drinking. Straightforwardly, he tells of his bittersweet memories of drinking and of his struggle, successful so far, to keep the thirsty "animal living inside" locked in its cage.

Words to Know

accouterments   the items and sensations accompanying a certain activity

Bordeaux   a type of French wine, usually red

lolling   lounging, relaxing

Getting Started

Can you describe some of the negative effects of alcohol on you or someone you know?

I was very young, but I still vividly remember how my father fascinated 1 my brothers and me at the dinner table by running his finger around the rim of his wineglass. He sent a wonderful, crystal tone wafting through the room, and we loved it. When we laughed too raucously, he would stop, swirl the red liquid in his glass and take a sip.

There was a wine cellar in the basement of the house we moved into 2 when I was eleven. My father put a few cases of Bordeaux down there in the dark. We played there with other boys in the neighborhood, hid there, made a secret place. It was musty and cool and private. We wrote things and stuck them in among the bottles and imagined someone way in the future baffled by our messages from the past.

Many years later, the very first time I drank, I had far too much. But I 3 found I was suddenly able to tell a girl at my high school that I was mad about her.

When I drank in college with the men in my class, I was trying to 4 define a self-image I could feel comfortable with. I wanted to be "an Irishman," I decided, a man who could drink a lot of liquor and hold it. My favorite play was Eugene O'Neill's *Long Day's Journey into Night*, my model the drunken Jamie Tyrone.

I got out of college, into the real world, and the drunk on weekends 5 started to slip into the weekdays. Often I didn't know when one drunk ended and another began. The years were measured in hangovers. It took a long time to accept, and then to let the idea sink in, that I was an alcoholic.

It took even longer to do anything about it. I didn't want to believe 6 it, and I didn't want to deny myself the exciting, brotherly feeling I had whenever I went boozing with my friends. For a long time, in my relationships with women, I could only feel comfortable with a woman who drank as much as I did. So I didn't meet many women and spent my time with men in dark barrooms, trying to be like them and hoping I'd be accepted.

It is now two years since I quit drinking, and that, as all alcoholics 7 know who have come to grips with their problem, is not long ago at all. The urge to have "just one" includes a genuine longing for all the accouterments of drink: the popping of a cork, the color of Scotch through a glass, the warmth creeping over my shoulders with the third glass of stout. Those were joys. Ever since I gave them up I remember them as delicious.

I go to parties now and start off fine, but I have difficulty dealing with 8 the changing rhythms as the night wears on. Everyone around me seems to be having a better time the more they drink, and I, not they, become awkward. I feel like a kid with a broken chain when everyone else has bicycled around the corner out of sight. I fight against feeling sorry for myself.

What were the things I was looking for and needed when I drank? I often 9 find that what I am looking for when I want a drink is not really the alcohol, but the memories and laughter that seemed possible only with a glass in my hand. In a restaurant, I see the bottle of vintage port on the shelf, and imagine lolling in my chair, swirling the liquid around in the glass, inhaling those marvelous fumes. I think of my neighbor, Eileen, the funniest woman I ever got smashed with, and I want to get up on a bar stool next to her to hear again the wonderful stories she told. She could drink any man under the table, she claimed, and I wanted to be one of those men who tried. She always won, but it made me feel I belonged when I staggered out of the bar, her delighted laughter following me.

I had found a world to cling to, a way of belonging, and it still attracts 10 me. I pass by the gin mills and pubs now and glance in at the men lined up inside, and I don't see them as suckers or fools. I remember how I felt sitting there after work, or watching a Sunday afternoon ball game, and I long for the smell of the barroom and that ease—toasts and songs, jokes and equality. I have to keep reminding myself of the wasting hangovers, the lost money, the days down the drain.

I imagine my problem as an animal living inside me, demanding a 11 drink before it dies of thirst. That's what it says, but it will never die of thirst. The fact an alcoholic faces is that this animal breathes and waits. It is incapable of death and will spring back to lustful, consuming life with even one drop of sustenance.

When I was eighteen and my drinking began in earnest, I didn't play 12 in the wine cellar at home anymore; I stole there. I sneaked bottles to my room, sat in the window and drank alone while my parents were away. I hated the taste of it, but I kept drinking it, without the kids from the neighborhood, without any thought that I was feeding the animal. And one day, I found one of those old notes we had hidden down there years before. It fell to the ground when I pulled a bottle from its cubbyhole. I read it with bleary eyes, then put the paper back into the rack. "Beware," it said, above a childish skull and crossbones, "all ye who enter here." A child, wiser than I was that day, had written that note.

I did a lot of stupid, disastrous, sometimes mean things in the years 13 that followed, and remembering them is enough to snap me out of the memories and back to the reality that I quit just in time. I've done something I had to do, something difficult and necessary, and that gives me satisfaction and the strength to stay on the wagon. I'm very lucky so far. I don't get mad that I can't drink anymore; I can handle the self-pity that overwhelmed me in my early days of sobriety. From time to time, I daydream about summer afternoons and cold beer. I know such dreams will never go away. The thirsty animal is there, getting a little fainter every day. It will never die. A lot of my life now is all about keeping it in a very lonely cage.

Questions about the Reading

1. What went along with drinking for the writer? Why did he need alcohol to get those effects?
2. Why are parties difficult for the writer?
3. Why did the writer stop drinking?
4. When you finished reading the essay, what opinions had you formed of the writer's personality and character? Cite specific details from the essay to support your opinions.

Questions about the Writer's Strategies

1. What is the main idea of this essay? In which sentences is it most clearly stated?
2. What are the causes in this essay? What are the effects? Do they overlap at all?

3. Other than cause and effect, what modes of development does the writer use? Cite paragraphs in which he uses other modes.
4. The "animal" introduced in paragraph 11 is a metaphor. What does it stand for? Interpret it in your own words.
5. Identify the simile in paragraph 8. Is it effective in helping you understand how the writer feels?

Writing Assignments

1. Describe in an essay the effects that alcohol has on you. If you do not drink, describe the effects that you have seen it have on others.
2. Do you know anyone who abuses alcohol or other substances? If not, you have surely come across the lure of drugs in the media or in school awareness programs. On the basis of what you know and what you have learned from reading this essay, write an essay describing the causes and effects of substance abuse.

ad·sno Shon

3rd person

More Than Words

Victor Flores (student)

Victor Flores is a native of the Northern Mariana Islands who grew up on the picturesque island of Saipan. He attends Leeward Community College and lives in Honolulu, Hawaii. In his essay, he tells us about a mistake he made.

Word to Know

enticed   lured, tempted

Getting Started

Do you remember a particular experience that taught you the importance of being dependable?

I stood there frozen. My feet feeling like they were rooted into the   1
ground, planted too deeply to be moved. My father, in his anger, was yelling at me, and during those minutes that passed, it felt like an eternity. To this day I still remember those words forcing their way into my mind while piercing my heart. My father's bronze, tanned face turned red right before my eyes, like a piece of hot glowing coal. He yelled, "I'm not your friend. I'm your father. Don't treat me like your friends." I was hurt, and I masked my pain over the fear and disappointment.

My father, a hard-working and diligent man who rarely, if ever, stood   2
idle, was furious with me. He was always ready to greet people with a smile. Caring about his appearance, he always neatly combed his thinning hair. He was well dressed and wore comfortable shoes. But on this day it didn't matter. I had exhausted his patience as he waited for me to return home from school. After school that day, with my parents' car, I had driven my friend home. Time had whisked by. When I got home, it was after 5 P.M. It was too late. My father needed me to do something important. At sixteen and with my parents' car, coming home after school wasn't my idea of enjoying the privileges of my free afternoon. Enticed by sitting behind the wheel, it was too easy to get wrapped up in friends and lose track of time.

For as long as I can remember, my parents have always been self-   3
employed. They ran a small retail store, just the two of them for the most part. It was a well-stocked store with fishing supplies, clothing, guitar supplies, sporting goods and comfortable shoes. Every day except

223

Sundays and holidays, going to the post office two and often three times a day was routine. Nearly everything that filled the store's shelves was sent through the post office. Maybe my father had promised a customer that his or her order would be in that afternoon. Or maybe he needed a certain part to repair a fishing reel. Whatever the reason, my father had depended on me to get to the post office, pick up the merchandise and bring it back to the store. Before that day when he yelled at me, I had not realized how important that simple task was and how much they needed me.

Questions about the Reading

1. What was the "task" that the writer's father expected the writer to do? Was the writer usually responsible for doing this task?
2. What did the writer do that made his father angry?
3. What did the writer learn from disappointing his father?

Questions about the Writer's Strategies

1. What is the point of view (person, time, tone) of the essay?
2. What modes of development does the writer use in the essay?
3. What is the simile in the first paragraph of the essay?

Writing Assignments

1. Write an essay in which you tell about a personal experience that taught you an important lesson.
2. Think of an invention or convenience that has had positive effects on your life. Identify the invention or convenience and write an essay explaining its effects on your life.

9

Definition

WHEN WRITERS USE words that they think may be unfamiliar to their readers, they usually will define the words. A **definition** is an explanation of the meaning of a word or term.

In its shortest form, the definition may be simply a **synonym**—a familiar word or phrase that has the same meaning as the unfamiliar word. For example, in "she shows more *empathy* for, or true understanding of, older people than her sister," the word understanding is a synonym for *empathy*. Or the writer may choose to use an **antonym**—a word or phrase that has the opposite meaning of the unfamiliar word—as in "she is a compassionate rather than an *inconsiderate* person." Here the word inconsiderate gives the reader the opposite meaning of *compassionate*.

The writer may also choose to use the kind of precise definition found in dictionaries, called a **formal definition.** In a formal definition, the writer first uses a form of **classification,** assigning the word to the **class** of items to which it belongs, and then describing the characteristics that distinguish it from other items of that class. Here is an example of a formal definition.

Word defined: tiger; class: cat family — A <u>tiger</u>, a member of the <u>cat family</u>, is native to Asia, usually weighs over 350 pounds, and has tawny and black-striped fur.
Description of characteristics

Connotation, which refers to the impressions or qualities we associate with a word, and **denotation,** the dictionary definition of a word, are important in writing a definition. Think of the word *pig*, for instance. The dictionary may tell you that a pig is simply a domestic animal with hooves, short legs, bristly hair, and a blunt snout; and a farmer may tell you that a pig is relatively smarter and cleaner than other farm animals. However, the negative connotations of this word are so strong that you are likely to have trouble thinking of a pig without thinking of filth, fat, and greed.

In writing definitions, it is particularly important to choose your words in such a way that their connotations as well as their denotations will give your readers the correct impression of what you are defining. As you are writing and **revising,** remember to search for the single best word for conveying your ideas.

When you search for connotative words and expressions to use in your writing, beware of **clichés.** Clichés are words or phrases—such as "rosy red," "silly goose," "bull in a china shop," "weird," or "outrageous"—which have become so overused that they indicate a lack of imagination and thought on the part of the writer who uses them. Symbols, too, can be clichés. If you are defining *courage,* for example, using Superman as a symbol to enhance your definition is unlikely to impress your readers. You should also be aware that many clichés take the form of **similes:** "as filthy as a pig," for example. Try to make sure your similes are always of your own creation, not ones you have heard before.

Many complex words and abstract ideas—such as *truth* and *justice*—require longer and more detailed explanations, which are called **extended definitions.** In an extended definition, the writer may use one or more of the methods of development—description, examples, classification, and so forth—that you have learned about in the earlier chapters of this book. For example, the writer might use **process, description,** or **narration**—or all three—as the method of development in an extended definition.

Topic sentence: formal definition	A glacier is an accumulation of snow and ice that continually flows from a mountain ice field toward sea level. Glaciers are
Process	formed when successive snowfalls pile up, creating pressure on the bottom layers. Gradually, the pressure causes the snow on the bottom to undergo a structural change into an extremely dense form of ice called glacier ice, a process that may take several years. Once the ice begins to accumu-
Extended definition: descriptive narration	late, gravity causes the mass to move downhill. Glaciers usually take the path of least resistance, following stream beds or other natural channels down the mountainside. As they move, they scrape along the surface of the earth, picking up rocks and other sediment on the way. The ice and the debris carve a deep U-shaped valley as they proceed down the mountain. If they advance far enough, they will eventually reach the sea and become tidewater glaciers that break off, or calve, directly into salt water. Southeast

Alaska is one of only three places in the world where tidewater glaciers exist. (They also are found in Scandinavia and Chile.) Other glaciers, called hanging glaciers, spill out of icy basins high up on valley walls and tumble toward the valley floor.

Sarah Eppenbach,
Alaska's Southeast

In the example that follows, the writer combines a formal definition with **classification, examples, comparison** and **contrast.**

Formal definition: map
Classification: conventional picture
Characteristics: area of land, sea, or sky

A map is a <u>conventional picture</u> of an <u>area of land, sea, or sky</u>. Perhaps the maps most widely used are the <u>road maps</u> given away by the oil companies. They show the cultural features such as states, towns, parks, and roads, especially paved roads. They show also natural features, such as rivers and lakes, and sometimes mountains. As <u>simple maps,</u> most automobile drivers have on various occasions used sketches drawn by service station men, or by friends, to show the best automobile route from one town to another. 1

Example: road maps

Example: simple maps

Contrast: chart represents water; map represents land

The distinction usually made between "maps" and "charts" is that a chart is a representation of an area consisting chiefly of water; a map represents an area that is predominantly land. It is easy to see how this distinction arose in the days when there was no navigation over land, but a truer distinction is that charts are specially designed for use in navigation, whether at sea or in the air. 2

Contrast: chart for navigation

Example: use of maps

Maps have been used since the earliest civilizations, and explorers find that they are used in rather simple civilizations at the present time by people who are accustomed to traveling. For example, Arctic explorers have obtained considerable help from maps of the coast lines showing settlements, drawn by Eskimo people. Occasionally maps show not only the roads, but pictures of other features. One of the earliest such maps dates from about 1400 B.C. It shows not only roads, but also lakes with fish, and a canal with crocodiles and a bridge over the canal. This is somewhat similar to the modern maps of a state which show for each large town some feature of interest or the chief products of that town. 3

Example: features of some maps

Comparison: features of early maps with ones of modern maps

C. C. Wylie, *Astronomy, Maps, and Weather*

As you can see, you may use any method of development that is appropriate when you need to extend the definition of a word or term.

Whether you are writing an extended definition or relying primarily on some other mode of development, always remember to define any words or terms you use that may be unfamiliar to your readers—particularly any words they must know to understand your meaning. You should also define words with any special or technical meaning.

Running with the Cardio-Bots

Walter Kirn

*Stop by any gym or health center and check out Walter Kirn's definition
of the people working out on the treadmills, StairMasters, and bicycles!*

Words to Know

oblivious   unaware
profoundly   deeply
simulated   imagined, feigned

Getting Started

Do you follow a regular exercise program?

I walk into the gym, and there they are, the cardio-bots, half human,
half machine, eyes fixed on banks of televisions and ears glued to iPods
as they scale imaginary mountains or jog down simulated country roads.
How driven they seem, how profoundly self-conscious. Digital monitors
strapped around their biceps register their blood pressures and heart
rates as their tissues absorb L-glutamine-laced protein drinks that taste
like the sort of thing computers would drink if computers got thirsty.
And though there must be 30 cardio-bots, lifting their sinewy thighs in
unison as their StairMasters and treadmills tick off the number of calories they've burned, each one of them seems to exist in his or her own
universe, oblivious to the rest.

Questions about the Reading

1. What is the writer's opinion of the "cardio-bots" in the gym?
2. Why does the writer describe the cardio-bots as being "half human,
   half machine"?

Questions about the Writer's Strategies

1. What is the main idea of the paragraph? State it in your own
   words.

2. What modes of development does the writer use in the paragraph to define the cardio-bots?

Writing Assignments

1. Write a paragraph in which you define one of the following terms: *walking, running,* or *sleeping.*
2. Write a paragraph in which you define the terms *grocery shopping, doing your laundry,* or *cleaning your room* (assuming you ever do!).

The Ultimate Kitchen Gadget

Robert Capon

> *Anyone who likes to cook owns a number of kitchen gadgets. What is your favorite: a garlic press, a food processor, or a blender? In the following selection, Robert Capon, an Episcopal priest and lover of cooking, defines the ultimate kitchen gadget.*

Word to Know

trice a very short time

Getting Started

What is your favorite gadget: a cell phone, an iPod, a Walkman, or some other device you carry with you?

It is the ultimate kitchen gadget. It serves as a juicier for lemons, oranges and grapefruit, and as a combination seed remover and pulp crusher for tomatoes. It functions as a bowl scraper, an egg separator and a remover of unwelcome particles—the stray bit of eggshell, the odd grain of black rice—from mixing bowl or saucepan. It is a thermometer capable of gauging temperatures up to 500 degrees Fahrenheit and, in addition, is a measuring device for dry ingredients in amounts from 1 tablespoon down to 1/8 teaspoon or less, and for whatever liquids may be called for in the cooking of grains and stocks. It can be used as tongs for removing hot cup custards from the oven, as a mixer of water into pastry dough and as a kneader of bread. Best of all, it cleans up in a trice, presents no storage problems, will not chip, rust or tarnish and, if it cannot be said to be unlosable or indestructible, it nevertheless comes with a lifetime guarantee to remain the one household convenience you will have the least desire either to lose or to destroy. It is, of course, the human hand.

Questions about the Reading

1. Temperatures above about 160 degrees will burn a person's hand. How can the hand be used to gauge temperatures up to 500 degrees?

2. What is the lifetime guarantee of the ultimate kitchen gadget?
3. At what point in the paragraph did you guess what the ultimate kitchen gadget is?

Questions about the Writer's Strategies

1. What is the predominant mode of development used to define the ultimate kitchen gadget?
2. Why doesn't the writer identify what he is defining until the very last sentence?
3. What is the tone of this paragraph?
4. What connotations does the word *gadget* have? Would you normally associate these connotations with the human hand?
5. What is the **irony** in this paragraph?

Writing Assignments

1. Write a paragraph in which you define a household appliance (such as a blender, a vacuum cleaner, or a toaster) by giving examples of its uses and the purposes it serves.

2. Write a definition of the human hand from another point of view. Instead of giving examples of what it can do in the kitchen, describe its physical anatomy—what it looks like underneath the skin. Use the Internet to get correct biological and anatomical information.
3. Write a definition of the human body by giving examples of some of the things it can do.

What Does It Mean to Be Creative?

S. I. Hayakawa

S. I. Hayakawa was a United States senator, the president of San Francisco State College, and an authority on semantics—the study of the development, structure, and changes of language. In this paragraph, he defines the creative person.

Word to Know

examining   investigating, looking at

Getting Started

What do you think it means to be creative?

A creative person, first, is not limited in his thinking to "what everyone knows." "Everyone knows" that trees are green. The creative artist is able to see that in certain lights some trees look blue or purple or yellow. The creative person looks at the world with his or her own eyes, not with the eyes of others. The creative individual also knows his or her own feelings better than the average person. Most people don't know the answer to the question, "How are you? How do you feel?" The reason they don't know is that they are so busy feeling what they are supposed to feel, thinking what they are supposed to think, that they never get down to examining their own deepest feelings.

Questions about the Reading

1. According to the writer, how does the creative person look at the world?
2. What distinguishes the creative individual from the average person?
3. Why do most people not know the answer to "How are you? How do you feel?"

Questions about the Writer's Strategies

1. What is the writer's definition of a creative person?
2. What are two transitional words the writer uses? Would the definition be clearer by changing one of the transitional words? What transitional words would you use in the definition?

Writing Assignments

1. Write a paragraph in which you define and give examples of a creative person.
2. Write a paragraph in which you explain how someone in a certain sport might be creative.

Nostalgia

Richard Shelton

What is the crepuscular? Richard Shelton misses it, along with the bucolic *and* idyllic. *Although he does not define the word, a careful reading tells us what it means.*

Words to Know

bucolic   pastoral, rural, rustic
carnage   slaughter, bloodshed
gentility   politeness, refinement
idyllic   pleasing, simple, picturesque
mayhem   mutilation

Getting Started

Is there something that you remember from your childhood and now miss?

Whatever happened to the crepuscular? It's never mentioned anymore. Years since I heard any reference to the crepuscular. I wonder if anybody notices it now as we once did, creeping in and out with silent majesty, leaving some of us with lumps in our throats. It would be a relief from the carnage and mayhem. I remember sometimes at that time of day in the autumn when there was a chill in the air and somebody was burning leaves somewhere, I could nearly die of happiness. But I am older now and it's illegal to burn leaves. So I guess nobody notices the crepuscular anymore. Or the bucolic. Nobody ever says, "Let's go spend a bucolic weekend in the country." And nobody calls anything idyllic. Whatever became of idyllic afternoons beside the river? And grand passions? Passions don't seem to be grand anymore, just sort of everyday affairs. I guess it's hard to have a grand passion without idyllic afternoons and crepuscular evenings, and we are just too busy to take the time for such things. And nightingales? I never heard one myself, but I certainly read about them, and they seemed to be almost everywhere at one time. Perhaps they were no longer needed and they died out or somebody shot them. Might be a few left in a zoo somewhere, I wouldn't know about that. But surely gentility has survived. You mean gentility is gone too? Lord! But whatever happened to peace and quiet? Somewhere there still must be some peace and quiet. And whatever happened to kindness . . . ?

Questions about the Reading

1. According to the writer, how did people feel when they noticed the crepuscular?
2. How did the writer feel when somebody was burning leaves somewhere?
3. What would a bucolic weekend in the country be like?
4. What would an idyllic afternoon be like?

Questions about the Writer's Strategies

1. What is the main idea of the paragraph? Is it stated or implied?
2. What does *crepuscular* mean? How did you figure out the meaning?
3. What modes of development does the writer use?
4. What is the tone of the paragraph?

Writing Assignments

1. Write a paragraph in which you define one of the following terms: *democracy, religion, ethics.* Include a formal definition from an online dictionary such as yourDictionary.com (**www.yourdictionary.com**), and use at least two other modes of development. Make a copy of the web page on which you find your definition and attach it to your paragraph.
2. Write a paragraph in which you define one of the following sports: baseball, football, basketball, soccer.
3. Write a paragraph about some holiday celebration that you remember and now miss.

What Is Poverty?

Jo Goodwin Parker

*In this powerful essay, Jo Goodwin Parker uses **parallelism** to leave us with an unforgettable definition of poverty—one that she hopes will stir us to action.*

Word to Know

malnutrition   insufficient nutrition, lack of food

Getting Started

What services does your town or city provide for homeless or impoverished people?

You ask me what is poverty? Listen to me. Here I am, dirty, smelly, and with no "proper" underwear on and with the stench of my rotting teeth near you. I will tell you. Listen to me. Listen without pity. I cannot use your pity. Listen with understanding. Put yourself in my dirty, worn out, ill-fitting shoes, and hear me. 1

Poverty is getting up every morning from a dirt- and illness-stained mattress. The sheets have long since been used for diapers. Poverty is living in a smell that never leaves. This is a smell of urine, sour milk, and spoiling food sometimes joined with the strong smell of long-cooked onions. Onions are cheap. If you have smelled this smell, you did not know how it came. It is the smell of the outdoor privy. It is the smell of young children who cannot walk the long dark way in the night. It is the smell of the mattresses where years of "accidents" have happened. It is the smell of the milk which has gone sour because the refrigerator long has not worked, and it costs money to get it fixed. It is the smell of rotting garbage. I could bury it, but where is the shovel? Shovels cost money. 2

Poverty is being tired. I have always been tired. They told me at the hospital when the last baby came that I had chronic anemia caused from poor diet, a bad case of worms, and that I needed a corrective operation. I listened politely—the poor are always polite. The poor always listen. They don't say that there is no money for iron pills, or better food, or worm medicine. The idea of an operation is frightening and costs so much that, if I had dared, I would have laughed. Who takes care of my children? Recovery from an operation takes a long time. I have three children. When I left them with "Granny" the last time I had a job, I 3 came home to find the baby covered with fly specks, and a diaper that had not been changed since I left. When the dried diaper came off, bits of my baby's flesh came with it. My other child was playing with a sharp bit of broken glass, and my oldest was playing alone at the edge of a lake. I made twenty-two dollars a week, and a good nursery school costs twenty dollars a week for three children. I quit my job.

Poverty is dirt. You can say in your clean clothes coming from your 　4 clean house, "Anybody can be clean." Let me explain about housekeeping with no money. For breakfast I give my children grits with no oleo or cornbread without eggs and oleo. This does not use up many dishes. What dishes there are, I wash in cold water and with no soap. Even the cheapest soap has to be saved for the baby's diapers. Look at my hands, so cracked and red. Once I saved for two months to buy a jar of Vaseline for my hands and the baby's diaper rash. When I had saved enough, I went to buy it and the price had gone up two cents. The baby and I suffered on. I have to decide every day if I can bear to put my cracked sore hands into the cold water and strong soap. But you ask, why not hot water? Fuel costs money. If you have a wood fire it costs money. If you burn electricity, it costs money. Hot water is a luxury. I do not have luxuries. I know you will be surprised when I tell you how young I am. I look so much older. My back has been bent over the wash tubs every day for so long, I cannot remember when I ever did anything else. Every night I wash every stitch my school-age child has on and just hope her clothes will be dry by morning.

Poverty is staying up all night on cold nights to watch the fire know- 　5 ing one spark on the newspaper covering the walls means your sleeping child dies in flames. In summer poverty is watching gnats and flies devour your baby's tears when he cries. The screens are torn and you pay so little rent you know they will never be fixed. Poverty means insects in your food, in your nose, in your eyes, and crawling over you when you sleep. Poverty is hoping it never rains because diapers won't dry when it rains and soon you are using newspapers. Poverty is seeing your children forever with runny noses. Paper handkerchiefs cost money and all your rags you need for other things. Even more costly are anti-histamines. Poverty is cooking without food and cleaning without soap.

Poverty is asking for help. Have you ever had to ask for help, know- 　6 ing your children will suffer unless you get it? Think about asking for a loan from a relative, if this is the only way you can imagine asking for help. I will tell you how it feels. You find out where the office is that you are supposed to visit. You circle that block four or five times. Thinking of your children, you go in. Everyone is very busy. Finally, someone comes out and you tell her that you need help. That never is the person you need to see. You go see another person, and after spilling the whole shame of your poverty all over the desk between you, you find that this isn't the right office after all—you must repeat the whole process, and it never is any easier at the next place.

You have asked for help, and after all it has a cost. You are again told   7
to wait. You are told why, but you don't really hear because of the red cloud of shame and the rising cloud of despair.

Poverty is remembering. It is remembering quitting school in junior   8
high because "nice" children had been so cruel about my clothes and my smell. The attendance officer came. My mother told him I was pregnant. I wasn't, but she thought that I could get a job and help out. I had jobs off and on, but never long enough to learn anything. Mostly I remember being married. I was so young then. I am still young. For a time, we had all the things you have. There was a little house in another town, with hot water and everything. Then my husband lost his job. There was unemployment insurance for a while and what few jobs I could get. Soon, all our nice things were repossessed and we moved back here. I was pregnant then. This house didn't look so bad when we first moved in. Every week it gets worse. Nothing is ever fixed. We now had no money. There were a few odd jobs for my husband, but everything went for food then, as it does now. I don't know how we lived through three years and three babies, but we did. I'll tell you something; after the last baby I destroyed my marriage. It had been a good one, but could you keep on bringing children in this dirt? Did you ever think how much it costs for any kind of birth control? I knew my husband was leaving the day he left, but there were no goodbyes between us. I hope he has been able to climb out of this mess somewhere. He never could hope with us to drag him down.

That's when I asked for help. When I got it, you know how much it   9
was? It was, and is, seventy-eight dollars a month for the four of us; that is all I ever can get. Now you know why there is no soap, no needles and thread, no hot water, no aspirin, no worm medicine, no hand cream, no shampoo. None of these things forever and ever and ever. So that you can see clearly, I pay twenty dollars a month rent, and most of the rest goes for food. For grits and cornmeal, and rice and milk and beans. I try my best to use only the minimum electricity. If I use more, there is that much less for food.

Poverty is looking into a black future. Your children won't play with   10
my boys. They will turn to other boys who steal to get what they want. I can already see them behind the bars of their prison instead of behind the bars of my poverty. Or they will turn to the freedom of alcohol or drugs, and find themselves enslaved. And my daughter? At best, there is for her a life like mine.

But you say to me, there are schools. Yes, there are schools. My chil- 11 dren have no extra books, no magazines, no extra pencils, or crayons, or paper and most important of all, they do not have health. They have worms, they have infections, they have pink-eye all summer. They do not sleep well on the floor, or with me in my one bed. They do not suffer from hunger, my seventy-eight dollars keeps us alive, but they do suffer from malnutrition. Oh yes, I do remember what I was taught about health in school. It doesn't do much good. In some places there is a surplus commodities program. Not here. The country said it cost too much. There is a school lunch program. But I have two children who will already be damaged by the time they get to school.

But, you say to me, there are health clinics. Yes, there are health clin- 12 ics and they are in the towns. I live out here eight miles from town. I can walk that far (even if it is sixteen miles both ways), but can my little children? My neighbor will take me when he goes; but he expects to get paid, *one way or another*. I bet you know my neighbor. He is that large man who spends his time at the gas station, the barbershop, and the corner store complaining about the government spending money on the immoral mothers of illegitimate children.

Poverty is an acid that drips on pride until all pride is worn away. 13 Poverty is a chisel that chips on honor until honor is worn away. Some of you say that you would do *something* in my situation, and maybe you would, for the first week or the first month, but for year after year after year?

Even the poor can dream. A dream of a time when there is money. 14 Money for the right kinds of food, for worm medicine, for iron pills, for toothbrushes, for hand cream, for a hammer and nails and a bit of screening, for a shovel, for a bit of paint, for some sheeting, for needles and thread. Money to pay *in money* for a trip to town. And, oh, money for hot water and money for soap. A dream of when asking for help does not eat away the last bit of pride. When the office you visit is as nice as the offices of other governmental agencies, when there are enough workers to help you quickly, when workers do not quit in defeat and despair. When you have to tell your story to only one person, and that person can send you for other help and you don't have to prove your poverty over and over and over again.

I have come out of my despair to tell you this. Remember I did not 15 come from another place or another time. Others like me are all around you. Look at us with an angry heart, anger that will help you help me. Anger that will let you tell of me. The poor are always silent. Can you be silent too?

Questions about the Reading

1. What does the writer want the reader to do about poverty?
2. How would you summarize the writer's definition of *poverty*?
3. Why, according to the writer, is she impoverished?
4. Why, according to the writer, is she unable to work?

Questions about the Writer's Strategies

1. What modes of development does the writer use to define *poverty*?
2. What is the technique the writer uses to add emphasis to her definition of *poverty*?
3. What is the point of view (person, tone) of the essay? Would any other point of view be as effective? Why or why not?

Writing Assignments

1. *Working Together* Join with some classmates to find out what services are provided in your city or state for homeless people. Write an essay in which you define the services and the criteria by which a person qualifies for those services.
2. *Working Together* Join with some classmates to write an essay in which you define what constitutes the "poverty level" according to the federal government and explain what services are available at that level for a single woman with children.
3. Write an essay in which you define the services in which you can or do participate to help impoverished people.

What Is Intelligence, Anyway?

Isaac Asimov

*Many of us think that intelligence is something one is simply born with
or that it has to do with doing well in school or getting high scores on IQ
tests. But did you ever stop to think about what IQ tests really measure?
In the essay that follows, Isaac Asimov asks us to rethink our definition
of intelligence.*

Words to Know

aptitude   ability, talent
arbiter   someone who has the power to judge
complacent   self-satisfied
intricate   elaborate
KP   kitchen patrol
oracles   wise expressions or answers
raucously   loudly

Getting Started

Do you think that tests can ever really measure intelligence?

What is intelligence, anyway? When I was in the army I received a   1
kind of aptitude test that all soldiers took and, against a normal of 100,
scored 160. No one at the base had ever seen a figure like that, and for
two hours they made a big fuss over me. (It didn't mean anything. The
next day I was still a buck private with KP as my highest duty.)

All my life I've been registering scores like that, so that I have the   2
complacent feeling that I'm highly intelligent, and I expect other people
to think so, too. Actually, though, don't such scores simply mean that I
am very good at answering the type of academic questions that are considered worthy of answers by the people who make up the intelligence
tests—people with intellectual bents similar to mine?

For instance, I had an auto-repair man once, who, on these intelligence   3
tests, could not possibly have scored more than 80, by my estimate. I
always took it for granted that I was far more intelligent than he was.
Yet, when anything went wrong with my car I hastened to him with it,
watched him anxiously as he explored its vitals, and listened to his pro-
nouncements as though they were divine oracles—and he always fixed
my car.

Well, then, suppose my auto-repair man devised questions for an 4
intelligence test. Or suppose a carpenter did, or a farmer, or, indeed,
almost anyone but an academician. By every one of those tests, I'd prove
myself a moron. And I'd *be* a moron, too. In a world where I could not
use my academic training and my verbal talents but had to do something
intricate or hard, working with my hands, I would do poorly. My intelligence, then, is not absolute but is a function of the society I live in and of
the fact that a small subsection of that society has managed to foist itself
on the rest as an arbiter of such matters.

Consider my auto-repair man, again. He had a habit of telling me jokes 5
whenever he saw me. One time he raised his head from under the automobile hood to say: "Doc, a deaf-and-dumb guy went into a hardware
store to ask for some nails. He put two fingers together on the counter
and made hammering motions with the other hand. The clerk brought
him a hammer. He shook his head and pointed to the two fingers he
was hammering. The clerk brought him nails. He picked out the sizes he
wanted, and left. Well, Doc, the next guy who came in was a blind man.
He wanted scissors. How do you suppose he asked for them?"

Indulgently, I lifted my right hand and made scissoring motions with 6
my first two fingers. Whereupon my auto-repair man laughed raucously
and said, "Why, you dumb jerk, he used his *voice* and asked for them."
Then he said, smugly, "I've been trying that on all my customers today."
"Did you catch many?" I asked. "Quite a few," he said, "but I knew
for sure I'd catch *you*." "Why is that?" I asked. "Because you're so god-
damned educated, Doc, I *knew* you couldn't be very smart."

And I have an uneasy feeling he had something there.   7

Questions about the Reading

1. What does the writer mean when he says, "My intelligence, then, is not
   absolute but is a function of the society I live in . . ." (paragraph 4)?
2. What distinction does the writer make between being educated and
   being smart?
3. Do you think the repairman is smarter than the writer? Why or why
   not?

Questions about the Writer's Strategies

1. What mode of development does the writer use in paragraphs 5 and 6?
   What is the purpose of these paragraphs?

2. Does the writer actually define *intelligence*? If so, state his definition in your own words. If not, explain why you think he didn't.
3. In paragraph 6, the writer says he made the scissoring motions "indulgently." What does this tell you about his attitude towards the joke? Why is his attitude ironic?
4. Does the essay contain a thesis statement? If so, where is it located? If not, state it in your own words.
5. Is the repairman a symbol? If so, what does he represent?

Writing Assignments

1. Imagine a society in which intelligence is measured by how well people can work with their hands and fix machinery. Write a definition of *intelligence* for that society.
2. Write an essay defining the term *joke*. Use examples to illustrate your definition.
3. Pick one of the following terms and define it in an essay: *beauty, truth, wisdom,* or *quality*.

Total Eclipse of the Son

Tiffany Kary

In Japan, a society long known for valuing and respecting parents and elders, young people are withdrawing from them in a phenomenon known as hikikomori.

Words to Know

agoraphobia   fear of being in the open or in public places
bastion   protector
controversial   debatable, arguable
ramifications   consequences
syndrome   illness, disease

Getting Started

How would you define *good parenting* and *bad parenting*?

A syndrome known as *hikikomori,* in which the outside world is 1
shunned, is wreaking havoc on young people in Japan, a country known
for its communal values. And an older generation—the very bastion of
those old-fashioned values—may be to blame, according to a controversial new theory.

Hikikomori (the term refers to the behavior itself and to those who 2
suffer from it) was first recognized in the early 1990s. One million Japanese, or almost 1 percent of the population, are estimated to suffer from
hikikomori, defined as a withdrawal from friends and family for months
or even years. Some 40 percent of *hikikomori* are below the age of 21,
according to a 2001 government report.

Western psychologists compare *hikikomori* with social anxiety and 3
agoraphobia, a fear of open places. The affliction has also been likened to
Asperger's syndrome, a mild variant of autism. But these theories carry
little weight in Japan, where the disorder is considered culturally unique
and is linked to violence.

Yuichi Hattori, MA, a psychologist currently treating 18 patients with the 4
disorder, believes that *hikikomori* is caused by emotionally neglectful parenting. Hattori argues that none of his patients had been sexually or physically abused, yet they all show signs of posttraumatic stress disorder.

As the cultural gap between Japan's youth and elders widens, some 5
young Japanese may view their parents as too stony-faced and reserved.

Hattori speaks of Japanese society's deep-rooted division between *hone* and *tatemae*—one's true feelings and one's actions—to illustrate the frustration his patients express toward aloof parents.

"Patients tell me their mothers have no emotions," says Hattori. "Six 6 patients have called their parents zombies."

Hattori's findings, presented in November to the International society 7 for the Study of Dissociation, are reminiscent of the now-discredited theory of the "refrigerator mother," which attributed autism to a detached style of parenting.

"*Hikikomori* looks more to me like an extreme case of social anxiety," 8 says David Kupfer, PhD, a psychologist with a private practice in Virginia. Emotionally unresponsive parents are only one of the factors involved in the development of this disorder, says Kupfer, who points out that "in Japan, the pressure to succeed is a unique cultural source of trauma."

For now, Eastern and Western psychologists agree only that *hikikomori* 9 is unique to Japan and has serious ramifications for both generations.

Questions about the Reading

1. What is *hikikomori*?
2. What percentage of the Japanese population suffer from *hikikomori*?
3. What is the age of 40 percent of the persons who suffer from *hikikomori*?
4. What is the cause of *hikikomori*, according to the psychologist Yuichi Hattori?

Questions about the Writer's Strategies

1. What is the definition of *hikikomori*?
2. What other modes of development does the writer use? Identify them.
3. Could the essay be classified under any other modes of development? If so, what are they?
4. What is the tone of the essay?

Writing Assignments

1. Write an essay in which you define *good parenting* and *bad parenting*. Identify the modes of development you use.
2. Write an essay in which you define *good teaching*. Identify the modes of development you use.

Earning Their Pinstripes

Rick Reilly

*It may look like an easy job and lots of fun, but Rick Reilly shows us that
being a batboy for a major league baseball team is a tough, demanding,
and low-paying job. (Rick Reilly, "Earning Their Pinstripes," Sports
Illustrated, Sept. 23, 2002, p. 92. Reprinted by permission of Sports
Illustrated.)*

Word to Know

volcanic   violent, explosive

Getting Started

What job would you like to have? Do you know what the requirements of the job are and what it pays?

So, kid, you want to be a New York Yankees batboy? Hang out with   1
Derek Jeter? Ride in the parades? Great. But, first, maybe you'd better
take a look at a batboy's typical day.

2 P.M.—Pete Shalhoub, 17, shows up for a 7:15 game and starts setting   2
up the dugout. Sure, most of the players won't be arriving for at least
two hours, but so what? Pete'll be here two hours after the players have
left, too.

You think batboys still only run out and get Johnny Blanchard's bat?   3
Get real. Pete and the six other Yankees batboys—clubhouse boys are
valets, cabbies, maids, deliverymen, shrinks and short-order cooks. And
they're not 12 years old anymore. They're all 16 and older because the
average sixth-grader doesn't do well when he's also working 75-hour
weeks.

Some nights Pete has to show up at 3 in the morning to help unload   4
the road-trip truck, do laundry and set up players' lockers. That takes
four hours. Then he goes straight to high school in Jersey City, and then
right back to the Stadium, where he'll work until about 1 A.M., go to bed
at 2 and get up again at 6 the next morning to go to class.

"It's like I tell him," says Joe Lee, another member of the crew. "In this   5
job you've got to sleep twice as fast."

3:45 P.M.—One of Pete's 1,000 jobs is mixing Gatorade for the dugout.   6
That can be dangerous. A few years ago former visiting team batboy
Joe Rocchio made green, not knowing volcanic Cleveland Indians star

Albert Belle drank only red. Belle spit it out, knocked the jug over in the dugout, and Joe had to clean it up. Glamorous job, no?

4 P.M.—When players arrive, batboys start hopping. They're each 7 player's little Jeeves. "Anything they ask for, they pretty much get," says Pete. That includes everything from, "Go get my wife a birthday present" to "Go get my brother-in-law at the airport." From going to a player's home to pack his bags to making dinner reservations. One player asked Lee to go to the ballpark every day during a 12-day road trip and idle his car for a half hour. "Keeps the engine clean," the player said.

Of course, there *are* rewards. When Jason Giambi was with Oakland, 8 he sent an A's batboy to McDonald's. Giambi got three hits that day, so he kept sending the kid for the rest of the season. When Giambi won the MVP, he tipped him $5,000.

4:30 P.M.—A new kid shows up, the winner of a contest to be a batboy 9 for a day. He's lucky he doesn't get the initiation Craig Postolowski got. To start, Jeter sent him off to look for the key to the batter's box. Then Joe Torre told him to go get the knuckleballs ready. Then Don Zimmer needed the lefthanded fungo bat. Finally, when Bernie Williams asked him to get a bucket of steam from the shower to clean home plate, he realized he'd been had.

5:45 P.M.—It's Pete's day to shag flies in the outfield and run the balls 10 back to the batting practice pitcher. This is a gas. There's other cool stuff too. Some nights the clubhouse is lousy with celebs. You get to be in the team photo. And players have been known to lend batboys their sweet sleds for the prom. Of course, two years ago Manny Alexander of the Boston Red Sox lent his car to a batboy. Problem is, the kid got pulled over and police found steroids in it. Oops. Always check the glove compartment, Kid.

7:05 P.M.—Tonight Pete works balls for the home plate umpire. 11 Another guy works the rightfield line, snagging foul balls, and another works bats in the dugout. (The rest are stuck in the clubhouse.) Problem is, sometimes a kid will be so tired from lack of sleep that he'll be out there nodding off in front of 50,000 people. "I've done it," says Lee. "I'm just glad a line drive didn't wake me up."

10:30 P.M.—Game's over. The real, nasty work starts. "Everybody 12 thinks this is when we go home," says Pete. "But we've still got two hours of work to do." They pick up dirty uniforms, vacuum, straighten lockers, make food runs, empty trash, clean and polish 40 pairs of shoes. And they've got to do it all while dodging flying jocks, socks and towels thrown at their heads by millionaires. *Fwomp!*

12:30 A.M.—O.K., everything's done. Pete's spent, but he'll be in bed 13 before 2 A.M. for once. At least he saw some baseball. The boys who worked the clubhouse have to watch the highlights later.

So there it is, Kid. And remember, don't ask for tickets, autographs or 14
a raise. With the Yankees, you get the minimum, $5.15 an hour, even if
you've been on the job 10 years. Hey, don't forget your boss is George
Steinbrenner!

So, you want the job? Kid? *Kid?*   15

Questions about the Reading

1. How many batboys do the Yankees have?
2. How old must a batboy be?
3. What are the responsibilities of the batboys?
4. Are there any "rewards" to being a batboy? What are the examples
   the writer provides?

Questions about the Writer's Strategies

1. What is the point of view of the essay?
2. Is the essay objective or subjective or both? Support your answer
   with examples from the essay.
3. What is the order of the essay?
4. What does the last sentence of the essay imply?

Writing Assignments

1. Write an essay in which you define the requirements of a job you
   would like to have.
2. *Working Together* Join with some classmates to select a term or terms
   related to government and write an essay in which you define the
   terms. Identify the modes of development you use.

10

Argumentation and Persuasion

ALL EFFECTIVE WRITING involves, to some extent, argumentation or persuasion. As you have learned from the preceding chapters, writers use various kinds of information to develop a **topic** or **thesis.** Such information can be said to "argue" or "persuade" in the sense that it convinces the reader that the writer's idea is true or believable. However, as **modes of development**, argumentation and persuasion have some particular characteristics that you should know about and be able to use in your own writing.

Let's look first at **persuasion** in its most obvious form—the advertisement. You should not use sentence fragments in your writing assignments, as the advertisement below does; and of course, you should continue to structure your writing according to a main (general) idea and to support it according to the various modes of development. But you will want to appeal to the emotions, qualities, or values that a reader is likely to share or find desirable, as advertisers do. One way to appeal to a reader is to use words for their **connotations**—explained in the preceding chapter as the feelings or qualities a reader may associate with a word—rather than for their **denotations** or dictionary definitions.

In the following example, the advertiser uses the words *clean, smooth, fresh,* and *pure innocence.* We associate such words with highly desirable qualities, and the advertiser intends to persuade us that a particular soap will give our skin these qualities. The word *new* implies that the product has been improved and, therefore, is better or more desirable than its predecessor or a competing product. Notice, too, that the ad appeals to our senses when it describes the soap's lather as *silky* and *soft.*

Connotation | Now. Clean skin with the touch of <u>innocence</u>. The joy of it.
Connotation | Of having skin <u>so clean</u>, <u>so smooth</u>, <u>so fresh</u>, it has the touch of <u>pure innocence</u>. Today, you can capture that feeling, sim-
Connotation | ply by cleansing with the extraordinary <u>new</u> Olay Beauty
Connotation | Bar. Its special Olay lather, <u>silky and soft</u>, creams up to clean
Connotation | when you work it in. The tinier bubbles work in <u>natural harmony</u> with your skin. They lift out impurities, then rinse
Connotation | <u>cleanly</u> away, leaving better skin even before you raise your eyes to the mirror—<u>fresher</u> skin each time, <u>smoother</u> skin at
Connotation | every touch. Again and again, new Olay Beauty Bar cleanses
Connotation | <u>innocence</u> into your skin.

The purpose of persuasion is to make the reader accept the writer's idea. That idea may be an opinion or judgment that the reader might not ordinarily share or have knowledge of. The idea may be controversial—as we shall see later, the idea of an argument must be—but it does not have to be. The idea may even be humorous. Whatever the idea, the writer will use words and information to appeal to the reader's emotions. Such information may be biased in favor of the writer's idea, but it should be honest and accurate. Notice the emotional strength of the writer's examples in the letter that follows.

R. J. Reynolds Tobacco Co.
4th and Main Street
Winston-Salem, NC 27102

Dear Sirs:

1   When my wife died of lung cancer in 1976, I wanted to write you about her love affair with Camel cigarettes. I concluded, however, that it would be an exercise in futility.

2   I take up the challenge now, because you have publicly announced an advertising campaign to cast doubt on medical reports that cigarettes are a public-health hazard. You call for an open debate. Okay, let's debate.

3   *Example 1: wife* — My wife died a painful death. She was just 56 and had smoked at least a pack of Camels a day for 40 years. Coincidentally, just 30 days before her demise her 47-year-old
Example 2: brother-in-law — brother died of the same illness. Both experienced unbearable pain. He, too, was a heavy smoker.

4   But there is more to this horror story. In 1958, my father died suddenly of a cardiovascular ailment. He'd been a two-pack-a-day man for years, and would "walk a mile for a Camel" when younger. Later in life, he could hardly walk at all. But he still puffed away, day and night, before
Example 3: father — breakfast and with his meals. He endured continual nasal and respiratory problems, and never enjoyed a day free of a hacking cough.

5   A popular pharmacist, he had many doctor friends who urged him to stop smoking. But he was firmly hooked and

had been since 1909. Ill with lung disease (emphysema and chronic bronchitis), he had long suffered intensely painful attacks of near-suffocation. In 1955 he was forced to retire and spend his "golden years" either lying on our sofa or propped up in a lounge chair.

In late summer of 1957, I took him to a specialist at the University of Maryland Hospital in Baltimore. There he was told there was no cure for his condition. But he could help himself. "How?" he asked. "Stop smoking," was the reply.   6

That is a tall order for anyone who has smoked for almost 50 years. But my father did not want to live the life of an invalid, so he determined to try. That he succeeded—cold turkey—is nothing short of a miracle. But he really had no other choice, except to suffer.   7

Within weeks he was breathing easier, and it was not long before he was walking about and driving his car. He got to enjoy life a bit. I'm convinced that giving up smoking added that near-year to his life.   8

Example 4: daughter

Today, I have a daughter—a working mother of two—who has been addicted to cigarettes since peer pressure in high school encouraged her to smoke. She wants desperately to quit. In fact, she has done so several times, only to be lured back by the smoking of others in her workplace.   9

Having presented four powerful extended examples, this writer goes on to a thorough persuasive conclusion. You will see next that he uses rhetorical questions to introduce and structure his conclusion. A **rhetorical question** is a question to which no real answer is expected because only one obvious reply can be made—and that reply will either support or restater the writer's point. Rhetorical questions are fairly common in persuasive writing and in argumentation because they offer a way for writers to emphasize the correctness of their viewpoints.

Okay, R. J. Reynolds, that's my story. What's yours? Are you prepared to tell us that the National Institutes of Health, the Surgeon General and the various voluntary health agencies are all wrong? Are the many scientific studies indicting smoking just so much hogwash?   10

For the sake of debate, let's assume smoking's critics are wrong. Can you deny that cigarette smoking is addictive? Isn't that fact precisely the reason why you sell so many cigarettes? Is it moral to manufacture and sell any product that causes addiction—even if it might otherwise be harmless? As bad as alcohol abuse is, alcohol is addictive to only a relatively small number of consumers. You can't say that about cigarettes. Smoking hooks nearly every consumer. And once hooked it is difficult to stop; for some, it seems impossible.   11

In a free society, people can't be forbidden to smoke. But government does have the obligation to warn the public of the dangers involved. It has the responsibility to hold R. J. Reynolds Tobacco Co. and others accountable for luring impressionable people to smoke, while suggesting that   12 medical findings establishing a relationship between smoking and cancer, cardiovascular diseases and respiratory ailments are inconclusive.

It's hard to fight the rich tobacco industry, but just maybe, through   13
education, we non-smokers will eventually win. As a witness to so much tragedy caused by smoking, I feel compelled to hope so.

Sincerely,

Gil Crandall

In summary, then, a persuasive paragraph or essay, like the other modes of development, is based on a **main (general) idea** developed by one or more of the modes of development and is characterized by the use of words or information that appeals to the reader's emotions. The information or evidence used in persuasion may be one-sided, but it should be honest and accurate. The topic, or thesis, of persuasion may be controversial, but it does not have to be.

Argumentation, on the other hand, must be based on a controversial idea—an idea that people have conflicting views or opinions about. Although argumentation may include some persuasion, its appeal to the reader should be rational and logical, as opposed to emotional, and **objective**, rather than one-sided. A classic or formal argument includes five elements:

- *Statement of the problem*
- *Solution*, the writer's thesis or answer to the problem
- *Evidence*, the information the writer presents to support or prove the thesis
- *Refutation*, the writer's acknowledgment of and response to opposing views
- *Conclusion*, the writer's summation of the evidence and, generally, a restatement of the thesis

Although you may seldom need to write a paragraph-length argument, it is helpful to examine an example of one. Notice in the following example that the writer has explained the problem, stated a solution or answer to the problem—which is the topic of the paragraph—provided evidence in support of the solution, refuted the opposing view, and summarized the position taken on the topic.

Statement of the problem

During the late sixties and early seventies, political and social activism was rampant on college campuses. Student protests—which were sometimes peaceful and other times violent—addressed issues related to civil rights, the environment, war, nuclear arms, and consumer protection and rights. In recent years, student protests have been much less frequent and, generally, peaceful, causing some writers and politicians to label present-day students as apathetic.

Solution

Nonsense! Today's students are not apathetic. They simply have different concerns from the ones of the sixties and seventies. They are more concerned about, for instance, employment and the quality of their own lives. They are assessing, confronting even, themselves—their hopes, plans, desires, ambitions, and values. They are fighting quietly for their causes—personal or otherwise—by pursuing training and retraining opportunities and by exercising their voting privileges. To say they are apathetic is to ignore the steadfastness with which they are pursuing their goals. To say they are apathetic is to imply that a person is not concerned about an issue unless that person takes to the streets or possibly engages in violent acts on behalf of that issue. The fact is, the current college population is older—the average age of community college students nationwide is about twenty-eight—more experienced, and in some ways wiser. As a consequence, they have perhaps learned that confrontation may win a battle but lose the war, that in the long run, they must live and work with those persons who hold opposing views. Thus, while they are indeed quieter than their predecessors, they continue to be concerned about such important issues as employment (their own and others), nuclear arms, the environment, civil rights, and war. We make a mistake if we write off today's college students as apathetic simply because we do not see overt evidence of their concern.

Evidence

Refutation

Conclusion

In a full-length essay, you can develop your argument more fully and convincingly than you can in a paragraph. The order in which you present the elements of an argument may differ from the classic organization represented by the preceding paragraph. For instance, you may want to state the refutation before presenting the evidence for your argument. And sometimes one of the elements of your argument may be **implied** rather than stated, just as the topic sentence of a paragraph or the main idea of an essay may be implied.

No matter what method is used to develop an argument, however, always remember that the evidence presented to support the solution and the conclusion must be valid—true, supported by facts, accurately expressed, and based on sound reasoning. This is something to watch for not only in your own writing but also when you are reading arguments composed by others. When you read or write an argument, analyze not only the main conclusion but also all the ideas that support it. A conclusion may seem quite sensible based on the evidence the writer supplies, but if the evidence itself is not true and not presented logically, the conclusion will be viewed as faulty.

In the essay below, the writer follows the classic model in presenting her argument and supports her opinion with facts that give the reader sound reasons to accept her conclusion. Notice that she uses several modes of development, such as **contrast** and **examples.**

Statement of the problem

Each year, from late spring to early fall, thousands of high school students and their parents spend a great deal of time and money driving around the country to visit expensive and prestigious colleges that the students think they might like to attend. Each year, thousands of students go through the ritual of applying to and being rejected by these colleges.   1

Solution

Instead, they should go to a community college and, after earning their associate degree, transfer to a four-year university to complete their education.

Evidence

Most community colleges offer a wide choice of career or technical programs as well as a curriculum paralleling that offered by a university. If the student has already made a career choice, an associate degree prepares the student to enter the workforce or to continue his or her career study in a four-year university. If the student has not decided on a career, a community college is an excellent place to learn more about many different career possibilities and to complete the general education courses required by either a career or university-parallel program.   2

Evidence

Most community colleges also have a more diverse population than that of the student's high school. In a community college the student has the opportunity to meet persons of all ages, abilities, and ethnic and racial backgrounds and to improve his or her knowledge and understanding of others.   3

Evidence

A community college is also much less expensive than most colleges. In addition to the lower cost of tuition and fees, the student can usually live at home and commute to classes, which also saves the high cost of dorm or apartment fees.   4

Refutation

It is true, of course, that a community college does not offer the prestige of the more famous universities. But if prestige is significant, the student could complete a baccalaureate and graduate work at a better-known school. Also, whether the education the student receives at a community college is equal to that provided by a more prestigious university can be determined only on a case-by-case basis, since much of the success of any education depends on the individual student.   5

Conclusion

The fact is, for most students a community college is a sound educational and economic choice. Instead of engaging in the expensive and time-consuming spring-to-fall ritual of college shopping, most students would be as well or better served by taking advantage of the educational opportunity offered by their local community college.   6

When you read an argument, remember, too, that a writer may present facts selectively. That is, the writer may not give you all the facts relating to an issue or problem. For this reason, it is advisable to read and consider arguments on both sides of the controversy and to carefully analyze the facts when you are trying to form an opinion about an important issue. It will then be up to you when writing an argumentation paper to interpret the facts and conclusions, to decide which ones are most valid, and to choose the ones you will use to support your own thesis.

Be alert, too, for **fallacies** in your reasoning. In addition to the fallacies identified in chapter 8 (p. 194), guard against the following:

- *False analogy.* A false analogy assumes that two things that are alike are alike in all respects. A Honda and a Cadillac are both cars, but they are not alike in all respects.
- *Circular argument.* A circular argument restates an idea in different words: "The airports are too crowded because too many people are traveling."
- *Argument to the man* (argument ad hominem). An argument to the man attacks the person rather than the issue: "He gets poor grades. After all, he's a computer nerd."
- *Bandwagon.* A bandwagon fallacy claims that something is true because the majority believe or act on it: "Everyone thinks she should be elected class president" or "We should go to the concert because everyone else is."
- *Either-or.* An either-or argument assumes that only two things are possible: "The submarine sank because of either poor maintenance or poor personnel training."
- *Begging the question.* Begging the question presents as a fact an idea or premise that is not proven: "If we removed all chat rooms from the Internet, children would not be enticed to meet people who could do them harm."

In summary, although argumentation and persuasion have a common **purpose**—to convince the reader to accept the writer's opinion—they differ principally in the way the writer appeals to the reader. In argumentation, the writer supports the topic or thesis by presenting objective, logical evidence that appeals to the reader's reason. In persuasion, the writer does not necessarily abandon objectivity or logic but uses words or other information that appeals to the reader's emotions. Also, although the thesis of persuasion *may* be controversial, the thesis of an argument *must* be. In both argumentation and persuasion, the writer makes use of whatever modes of development are effective and appropriate.

In school and beyond, there will be occasions when you will want to use argumentation or persuasion to make a point to your **audience.** Whether you are doing so orally or in writing, being familiar with techniques used in argumentation and persuasion will help you.

Tax Junk Food? Yes

Michael F. Jacobson

The writer claims that taxing junk food would raise billions that could be used to promote healthy eating and improve our health.

Word to Know

subsidized   funded, paid for

Getting Started

Would a tax on junk food and sugary drinks discourage you from buying them?

Heart disease, cancer, stroke, and other diet-related conditions (together with too little physical activity) prematurely kill several hundred thousand Americans each year, and treatment of those conditions costs taxpayers more than $100 billion each year. Yet the government spends almost nothing to promote better diet and more exercise, which would prevent disease. A one-cent-per-can tax on sugary soft drinks, though, or small taxes on other disease-promoting foods could raise billions of dollars to

- Put more fresh fruits and vegetables on the plates of school-age kids
- Encourage Americans to switch from high-fat milk to 1 percent or skim
- Fund after-school athletic programs now sometimes subsidized by the shameful practice of selling junk food to schools
- Fund major media campaigns designed to encourage kids to take up physical activity (the Bush administration recently urged zeroing out the only such government program along these lines)

Questions about the Reading

1. What are the consequences of an unhealthy diet and lack of exercise?
2. What is the cost of treatment of diet-related conditions to taxpayers?
3. What could a tax on junk food and sugary soft drinks be used for?

Questions about the Writer's Strategies

1. What is the problem the writer is addressing?
2. What is the writer's solution to the problem?
3. What evidence does the writer provide to support his solution to the problem?
4. Does the writer acknowledge any opposing views? If so, what are they?

Writing Assignments

1. Write a persuasive or argumentative paragraph for or against a tax on junk food. Be sure to define what you mean by the term *junk food*.
2. Write a persuasive or argumentative paragraph for or against a fee for parking your car on your school grounds.

Frightening—and Fantastic

Anna Quindlen

It's a scary world out there, with bad people seemingly everywhere. Every hour the television news makes us aware of that fact. But Anna Quindlen reminds us that we should also let the children know that there are good people out there, too.

Words to Know

Good Samaritan   someone who helps another person
Oscar Wilde   Nineteenth-century British playwright, poet, and
  novelist

Getting Started

What precautions do you take if you go out by yourself at night?

So this is a plea for parents to remember to have That Talk with their kids. No, not the one about smoking cigarettes or driving under the influence. That's the one they will certainly get. What they need to hear occasionally is about the pleasures, not just the perils. Even when we talk about September 11, we can tell a tale of human goodness as well as evil, a tale of those who saved strangers as well as those who murdered them. For all the sleazebags who will try to lure a kid into a car, there are many Good Samaritans who are just concerned when they see a 12-year-old trudging along the road in the rain. I suppose we live at a time when we can't afford to let them accept the Samaritan's ride. But we also can't afford to have them think that Samaritans no longer exist. All these lectures, lessons and cautionary tales can't be to preserve a lifetime of looking over one shoulder. As Oscar Wilde wrote, "We are all in the gutter, but some of us are looking at the stars."

Questions about the Reading

1. What is "That Talk" the writer wants parents to have with their kids?
2. What should the kids hear about the September 11 terrorist attacks on the World Trade Center?

3. Why must parents tell their kids about the Good Samaritans?
4. What is the meaning of the Oscar Wilde quotation? Why is it appropriate to the main idea of the paragraph?

Questions about the Writer's Strategies

1. What is the main idea of the paragraph? State it in your own words.
2. Is the paragraph persuasion or argumentation? Explain your answer.
3. What modes of development does the writer use in the paragraph?

Writing Assignments

1. Write an argumentative or persuasive paragraph in which you explain the main "cautions" your parents have taught you and why you do or do not follow them.
2. Write an argumentative or persuasive paragraph for or against abolishing some rule or regulation established by your school or your town.

Drinking—What Age?

Barrett Seaman

> *Sixteen is old enough to drive a car, and eighteen is old enough to vote and join the army, but you have to be twenty-one to buy an alcoholic drink. Barrett Seaman says that eighteen-year-old college students may "go overboard" initially if permitted to drink but that most of them will soon "put drinking in its proper place."*

Words to Know

exploiting   using, taking advantage of
savored   tasted, enjoyed

Getting Started

Is a person's age a reliable measure for whether he or she will drink responsibly?

What would happen if the drinking age was rolled back to 18 or 19? Initially, there would be a surge in binge drinking as young adults savored their new-found freedom. But over time, I predict, U.S. college students would settle into the saner approach to alcohol I saw on the one campus I visited where the legal drinking age is 18: Montreal's McGill University, which enrolls about 2,000 American undergraduates a year. Many, when they first arrive, go overboard, exploiting their ability to drink legally. But by midterms, when McGill's demanding academic standards must be met, the vast majority have put drinking into its practical place among their priorities.

Questions about the Reading

1. What would happen initially if the legal age for drinking were lowered to eighteen?
2. How did McGill University students handle being able to drink legally at age eighteen? Did their behavior change over time? Why?
3. What does the writer mean by "put drinking into its practical place"? What do you think is the "practical place" for drinking?

Questions about the Writer's Strategies

1. What is the main idea of the paragraph? State it in your own words.
2. What modes of development does the writer use in the paragraph?

Writing Assignments

1. Write a paragraph in which you argue or persuade your reader that the legal age for driving a car should be lowered or raised or that there should be a maximum age at which a person is allowed to drive.
2. Do you object to some of the courses required for your major? Write an argumentation or persuasion paragraph for the changes you want in the curriculum for your major.

The Measure of Our Success

Marian Wright Edelman

"Children—my own and other people's—became the passion of my personal and professional life. For it is they who are God's presence, promise, and hope for humankind." These are the words of Marian Wright Edelman, the African American civil rights lawyer and founder of the Children's Defense League. In the following paragraph from her book The Measure of Our Success: A Letter to My Children and Yours, *Edelman urges her readers to face the mounting crisis of our country's impoverished children and families by taking action themselves.*

Words to Know

empathy   understanding
mentoring   being a counselor or teacher
neonatal   having to do with infants

Getting Started

What are some things you can do to help build a stronger community for all our children and their children's children?

The place to begin is with ourselves. Care. As you read about or meet some of the children and families in this country who need your help, put yourself in their places as fellow Americans. Imagine you or your spouse being pregnant, and not being able to get enough to eat or see a doctor or know that you have a hospital for delivery. Imagine your child hungry or injured, and you cannot pay for food or find health care. Imagine losing your job and having no income, having your unemployment compensation run out, not being able to pay your note or rent, having no place to sleep with your children, having nothing. Imagine having to stand in a soup line at a church or Salvation Army station after you've worked all your life, or having to sleep in a shelter with strangers and get up and out early each morning, find some place to go with your children, and not know if you can sleep there again that night. If you take the time to imagine this, perhaps you can also take the time to do for them what you would want a fellow citizen to do for you. Volunteer in a homeless shelter or soup kitchen or an afterschool tutoring or mentoring program. Vote. Help to organize your community to speak out for the children who need you.

Visit a hospital neonatal intensive care nursery or AIDS and boarder baby ward and spend time rocking and caring for an individual child. Adopt as a pen pal a lonely child who never gets a letter from anyone. Give a youth a summer job. Teach your child tolerance and empathy by your example.

Questions about the Reading

1. According to the writer, how can people begin to make a difference in this country? Do you agree or disagree with her argument? Why?
2. What different methods of action does Edelman describe? Pick out some of the examples she uses.
3. What do you think Edelman means by the last sentence? Do you agree or disagree with her statement? Why?
4. Think about all the different suggestions Edelman makes. Which have you tried? Which might you consider trying?

Questions about the Writer's Strategies

1. Is there a topic sentence in the paragraph? If so, where is it? If not, state the main idea in your own words.
2. Is this a paragraph of argumentation, persuasion, or both? Support your answer with details from the paragraph.
3. Besides persuasion, what other mode of development does the writer use? Support your answer with details from the text.
4. Edelman uses numerous powerful images to support her thesis that we all need to work together to rebuild this country. What are some of the images Edelman uses when she asks us to imagine trading places with our less fortunate fellow Americans? What impact do the images have on you?
5. What is the tone of the paragraph? Why does Edelman use this tone?

Writing Assignments

1. Do you agree or disagree with Edelman's argument that all responsible people need to be active in their communities and their nation? Write a persuasive paragraph on your answer.
2. Do you agree or disagree that children learn tolerance and empathy— or, for that matter, prejudice and hate—by the example of their parents? Write a paragraph in which you argue for or against that statement. Use examples and details to support your position.

Hang It Up

Jesse Scaccia

Imagine you are the teacher facing a classroom of students with cell phones at their ears or in their hands. Jesse Scaccia tells us how that feels.

Words to Know

appendages attachments, add-ons
confiscated taken away

Getting Started

What is the policy of your school regarding having cell phones in the classroom?

You're a teacher in the New York City public school system. It's 1
September, and you're lecturing the class on the structure of an essay. Your students need to know this information to pass your class and the Regents exam, and you, of course, hope that one day your talented students will dazzle and amaze English professors all over the country.

You turn your back to write the definition of *thesis* on the chalkboard. 2
It takes about 15 seconds. You turn around to the class expecting to see 25 students scribbling the concept in their notebooks. Instead, you see a group of students who have sprung appendages of technology.

Jose has grown an earphone. Maria's thumbs have sprouted a two- 3
way. Man Keung, recently arrived from China, is texting away on a cell phone connected to his wrist. And Christina appears to be playing Mine Sweeper on a Pocket PC on her lap.

Come the end of the term, a handful will fail the class. A number will 4
never pass the Regents exam. As we all know, far too many will drop out of school. And I can tell you with no hint of pride that it isn't the teacher's fault. As much as any other problem plaguing our schools, the onus for failure should be placed on distractions in the classroom, specifically the cell phone.

Though electronic devices have been banned in public schools for 5
years, the issue came to the forefront last month when Chancellor Joel

Klein announced the random placement of metal detectors in schools. The result: More than 800 cell phones have been confiscated.

Students and their parents, who say they rely on cell phones for safety 6 reasons, are outraged. There's even talk of a lawsuit arguing that the rule should be struck down.

But as a former New York City public school teacher, I can tell you 7 that cell phones don't belong in the classroom. A student with a cell phone is an uninterested student, one with a short attention span who cares more about his social life than education.

Parents think of cell phones as a connection to their children in an 8 emergency. I have a few questions for those parents: First, when was the last situation that genuinely called for immediate interaction with your child? In most cases, the hospital or the police would seem more urgent. Second, is phoning the main office and having it patch you through to your child not quick enough? And third, do you know why your children really want to take cell phones to school?

Because, just like the new Jordans and Rocawear they desire, cell 9 phones are status symbols. Because when their cell phone rings while the teacher is talking, everyone laughs. Because playing video games on their cell makes them look cool. Because text messaging their friend in the next room is more fun than learning about the topic sentence. So is listening to the new Three 6 Mafia song they just downloaded onto their cell.

And saying students can store their phones in the locker is a joke. If 10 they have cell phones, they're going to bring them into class.

There are legitimate causes that parents should be taking on. Rally 11 against crowding in the classroom. Fight against the oppressive and culturally biased Regents tests. But you're wrong on this cell phone issue. In this case, you are part of the problem, not the solution.

Questions about the Reading

1. What is the teacher trying to teach?
2. What are the students doing?
3. What are the consequences, according to the writer, of the students' actions?

Questions about the Writer's Strategies

1. What is the problem the writer addresses?
2. What is the writer's thesis or answer to the problem?

3. What evidence does the writer present to prove the thesis? Is the evidence adequate? Why or why not?
4. What modes of development does the writer use?

Writing Assignments

1. *Working Together* Join with some classmates to write an essay in which you argue for or against student use of laptop computers in the classroom.
2. Write an essay in which you argue for or against prohibiting cell phones in schools.

Excuses, Excuses

Helen C. Vo-Dinh

> *In its report,* A Nation at Risk, *the National Commission on Excellence in Education warns that "for the first time in the history of our country, the educational skills of one generation will not surpass, will not equal, will not even approach, those of its parents." Not surprisingly, this prediction has caused considerable discussion of educational reform, much of it focused on the quality of the teaching in our schools. Here, Helen C. Vo-Dinh, a teacher in a school near Washington, D.C., argues that the* quantity *of teaching in American schools may be at least equally to blame for the decline in student achievement.*

Words to Know

charade imitation of a real activity
competency ability to do a job
consensus general opinion
culmination climax, most extreme point
depleted made smaller, reduced
en masse in a group or body
guise false appearance
merit pay wages based on the quality of the work performed
plethora an excessive amount, superabundance
rationale line of reasoning
sanctioned approved, accepted
Second Coming return of Christ at the end of the world
state-mandated required or decreed by the state

Getting Started

Are too many of your classes dismissed for extracurricular activities or special events?

By and large, the report of the National Commission on Educational 1 Excellence has been received favorably by those of us in the teaching profession, even though the blame for a shoddy educational system falls so often on our shoulders. For example, recently we have been hearing a lot about teacher competency and the need for merit pay, as if this would solve our problems.

Somewhere in the commission's report and lost to sight in the hue and 2 cry is a recommendation that received little publicity. This is the suggestion that schools make more effective use of the existing school day.

As a teacher I understand this to mean that I had better make sure my 3
students spend every minute they have with me studying and learning
the subject I teach. Now, we teachers have some control over time on
task. We have no one to blame but ourselves if we fill up half a period
Monday entertaining our classes with stories about what we did over the
weekend. However, even those of us with the best intentions find our
classes interrupted, depleted or canceled by forces beyond our control
day after day after day. For under the guise of "education," a plethora of
social activities has sprouted in our schools which draw students from
our rooms. This situation is particularly destructive at the high-school
level where I am now teaching.

Sometime in the summer, our school district, like others across the 4
country, will publish a school calendar for the coming year. In my state,
students must attend school 180 days. This means that each of the students assigned to me will have 180 periods of classroom instruction in
the subject I teach. However, I know that this will never happen. If I
consider only the classes I lose to "necessities" such as fire drills, bomb
scares, three days of state-mandated testing, three days of registration
and one entire day for school photos, my students have already missed
10 periods out of the 180. Now, depending upon how many pep rallies
are needed, how many assemblies we can afford and the degree to which
my students participate in a host of activities offered during schooltime,
I will lose all of them again, and most of them again and again.

It might be helpful to compare the situation in our high schools with 5
that in our colleges, where an intellectual atmosphere still prevails. Think
back a moment. Do you remember your college classes being canceled
for pep rallies, assemblies or class meetings? Not once, but often during a
semester? When you wanted to attend some social function or help prepare for a dance were you excused with the blessings of the administration, or did you cut? Do you remember lectures interrupted routinely by
a hidden sound system? Did office aides make it a practice to appear with
urgent memos which your professors had to read and respond to while
you waited impatiently? Was it a common occurrence for football players
to rise en masse in the middle of a discussion to go to practice or a game?

And yet this is precisely the kind of situation we high-school teachers 6
put up with day after day. Is it any wonder that many students don't
value much of what goes on in the classroom?

At the latest count my syllabus is at the mercy of 45 different activi- 7
ties sanctioned by our school system. I lost students this past year for
the following reasons: club trips to Atlantic City, student-council elec-
tions, bloodmobile, appointments with guidance counselors and Army
representatives, an art show, community show, tennis, track, baseball,
swimming, football, cheerleading, club meetings, class meetings, drama

and band workshops, yearbook, PSAT, chorus and orchestra rehearsals, science day, cattle judging, attendance at the movie "Gandhi" and graduation rehearsal.

This list is by no means complete.   8

The rationale which allows this charade to continue is that if students   9
miss classes they can make up the work and no harm is done. Of course, this idea carried to its logical conclusion means that we need less school for students, not more as the president's commission recommended. It is true that many students can read assignments outside of class, copy notes and keep up with their work. Others may opt for lower grades. But much of what takes place during class cannot be made up. How do you make up a class discussion where you have a chance to test and clarify your ideas on a subject? A group discussion where you must come to a consensus? An oral reading?

When I cannot organize a group discussion in advance because I am   10
never sure who will show up, when "Romeo" is off to a band rehearsal and "Juliet" has a swim meet on the day the class reads "Romeo and Juliet" aloud, how can I generate seriousness of purpose and respect for intellectual effort?

Obviously many of these activities are worthwhile. But there is no   11
pressing reason why any of them have to take place during class hours. Days could be added to the school calendar for state-mandated testing and registration. And why not let communities sponsor dances, sports, college and Army representatives and clubs after school hours? At the very least we would then discover which students wanted to participate in activities and which simply wished to escape from class.

The culmination of this disrespect for intellectual effort occurs in   12
my school when the seniors are allowed to end classes and prepare for graduation three weeks before the rest of the student body. The message which comes across is that the senior curriculum is so negligible it can be cut short, and that when you get older, you have it easier than anybody else, not harder.

I am not a kill-joy. I know that kids need fun just as much as adults do   13
and that clubs are educational in their own way. But as a member of a profession which is accorded only the most grudging respect and which is continually suspected of not doing its job, I say start by giving us a chance. Guarantee me those 180 periods I'm supposed to have. I'll know the public and the people who run the schools are serious about improving them the year my classes have not been shortened, delayed, canceled, interrupted or depleted for any reason short of illness, an emergency or the Second Coming.

Questions about the Reading

1. According to Vo-Dinh, who is usually considered to blame for the declining quality of American education? Which remedies for this decline receive most attention?
2. How does Vo-Dinh define "effective use of the existing school day"?
3. What are some of the interruptions and activities for which class time is lost?
4. Why does Vo-Dinh feel that unified class time and consistent attendance are important?
5. What specific recommendations does the writer make for scheduling activities that now take place during the school day?

Questions about the Writer's Strategies

1. Identify the five elements of argumentation in Vo-Dinh's essay. (See Glossary for *statement of the problem, solution, evidence, refutation,* and *conclusion.*)
2. What different *modes of development* does the writer use to support her argument? (See Glossary for *mode of development.*)
3. A *rhetorical question* is a question to which no real answer is expected because only one obvious reply can be made. Writers often use rhetorical questions to emphasize their points by suggesting that there is only one possible response to a situation—their own. Where does Vo-Dinh use rhetorical questions in this essay? How do they influence your acceptance of her argument?
4. The writer has an insider's position with respect to her topic. How can this be both an advantage and a disadvantage in writing an argument? How does the writer establish herself as a fair observer?

Writing Assignments

1. Some critics of the American educational system feel that its quality can be improved by rating teachers individually according to various criteria and paying them only as much as that evaluation suggests they deserve (merit pay). Consider the pros and cons of this proposal, and write an essay supporting or rejecting it.
2. Many colleges require a certain minimum of class attendance for course credit. Attack or defend this practice.
3. Colleges frequently have distribution requirements that control the kinds of courses students take and the amount of time they spend in particular areas of study. Evaluate the distribution policies of your school or major department, and write an essay supporting them or recommending specific changes.

So That Nobody Has to Go to School if They Don't Want To

Roger Sipher

Roger Sipher, a professor of history at the State University of New York, has a different solution to the problem of the declining quality of American schools. Instead of increasing the quantity of teaching, as Helen Vo-Dinh recommends (see pp. 267–270), he suggests that mandatory attendance laws be abolished. The effect, he argues, will be to improve dramatically the quality of education for those children who choose to go to school.

Words to Know

antagonistic opposing
archaic old-fashioned
assertion strong statement
conventional customary
enacted made law
homage honor
homily sermon
mandatory required by rule or law
oust force out
recalcitrant hard to control
repeal abolish
tangentially superficially relevant
undermines weakens

Getting Started

Should students be required to attend school through high school?

A decline in standardized test scores is but the most recent indicator 1
that American education is in trouble.

One reason for the crisis is that present mandatory-attendance laws 2
force many to attend school who have no wish to be there. Such children
have little desire to learn and are so antagonistic to school that neither
they nor more highly motivated students receive the quality education
that is the birthright of every American.

The solution to this problem is simple: Abolish compulsory-attendance 3
laws and allow only those who are committed to getting an education
to attend.

This will not end public education. Contrary to conventional belief, 4 legislators enacted compulsory-attendance laws to legalize what already existed. William Landes and Lewis Solomon, economists, found little evidence that mandatory-attendance laws increased the number of children in school. They found, too, that school systems have never effectively enforced such laws, usually because of the expense involved.

There is no contradiction between the assertion that compulsory atten- 5 dance has had little effect on the number of children attending school and the argument that repeal would be a positive step toward improving education. Most parents want a high school education for their children. Unfortunately, compulsory attendance hampers the ability of public school officials to enforce legitimate educational and disciplinary policies and thereby make the education a good one.

Private schools have no such problem. They can fail or dismiss stu- 6 dents, knowing such students can attend public school. Without compulsory attendance, public schools would be freer to oust students whose academic or personal behavior undermines the educational mission of the institution.

Has not the noble experiment of a formal education for everyone 7 failed? While we pay homage to the homily, "You can lead a horse to water but you can't make him drink," we have pretended it is not true in education.

Ask high school teachers if recalcitrant students learn anything of 8 value. Ask teachers if these students do any homework. Ask if the threat of low grades motivates them. Quite the contrary, these students know they will be passed from grade to grade until they are old enough to quit or until, as is more likely, they receive a high school diploma. At the point when students could legally quit, most choose to remain since they know they are likely to be allowed to graduate whether they do acceptable work or not.

Abolition of archaic attendance laws would produce enormous 9 dividends.

First, it would alert everyone that school is a serious place where one 10 goes to learn. Schools are neither day-care centers nor indoor street corners. Young people who resist learning should stay away; indeed, an end to compulsory schooling would require them to stay away.

Second, students opposed to learning would not be able to pollute 11 the educational atmosphere for those who want to learn. Teachers could stop policing recalcitrant students and start educating.

Third, grades would show what they are supposed to: how well a stu- 12 dent is learning. Parents could again read report cards and know if their children were making progress.

Fourth, public esteem for schools would increase. People would stop 13
regarding them as way stations for adolescents and start thinking of
them as institutions for educating America's youth.

Fifth, elementary schools would change because students would find 14
out early that they had better learn something or risk flunking out later.
Elementary teachers would no longer have to pass their failures on to
junior high and high school.

Sixth, the cost of enforcing compulsory education would be eliminated. 15
Despite enforcement efforts, nearly 15 percent of the school-age children
in our largest cities are almost permanently absent from school.

Communities could use these savings to support institutions to deal 16
with young people not in school. If, in the long run, these institutions
prove more costly, at least we would not confuse their mission with that
of schools.

Schools should be for education. At present, they are only tangentially 17
so. They have attempted to serve an all-encompassing social function,
trying to be all things to all people. In the process they have failed miserably at what they were originally formed to accomplish.

Questions about the Reading

1. What evidence is given that the American educational system is in
   trouble?
2. What did economists William Landes and Lewis Solomon find out?
3. List at least three benefits of abolishing mandatory-attendance laws.
4. What does the writer mean by the statement, "You can lead a horse
   to water but you can't make him drink"? How have we pretended
   that this isn't true for education?

Questions about the Writer's Strategies

1. Locate the *statement of the problem* and the *solution*. (See Glossary for
   statement of the problem and *solution*.)
2. What is the function of paragraphs 4 and 5?
3. Many writers refer to expert testimony to support their arguments.
   Does the writer of this essay refer to expert testimony? If so, in which
   paragraphs does he do so? Which experts does he cite?
4. What *mode of development* does the writer use in paragraphs 9 through
   15? (See Glossary for *mode of development*.)

Writing Assignments

1. In her essay "Excuses, Excuses" (pp. 267–270), Helen Vo-Dinh provides another solution for our troubled school systems. Which solution do you think is more likely to improve the quality of education? Write a paper explaining your position and providing evidence to support your view.

2. Many colleges require that students score at a certain level on the Scholastic Aptitude Test (SAT) before admission to the college. Standardized tests have recently come under attack for not measuring aptitude or ability but for measuring information that students have learned in school. Some people think that such tests are biased in favor of white, middle-class students. Do you think colleges should require the SAT as a prerequisite for admission? Write an essay that explains and provides evidence for your position.

3. Some states, such as New York, require that students pass a competency exam before they can graduate from high school. If students can't read and write at a certain minimum level, as measured by the test, they aren't allowed to graduate. Write a paper in which you support or reject the use of such tests.

Keep the Drinking Age at Twenty-One

Robert Voas

> *Robert Voas, a senior research scientist at the Pacific Institute for Research and Evaluation, counters Barrett Seaman's argument for lowering the drinking age.*

Words to Know

conjecture   guess, inference
glib   easy, smooth, slick
revanchist   move to turn back or regain something lost

Getting Started

When was eighteen made the legal age for voting?

After nearly four decades of exacting research on how to save lives and 1 reduce injuries by preventing drinking and driving, there is a revanchist attempt afoot to roll back one of the most successful laws in generations: the minimum legal drinking age of 21.

This is extremely frustrating. While public health researchers must 2 produce painstaking evidence that's subjected to critical scholarly review, lower-drinking-age advocates seem to dash off remarks based on glib conjecture and self-selected facts.

It's startling that anybody—given the enormous bodies of research 3 and data—would consider lowering the drinking age. And yet, legislation is currently pending in New Hampshire and Wisconsin to lower the drinking age for military personnel and for all residents in Vermont.

I keep hearing the same refrains: "If you're old enough to go to war, 4 you should be old enough to drink," or "the drinking-age law just increases the desire for the forbidden fruit," or "lower crash rates are due to tougher enforcement, not the 21 law," or "Europeans let their kids drink, so they learn how to be more responsible," or finally, "I did it when I was a kid, and I'm OK."

First, I'm not sure what going to war and being allowed to drink 5 have in common. The 21 law is predicated on the fact that drinking is more dangerous for youth because they're still developing mentally and physically, and they lack experience and are more likely to take risks.

Ask platoon leaders and unit commanders, and they'll tell you that the last thing they want is young soldiers drinking.

As for the forbidden-fruit argument, the opposite is true. Research 6 shows that back when some states still had a minimum drinking age of 18, youths in those states who were under 21 drank more and continued to drink more as adults in their early 20s. In states where the drinking age was 21, teenagers drank less and continue to drink less through their early 20s.

And the minimum 21 law, by itself, has most certainly resulted in 7 fewer accidents, because the decline occurred even when there was little enforcement and tougher penalties had not yet been enacted. According to the National Highway Traffic Safety Administration, the 21 law has saved 23,733 lives since states began raising drinking ages in 1975.

Do European countries really have fewer youth drinking problems? 8 No, that's a myth. Compared to [those for] American youth, binge drinking rates among young people are higher in every European country except Turkey. Intoxication rates are higher in most countries; in Britain, Denmark, and Ireland they're more than twice the U.S. level.

But you drank when you were a kid, and you're OK. Thank good- 9 ness, because many kids aren't OK. An average of 11 American teens die each day from alcohol-related crashes. Underage drinking leads to increased teen pregnancy, violent crime, sexual assault, and huge costs to our communities.

Among college students, it leads to 1,700 deaths, 500,000 injuries, 10 600,000 physical assaults, and 70,000 sexual assaults each year.

Recently, New Zealand lowered its drinking age, which gave research- 11 ers a good opportunity to study the impact. The result was predictable: The rate of alcohol-related crashes among young people rose significantly compared to [the rate for] older drivers.

I've been studying drinking and driving for nearly 40 years and have 12 been involved in public health and behavioral health for 53 years. Believe me when I say that lowering the drinking age would be very dangerous; it would benefit no one except those who profit from alcohol sales.

If bars and liquor stores can freely provide alcohol to teenagers, par- 13 ents will be out of the loop when it comes to their children's decisions about drinking. Age 21 laws are designed to keep such decisions within the family where they belong. Our society, particularly our children and grandchildren, will be immeasurably better off if we not only leave the minimum drinking age law as it is, but enforce it better, too.

Questions about the Reading

1. When was the drinking age raised to twenty-one?
2. At the time the essay was written, which states had legislation pending to lower the drinking age?
3. Why is drinking more dangerous for youth?
4. Who would profit, according to the writer, if the drinking age were lowered?

Questions about the Writer's Strategies

1. What is the thesis of the essay? State it in your own words.
2. What are the false analogies in the essay that the writer refutes?
3. What modes of development does the writer use?

Writing Assignments

1. *Working Together* Join with some classmates to interview restaurant owners, health professionals, and others in your town to determine their opinion of the appropriate drinking age. Write an essay in which you argue for or against a drinking age of eighteen, twenty-one, or higher, based on the information from your interviews.

2. Use the Internet to determine the ages in the different states at which persons under eighteen are legally allowed to marry. Write an essay in which you argue for or against allowing marriage under age eighteen.
3. Write an essay in which you argue for or against allowing persons to vote at age eighteen.

Facts about Global Warming You Should Know

Nathalie Fiset

We're told it's a threat to our planet, but just what is "global warming?"

Words to Know
phenomenon   an unusual or extraordinary occurrence

Getting Started
What are the facts you need to know about global warming?

Global warming is not a 20th century phenomenon. It has, in fact, 1
occurred in the past more than once, along with periods of extreme cold
known as the ice ages. With so much written and reported about global
warming, sometimes it's difficult to detect which is fact and which is just
part of scientific scare tactics. Here are some facts about global warming
that might help:

What exactly is global warming? Global warming is basically the 2
increase in the temperatures of the Earth's atmosphere, land masses and
oceans. The Earth's surface temperature is at an average of 59F and over
the last hundred years, this figure has risen to about 1F. By the year 2100,
the average change in the temperature of the Earth could range from 2.5F
to about 10F, enough to melt glaciers and polar ice caps.

The cause of global warming: Global warming has and will always 3
occur naturally. Why it has become such a concern in our lifetime is due
to the fact that human activities and practices have contributed significantly to its occurrence and severity. With the advent of industrialization
and careless environmental practices, we have caused the increase in the
average global temperatures by contributing negatively to the greenhouse effect.

This began about 240 years ago, when the Industrial Revolution was 4
born. As more and more fossil fuels in the form of oil were mined and
burned, gases as the by-product of that process began to be released in
the atmosphere. Currently, it is estimated that 75% of the increase in the
carbon dioxide content of the Earth's atmosphere is caused by the burning of these fossil fuels.

Global warming and the greenhouse effect: Global warming is related   5
to changes in the Earth's greenhouse effect. Gases naturally occur in
the Earth's atmosphere and act both to protect and retain heat. These
gases included carbon dioxide, methane, nitrous oxide and water vapor.
Of these, water vapor is the most dominant and abundant greenhouse gas.

Global warming and the greenhouse effect are not the same thing. The   6
greenhouse effect refers to a natural process that occurs in the Earth's
atmosphere. If this process is disrupted, then it could contribute to global
warming.

As the sun's rays hit the Earth, heat is bounced back to the atmosphere   7
where these gases contain the heat and keep it there to warm the planet.
This is an important natural process and allows life forms to flour-
ish and survive. Problems only occur when these gases multiply and
build-up, containing heat too efficiently and thus warming the Earth's
atmosphere.

As the Earth's average temperature rises, effects in its landmasses and   8
sea water level become apparent. Polar ice caps melt along with glaciers,
contributing to higher and warmer seas levels. By the end of the century,
it is estimated that sea levels can increase from 4 inches to a high of about
40 inches if global warming continues unabated.

Global warming can also affect the behavior of the winds and can also   9
contribute to a harsher and drier climate, with frequent visitings of strong
hurricanes. Water from heavier rainfall will not stay long to irrigate the
land, however because with a warmer climate, water on the Earth's surface will evaporate quickly. This has a significant effect on agricultural
practices not only in the US but also for the rest of the world.

Another phenomenon that is equated with global warming is the El   10
Nino. The El Nino phenomenon has occurred for probably thousands of
years and is not caused directly by global warming. However, changes
in the average temperature of the planet can contribute to its severity
and frequency.

Other human practices that contribute to global warming: The agri-   11
cultural revolution has also contributed to global warming. As more and
more communities need lands converted from forest to residential and
commercial areas, biomass is reduced, contributing to the increase in the
presence of carbon dioxide in those regions. Since carbon dioxide is pro-
cessed by plants and trees, their absence contributed to its increase.

It is estimated that about 25% of the annual increase in the carbon   12
dioxide found in the Earth's atmosphere is caused by extreme changes
and usage on the Earth's natural resources. Other practices also include
deforestation, salinization, desertification and overgrazing also contribute to global warming. However, many scientists surmise and agree that
the contribution is slight and indirect.

Facing the facts of global warming. Countries all over the world   13
have just begun to acknowledge the negative effects of global warming
not only to the world's politics and economy but also to humankind in
general. Many of the world's governments have encouraged implemen-
tation of measures to try to counteract the problem of global warming
through careful measures and practices designed to protect and respect
the environment.

How these measures will fare and contribute to the long-term mainte-   14
nance of our planet, though, remains to be seen.

Questions about the Reading

1. What is global warming?
2. According to the author, what has contributed to the increase in
   global warming?
3. How does global warming affect sea levels and winds?
4. How does deforestation—the clearing of trees and plants—contribute
   to global warming?

Questions about the Writer's Strategies

1. What is the thesis of the essay? Is it stated or implied? If stated, identify the sentences. If implied, state the thesis in your own words.
2. Is the essay argumentation or persuasion? If argumentation, identify
   the elements. If persuasion, identify the persuasive sentences and
   words.
3. What other modes of development does the writer use?

Writing Assignments

1. Join with some classmates and write an essay in which you argue for
   or against the contribution of urbanization to global warming.
2. Use the Internet to locate information related to the production of
   energy by sources other than oil and write an essay arguing for or
   against the development of one of the sources as a means of reducing
   greenhouse gases and global warming.
3. Write an essay in which you argue for or against allowing windmills
   to be erected in your neighborhood in order to produce energy to
   power lighting at night in your neighborhood.

What If Global-Warming Fears Are Overblown?

Jon Birger

> *Jon Birger, senior writer for* Fortune Magazine, *interviewed John Christy, director of The Earth System Science Center at the University of Alabama-Huntsville, about Christy's argument that global warming theory has been distorted by urbanization.*

Words to Know

climatologist   person who studies the science of the climate and climatic phenomena

controversial   argumentative, debatable

draconian   harsh or cruel requirement

Getting Started

Why would you want or not want a nuclear power plant or a windmill farm built in your town?

With Congress about to take up sweeping climate-change legislation, 1 expect to hear more in coming weeks from John Christy, director of the Earth System Science Center at University of Alabama-Huntsville.

A veteran climatologist who refuses to accept any research funding 2 from the oil or auto industries, Christy was a lead author of the 2001 Intergovernmental Panel on Climate Change report as well as one of the three authors of the American Geophysical Union's landmark 2003 statement on climate change.

Yet despite those green-sounding credentials, Christy is not calling 3 for draconian cuts in carbon emissions. Quite the contrary. Christy is actually the environmental lobby's worst nightmare—an accomplished climate scientist with no ties to Big Oil who has produced reams and reams of data that undermine arguments that the earth's atmosphere is warming at an unusual rate and question whether the remedies being talked about in Congress will actually do any good.

Christy's critics in the blogosphere assume his research is funded by 4 the oil industry. But Christy has testified in federal court that his research is funded by the National Oceanic & Atmospheric Administration and that the only money he has ever received from corporate interests— $2,000 from the Competitive Enterprise Institute for penning a chapter of a global warming book in 2002—he gave away to a charity, the Christian Women's Job Corps.

His most controversial argument is that the surface temperature read-   5
ings upon which global warming theory is built have been distorted by urbanization. Due to the solar heat captured by bricks and pavement and due to the changing wind patterns caused by large buildings, a weather station placed in a rural village in 1900 will inevitably show high temperature readings if that village has, over time, been transformed into small city or a suburban shopping district, Christy says.

The only way to control for such surface distortions is by mea-   6
suring atmospheric temperatures. And when Christy and his co-researcher Roy Spencer, a former NASA scientist now teaching at US-Huntsville, began analyzing temperature readings from NOAA and NMASA satellites, they found much slighter increases in atmospheric temperatures than what was being recorded on the surface. Clark and Spencer also found that nearly all the increases in average surface temperatures are related to nighttime readings—which makes sense if bricks and pavement are in fact retaining heat that would otherwise by dispersed.

In testimony to the House Ways and Means Committee in February,   7
Christy displayed a chart showing central California temperature trends for both the developed San Joaquin Valley and the largely undeveloped Sierra foothills. "The daytime temperatures of both regions show virtually no change over the past 200 years, while the nighttime temperatures indicate the developed Valley has warmed significantly while the undeveloped Sierra foothills have not" Christy told the committee.

I recently spoke with Christy about his controversial research.   8

**Why did you help write the 2001 IPCC report and the 2003 AGU   9
statement on climate change if you disagreed with their fundamental conclusions?**

With the 2001 IPCC report, the material in there over which I had   10
control was satisfactory to me. I wouldn't say I agreed with other parts. As far as the AGU, I thought that was a fine statement because it did not put forth a magnitude of the warming. We just said that human effects have a warming influence, and that's certainly true. There was nothing about disaster or catastrophe. In fact, I was very upset about the latest AGU statement (in 2007) it was about alarmist as you can get.

**When you testified before Ways and Means, did you have any sense   11
that committee members on either side were open to having their minds changed? Or are views set in stone at this point?**

Generally people believe what they want to believe, so their minds 12
will not change. However, as the issue is exposed in terms of economics
and cost benefit—in my view, it's all cost and no benefit—I think some
of the people will take one step backward and say Let me investigate the
science a little more closely.

In laymen's terms, what's wrong with the surface temperature read- 13
ings that are widely used to make the case for global warming?

First is the placement of the temperature stations. They're placed in 14
convenient locations that might be a parking lot or near a house and thus
get extra heating from these human structures. Over time, there's been
the development of areas into farms or buildings or parking lots. Also, a
number of these weather stations have become electronic, and many of
them were moved to a place where there is electricity, which is usually
right outside a building. As a result, there's a natural warming tendency,
especially in the nighttime temperatures, that has been misinterpreted as
greenhouse warming.

Are there any negative consequences to this localized warming? 15

It's a small impact, but there is an indication that major thunderstorms 16
are more likely to form downwind of major cities like St. Louis and
Atlanta. The extra heating of the city causes the air to rise with a little
more punch.

Have you been able to confirm your satellite temperature readings 17
by other means?

Weather balloons. We take satellite shots at the same place where the 18
balloon is released so we're looking at the same column of air. Our satellite data compares exceptionally well to the balloon data.

During your House Ways and Means testimony, you showed 19
a chart juxtaposing predictions made by NASA's Jim Hansen in
1988 for future temperature increases against the actual recorded
temperature increases over the past 20 years. Not only were the
actual increases much lower, but they were lower than what Hansen
expected if there were drastic cuts in CO2 emissions—which of
course there haven't been. [Hansen is a noted scientist who was
featured prominently in Al Gore's global warming documentary,
"An Inconvenient Truth."] Hansen was at that hearing. Did he say
anything to you afterwards?

We really don't communicate. We serve on a committee for NASA 20
together, but it only deals with specific satellite issues. At the Ways and
Means hearing, he was sitting two people down from me, but he did not
want to engage any of the evidence I presented. And that seems to be the
preferred tactic of many in the alarmist camp. Rather than bring up these
issues, they simply ignore them.

[Contacted by *Fortune*, Hansen acknowledges that his 1988 projections   21
were based on a model that "slightly" overstated the warming created
by a doubling in CO2 levels. His new model posits a rise of 3 degrees
Celsius in global temperatures by 2100, vs. 4.2 degrees in the old one.
Says Hansen, "The projections that the public has been hearing about
are based on a climate sensitivity that is consistent with the global warming rate of the past few decades." Christy's response: "Hansen at least
admits his 1988 forecasts were wrong, but doesn't say they were way
wrong not "slightly" as he states." Christy also claims that even Hansen's revised models grossly overestimated the amount of warming that
has actually occurred.]

I know you think there's been something of a hysteria in the media   22
about melting glaciers. Could you explain?

Ice melts. Glaciers are always calving. This is what ice does. If ice did   23
not melt, we'd have an ice-covered planet. The fact is that the ice cover
is growing in the southern hemisphere even as the ice cover is more
or less shrinking in the northern hemisphere. As you and I are talking
today, global sea ice coverage is about 400,000 square kilometers above
the long-term average—which means that the surplus in the Antarctic is
greater than the deficit in the Arctic.

What about the better-safe-than-sorry argument? Even if there's a   24
chance Gore and Hansen are wrong, shouldn't we still take action in
order to protect ourselves from catastrophe, just in case they're right?

The problem is that the solutions being offered don't provide any   25
detectable relief from this so-called catastrophe. Congress is now discussing an 80% reduction in U.S. greenhouse emissions by 2050. That's
basically the equivalent of building 1,000 new nuclear power plants all
operating by 2020. Now I'm all in favor of nuclear energy, but that would
affect the global temperature by only seven-hundredths of a degree by
2020 and fifteen hundredths by 2100. We wouldn't even notice it.

Questions about the Reading

1. What is John Christy's opinion of the accuracy of temperature readings taken in developed areas?
2. What does John Christy say is the problem with the solutions being
   offered to reduce greenhouse emissions?
3. What is John Christy's opinion of the concerns frequently expressed
   by the media about the glaciers melting?

Questions about the Writer's Strategies

1. What is the "thesis" or argument that John Christy expresses related to global warming temperature readings?
2. What modes of development are used in the interview by the writer (Jon Birger) and by the person being interviewed (John Christy)?

Writing Assignments

1. Join with some classmates and interview the weather reporters at your local television, newspaper, and radio stations to determine their opinions related to global warming and, if occurring, what corrective measures they think should be taken to offset it. Write an essay in which you and your classmates argue that global warming is/is not occurring and, if occurring, what measures should be taken to counteract it.
2. Write an essay in which you argue for or against having a nuclear energy power plant built in your town.
3. Write an essay in which you argue for or against installing windmills as a source of energy in your town.

Questions about the Reading

1. Why does Christy think global warming fears have been "overblown"?
2. How has urbanization affected global warming theory, according to Christy?
3. What has been the impact, according to Christy, of the placement of the temperature stations? Why?
4. What is Christy's opinion of the solutions currently being offered to relieve global warming?

Questions about the Writer's Strategies

1. What is the thesis of the interview? State it in your own words.
2. What modes of development are used in the interview by the writer (Jon Birger) and by the person being interviewed (John Christy)?

Writing Assignments

1. Join with some classmates and take the temperature by one of your school buildings early in the morning, at noon on a sunny day, and at night. Write an essay in which you argue for or against the influence of the building on the temperature.

2. Ask your local television weather reporters their opinions of whether the temperatures have warmed in your town and write an essay in which you argue for or against an increase in temperature and, if it has increased, discuss the possible causes.

11

Combining the Strategies

IN THIS CHAPTER, you will find some additional reading selections. Although some of the readings have one dominant **mode of development,** most of them illustrate combinations of the different modes.

As you read, keep in mind what we have stressed in earlier chapters. Determine the

- topic of each paragraph
- thesis of each essay
- structure of the reading (introduction, development, conclusion)
- supporting details
- modes of development
- point of view (person, time, tone)
- method of organization (time, space, order of importance)
- transitional words
- effective words and sentences

Then make use of these same strategies to write paragraphs and essays that are as clear and effective as those you have read.

A Trip to Honduras

Daniel Boehmer (student)

A trip to Honduras convinced Daniel Boehmer that he wanted a career that would have a positive effect on other people's lives. He is realizing that desire as a student at George Washington University, majoring in international affairs.

Words to Know

concurrently at the same time
disparity difference
docile obedient, accepting
effervescent lively, high-spirited
ensnare trap
immersed absorbed, deeply involved

Getting Started

Do you participate in some community or volunteer service?

It was a sizzling day in August as I stood watching the four-or-five-year-old girl placidly eating the fly-covered, white-breaded peanut butter and jelly sandwich I had just given her. As I watched, immersed in the unfamiliar surroundings, I began to think about why I was there. What had brought me to this impoverished Honduran community, Rincon de Dolores, a village so strikingly named "Corner of Pain"? At first glance, the little girl looked like any ordinary child her age. As I studied her more closely, however, her frayed clothing, disheveled hair, and tiny shoeless feet revealed her poverty to me. Though the exchange was undoubtedly simple for her, for me it had a significantly deeper meaning. I began to reconsider roles: Who was the giver and who was the receiver here?

I arrived in Honduras through my church, which was continuing its tradition of sending a youth and medical team to this secluded nook of Honduras to work with the people to improve their community in ways that their government could or would not. That year we were assigned to begin construction on a church in Rincon, and I jumped at the opportunity to go. I really had no idea what I was in for.

I presumed I was prepared to witness the widespread poverty that runs rampant in the region. After all, I had seen documentaries, read articles in *National Geographic,* and had been active in efforts of international aid before, but no amount of mental preparation could prepare me for my surprising visit to this corner of the world.

At first I was greeted with what I had expected: a constant barrage of 4 insects, bacterially infected water, the reality of life in a tin-roofed hut, and inescapable heat. As time went on, however, I began to see a side of Honduras I had not expected. Instead of seeing only the dramatic disparity in wealth between the Hondurans and me, I began to see the disparity in spirit between my comparatively rigid community back in the States and the Honduran community I experienced there. I was stunned by the undiscriminating kindness and the incredible work ethic of those people—the determination of a boy who woke at 4 A.M. every morning to trek several miles to school; the steadfast, vibrant piety of the Hondurans at their effervescent church services; and the sense of collective joy I saw in their faces when they greeted us to thank us for being there. Looking back, I wish I had been able to say how grateful I was for the inspiration they gave me. Honduras is very different from the relatively affluent Massachusetts community where I live. Though I had considered myself before my trip to Honduras to be a politically oriented and globally "aware" person, I soon realized that I had a great deal to learn about the nature of poverty—and the human spirit. I began to ask, "How had I intellectualized something as human as the daily struggle for life faced by 85 percent of our world's population?" Seeing was believing that summer of 2004.

My decision about the type of work I wanted to go into was a long and 5 thoughtful process. That moment—looking into the little girl's docile and composed but concurrently resolute face—as well as my trip to Honduras as a whole, had a profound effect on my decision about what I want to accomplish in life. I saw the effort exerted just to stay alive—faced by so many—embodied by the girl. It has given me a definitive direction in ways that a high school education or a book of majors could only hope to give. I discovered that I would be unable to feel accomplished in any career without getting the sense that what I did would have a constructive effect on the lives of others. In the weeks and months following my trip to Honduras, I slowly realized that the world was smaller and humanity more universal than I had previously imagined by more than a hundred thousand fold.

Honduras was a turning point for me and will be a cornerstone for 6 my future endeavors in life and vocation. Social action has moved me, and social action is my aim. International relations and government are areas of study that I know will allow me to have a constructive effect on the world. May I, throughout my life, ever be removed from the nets that ensnare those possessed by self-serving ambition, for success is truly fruitless unless it is in the conquest of helping one's fellow man.

The Dare

Roger Hoffmann

Roger Hoffmann recounts an episode from his adolescence when approval from his peers was more important than his personal safety. No matter our age or particular adolescent experience, we are able to relate to the pressure Hoffmann felt as a child. The desire for acceptance by friends and colleagues is something we never outgrow.

Words to Know

ambiguous not clear, having many interpretations

escalated increased

guerrilla act warfare carried out by an independent military force

implicit understood although not directly stated

provoke to cause anger or resentment

silhouette an outline of something that appears dark against a light background, a shadow

Getting Started

Have you ever taken a risk because of a dare?

The secret to diving under a moving freight train and rolling out the other side with all your parts attached lies in picking the right spot between the tracks to hit with your back. Ideally, you want soft dirt or pea gravel, clear of glass shards and railroad spikes that could cause you instinctively, and fatally, to sit up. Today, at thirty-eight I couldn't be threatened or baited enough to attempt that dive. But as a seventh grader struggling to make the cut in a tough Atlanta grammar school, all it took was a dare.

I coasted through my first years of school as a fussed-over smart kid, the teacher's pet who finished his work first and then strutted around the room tutoring other students. By the seventh grade, I had more A's than friends. Even my old cronies, Dwayne and O.T., made it clear I'd never be one of the guys in junior high if I didn't dirty up my act. They challenged me to break the rules, and I did. The I-dare-you's escalated: shoplifting, sugaring teachers' gas tanks, dropping lighted matches into public mailboxes. Each guerrilla act won me the approval I never got for just being smart.

Walking home by the railroad tracks after school, we started playing   3
chicken with oncoming trains. O.T., who was failing that year, always
won. One afternoon he charged a boxcar from the side, stopping just
short of throwing himself between the wheels. I was stunned. After the
train disappeared, we debated whether someone could dive under a
moving car, stay put for a 10-count, then scramble out the other side. I
thought it could be done and said so. O.T. immediately stepped in front
of me and smiled. Not by me, I added quickly, I certainly didn't mean
that I could do it. "A smart guy like you," he said, his smile evaporating,
"you could figure it out easy." And then, squeezing each word for effect,
"I . . . DARE . . . you." I'd just turned twelve. The monkey clawing my
back was Teacher's Pet. And I'd been dared.

As an adult, I've been on both ends of life's implicit business and   4
social I-dare-you's, although adults don't use those words. We provoke
with body language, tone of voice, ambiguous phrases. I dare you to:
argue with the boss, tell Fred what you think of him, send the wine
back. Only rarely are the risks physical. How we respond to dares
when we are young may have something to do with which of the truly
hazardous male inner dares—attacking mountains, tempting bulls at
Pamplona—we embrace or ignore as men.

For two weeks, I scouted trains and tracks. I studied moving boxcars   5
close up, memorizing how they squatted on their axles, never getting
used to the squeal or the way the air felt hot from the sides. I created
an imaginary, friendly train and ran next to it. I mastered a shallow,
head-first dive with a simple half-twist. I'd land on my back, count to
ten, imagine wheels and, locking both hands on the rail to my left, heave
myself over and out. Even under pure sky, though, I had to fight to keep
my eyes open and my shoulders between the rails.

The next Saturday, O.T., Dwayne and three eighth graders met me   6
below the hill that backed up to the lumberyard. The track followed a
slow bend there and opened to a straight, slightly uphill climb for a solid
third of a mile. My run started two hundred yards after the bend. The
train would have its tongue hanging out.

The other boys huddled off to one side, a circle on another planet, and   7
watched quietly as I double-knotted my shoelace. My hands trembled.
O.T. broke the circle and came over to me. He kept his hands hidden in
the pockets of his jacket. We looked at each other. BB's of sweat appeared
beneath his nose. I stuffed my wallet in one of his pockets, rubbing it
against his knuckles on the way in, and slid my house key, wired to
a red-and-white fishing bobber, into the other. We backed away from
each other, and he turned and ran to join the four already climbing up
the hill.

I watched them all the way to the top. They clustered together as if I   8
were taking their picture. Their silhouette resembled a round shouldered
tombstone. They waved down to me, and I dropped them from my mind
and sat down on the rail. Immediately, I jumped back. The steel was
vibrating.

The train sounded like a cow going short of breath. I pulled my shirt-   9
tail out and looked down at my spot, then up the incline of track ahead
of me. Suddenly the air went hot, and the engine was by me. I hadn't
pictured it moving that fast. A man's bare head leaned out and stared at
me. I waved to him with my left hand and turned into the train, bury-
ing my face into the incredible noise. When I looked up, the head was
gone.

I started running alongside the boxcars. Quickly, I found their pace,   10
held it, and then eased off, concentrating on each thick wheel that cut
past me. I slowed another notch. Over my shoulder, I picked my car as
it came off the bend, locking in the image of the white mountain goat
painted on its side. I waited, leaning forward like the anchor in a 440-
relay, wishing the baton up the track behind me. Then the big goat fired
by me, and I was flying and then tucking my shoulder as I dipped under
the train.

A heavy blanket of red dust settled over me. I felt bolted to the earth.   11
Sheet-metal bellies thundered and shook above my face. Count to ten,
a voice said, watch the axles and look to your left for daylight. But I
couldn't count, and I couldn't find left if my life depended on it, which it
did. The colors overhead went from brown to red to black to red again.
Finally, I ripped my hands free, forced them to the rail, and, in one con-
vulsive jerk, threw myself into the blue light.

I lay there face down until there was no more noise, and I could feel   12
the sun against the back of my neck. I sat up. The last ribbon of train
was slipping away in the distance. Across the tracks, O.T. was leading a
cavalry charge down the hill, five very small, galloping boys, their fists
whirling above them. I pulled my knees to my chest. My corduroy pants
puckered wet across my thighs. I didn't care.

Poetry

Kirsten Bauman (student)

That scary poetry assignment in an English class doesn't frighten Kirsten Bauman, a student at the University of Cincinnati Raymond Walters College in Blue Ash, Ohio. Here, she tells us about her good and bad poetry assignments.

Words to Know
boundaries limits, confines
confused lacking understanding
self-conscious ill-at-ease

Getting Started
What is your favorite poem? Have you ever written a poem?

P oetry is a form of free-thought expressed on paper. No boundaries or 1 limitations are set on the poet.

Many people think a poem has to rhyme or have a pattern, but that 2 is not the case. Poetry sets a mood or a tone by being humorous, sad, or serious. Poetry lets readers make their own inferences about the meaning of the poem. For that reason, a poem may be more meaningful or special to one person than to another.

Many of my fellow students, as well as some adults, say they don't 3 like poetry. Maybe the reason I do is because of my early experiences with poetry.

I can remember sitting on my bed with my Dad as he read aloud to 4 me from an old story book he had when he was a child. I remember that it was a collection of children's poems that I loved, no matter how many times my Dad read them to me. I liked the simple nature of the poems. I liked the fact that I could memorize them so I could "read along" with my Dad. I still remember what the book looked like. It was a tall, narrow book with a wood cover. Because it looked different from all my other books, I still remember it so clearly today.

I can also remember reading aloud from a wide, white poem book 5 called *A Light in the Attic* by Shel Silverstein. I remember liking the poems because I could relate to them as a child, and they made me laugh.

Some of my later experiences with poetry weren't as pleasant. In ninth 6 grade English class, we read Shakespeare's *Romeo and Juliet*. I remember having to read aloud and being confused by Shakespeare's use of words. I remember wondering why we were being tortured by reading something that everyone in the class clearly didn't understand.

In a later high school English class, we were divided into groups of 7 three. Our assignment was for each of us to write a poem that illustrated a different element of poetry. Our group was to illustrate the simile.

I had difficulty getting started on my poem; but once I had a begin- 8 ning place, thoughts and ideas just came naturally to me. I actually liked writing the poem. But we still had to present our poems in front of the class, and I was self-conscious about sharing my ideas with other people. It was hard to get in front of the class and read my poem aloud, but my turn was soon over. The class seemed to like my poem, so I decided that writing poetry was almost as pleasant as reading it.

I Won't Twitter My Life Away

Leonard Pitts, Jr.

> *A writer for the* Miami Herald, *Leonard Pitts questions whether our easier ways of communicating with each other have led to our communicating information that is of little importance.*

Words to Know

banality   trivial remark
crudity   crude, tasteless, uncultured remark

Getting Started

Are you wasting too much time Twittering or on unimportant e-mail messages?

Today, I make you a solemn promise: I will never Twitter you. Or is it 1
tweet? I'm never sure.

And here, let me pause to help the technologically illiterate catch 2
up. One uses Twitter to send tweets (no, I am *not* making that up!) i.e.,
electronic notes, to one's online friends, family and other subscribers.
A tweet, which is limited to 140 characters, (i.e., shorter than this very
sentence) is supposed to bring interested parties up to date on what you
are doing, seeing, thinking, in that exact moment.

When I first heard of this latest advance (?) in interpersonal commu- 3
nication, I pegged it as a fad that would be big among high school and
college students—i.e., young people, who frequently have the attention span of a squirrel on cocaine. Last week's presidential speech to a
joint session of Congress shows how wrong I was. It turns out that, as
the leader of the free world was addressing them on matters of urgent
national importance, some of our elected representatives were hunched
over their handheld devices madly tweeting, like 5th graders passing
notes in the back of the class.

For instance, The Washington Post reported that Republican Rep. 4
Robert Wittman tweeted the following urgent observation: "I am sitting
behind Sens. Graham and McCain."

"Place is on fire," said Rep. Denny Rehberg, a Republican from 5
Montana.

Which is not to imply that only pols have gone Twitter mad. CNN's 6
Roland Martin is stuck at an airport in Chicago, trying to get to

snowbound New York City even as I write this: "No flights allowed in," he tweets. "I was on plane in Chicago, we pulled out, got word, now back at gate."

NBC's Ann Curry, meantime, is in New York enjoying the snow: "All 7 stars are not the proper shoes for NYC today. But seeing this dark city frosted in white is worth my cold toes."

And you need to know this because..."   8

No, we are not being forced to look. But if you choose to, please reflect 9 on the fact that life is short and you just spent some irretrievable fraction of yours learning that Roland Martin's flight is delayed and Ann Curry's feet are cold.

In the '90s, you often heard people complain of how memoir writers 10 and afternoon talk shows had turned our public spaces into a communal confessional, Intimate secrets once necessary for whispering are now shouted into the ether like an order at a fast-food joint. Ten years later, we are not just sharing secrets; we are sharing lives. And not the good parts, either, but the banal, the mundane, the everyday.

I'm darned if I can see the fascination. I mean, I'm not surprised 11 that technology allows this. But I am surprised that people—by the thousands—buy into it.

Take it as one more example of the medium becoming its own mes- 12 sage. After all, every new advance in communications from telegraphs to Twitter has been sold as a means of perfecting human relationships, allowing us to interact more easily, understand one another more read- ily. But it hasn't happened yet.

Indeed, you have to wonder if, as communication becomes ever 13 easier, we have not gone in the opposite direction, crossing the point of diminishing returns as we did. More people have more ways to reach more people than at any point in history. But it turns out—read a mes- sage board or an unsolicited email, if you don't believe me—many of us don't have a whole lot to say. Unless, that is, you find some socially redeeming value in banality, cruelty, and crudity, which have become ubiquitous.

You have to wonder what that says about us.   14

Now here is Twitter, which encourages you to narrate your life in real 15 time as opposed to, well. . . living it. I'm sorry, but include me out.

I will never Twitter you.   16

In the first place, you have better things to do. In the second, I am not 17 that interesting.

No one is.   18

Time to Look and Listen

Magdoline Asfahani (student)

Magdoline Asfahani, an Arab and a Muslim, gives us a sensitive and thoughtful account of the effect of discrimination on her life. Asfahani is a student at the University of Texas, El Paso.

Words to Know

alluding referring, suggesting
incompatible not in agreement
medley mixture, assortment
monotheistic having a belief in one God
nuances subtleties, slight variations or differences

Getting Started

Do you feel that you discriminate against a group of people?

I love my country as many who have been here for generations can- 1 not. Perhaps that's because I'm the child of immigrants, raised with a conscious respect for America that many people take for granted. My parents chose this country because it offered them a new life, freedom and possibilities. But I learned at a young age that the country we loved so much did not feel the same way about us.

Discrimination is not unique to America. It occurs in any country that 2 allows immigration. Anyone who is unlike the majority is looked at a little suspiciously, dealt with a little differently. The fact that I wasn't part of the majority never occurred to me. I knew that I was an Arab and a Muslim. This meant nothing to me. At school I stood up to say the Pledge of Allegiance every day. These things did not seem incompatible at all. Then everything changed for me, suddenly and permanently, in 1985. I was only in seventh grade, but that was the beginning of my political education.

That year a TWA plane originating in Athens was diverted to Beirut. 3 Two years earlier the U.S. Marine barracks in Beirut had been bombed. That seemed to start a chain of events that would forever link Arabs with terrorism. After the hijacking, I faced classmates who taunted me with cruel names, attacking my heritage and my religion. I became an outcast and had to apologize for myself constantly.

After a while, I tried to forget my heritage. No matter what race, 4
religion or ethnicity, a child who is attacked often retreats. I was the
only Arab I knew of in my class, so I had no one in my peer group as
an ally. No matter what my parents tried to tell me about my proud cultural history, I would ignore it. My classmates told me I came from an
uncivilized, brutal place, that Arabs were by nature anti-American, and
I believed them. They did not know the hours my parents spent studying, working, trying to preserve part of their old lives while embracing,
willingly, the new.

I tried to forget the Arabic I knew, because if I didn't I'd be forever 5
linked to murderers. I stopped inviting friends over for dinner, because
I thought the food we ate was "weird." I lied about where my parents
had come from. Their accents (although they spoke English perfectly)
humiliated me. Though Islam is a major monotheistic religion with many
similarities to Judaism and Christianity, there were no holidays near
Chanukah or Christmas, nothing to tie me to the "Judeo-Christian" tradition. I felt more excluded. I slowly began to turn into someone without
a past.

Civil war was raging in Lebanon, and all that Americans saw of that 6
country was destruction and violence. Every other movie seemed to
feature Arab terrorists. The most common questions I was asked were if
I had ever ridden a camel or if my family lived in tents. I felt burdened
with responsibility. Why should an adolescent be asked questions like
"Is it true you hate Jews and you want Israel destroyed?" I didn't hate
anybody. My parents had never said anything even alluding to such
sentiments. I was confused and hurt.

As I grew older and began to form my own opinions, my embar- 7
rassment lessened and my anger grew. The turning point came in high
school. My grandmother had become very ill, and it was necessary for
me to leave school a few days before Christmas vacation. My chemistry
teacher was very sympathetic until I said I was going to the Middle East.
"Don't come back in a body bag," he said cheerfully. The class laughed.
Suddenly, those years of watching movies that mocked me and listening
to others who knew nothing about Arabs and Muslims except what they
saw on television seemed like a bad dream. I knew then that I would
never be silent again.

I've tried to reclaim those lost years. I realize now that I come from 8
a culture that has a rich history. The Arab world is a medley of people
of different religions; not every Arab is a Muslim, and vice versa. The
Arabs brought tremendous advances in the sciences and mathematics,
as well as creating a literary tradition that has never been surpassed.
The language itself is flexible and beautiful, with nuances and shades
of meaning unparalleled in any language. Though many find it hard to

believe, Islam has made progress in women's rights. There is a specific provision in the Koran that permits women to own property and ensures that their inheritance is protected—although recent events have shown that interpretation of these laws can vary.

My youngest brother, who is 12, is now at the crossroads I faced. 9 When initial reports of the Oklahoma City bombing pointed to "Arab-looking individuals" as the culprits, he came home from school crying. "Mom, why do Muslims kill people? Why are the Arabs so bad?" She was angry and brokenhearted, but tried to handle the situation in the best way possible: through education. She went to his class, armed with Arabic music, pictures, traditional dress and cookies. She brought a chapter of the social-studies book to life, and the children asked intelligent, thoughtful questions, even after the class was over. Some even asked if she was coming back. When my brother came home, he was excited and proud instead of ashamed.

I only recently told my mother about my past experience. Maybe if I 10 had told her then, I would have been better equipped to deal with the thoughtless teasing. But, fortunately, the world is changing. Although discrimination and stereotyping still exist, many people are trying to lessen and end it. Teachers, schools and the media are showing greater sensitivity to cultural issues. However, there is still much that needs to be done, not for the sake of any particular ethnic or cultural group but for the sake of our country.

The America that I love is one that values freedom and the differences 11 of its people. Education is the key to understanding. As Americans we need to take a little time to look and listen carefully to what is around us and not rush to judgment without knowing all the facts. And we must never be ashamed of our pasts. It is our collective differences that unite us and make us unique as a nation. It's what determines our present and our future.

Glossary

Various terms are used throughout this edition of *Patterns Plus* to explain the basic strategies of writing. These terms are boldfaced in the chapter introductions, and they are boldfaced and defined here in the following pages. Terms in bold type within the definitions are also defined in the Glossary.

Alternating Method   The alternating method of **comparison** and **contrast**, also called point-by-point method, compares and contrasts two subjects item by item. (See also **Block Method** and **Mixed Method**.)

Antonym   An antonym is a word that has a meaning *opposite* that of another word. For example, *pleasure* is an antonym of *pain*. Using an antonym is one method writers use to define an unfamiliar word.

Argumentation   Argumentation is a **mode of development** used to express a controversial idea. A classic or formal argument includes five elements: statement of the problem, solution, evidence, refutation, and conclusion. Argumentation may or may not include some persuasion, but should be rational, logical, and objective rather than emotional. (See also **Persuasion**.)

Audience   A reader or readers of a piece of writing. More specifically, an audience is that reader or group of readers toward which a particular piece of writing is aimed. (See also **Purpose** and **Occasion**.)

Block Method   In the block method of **comparison** and **contrast**, the writer first explains the characteristics of the first item in a block and then explains the characteristics of the second item in a block. (See also **Alternating Method** and **Mixed Method**.)

Body   The body is the development of the **thesis** in a group of related paragraphs in an **essay**. (See also **Introduction** and **Conclusion**.)

Brainstorming   A prewriting technique that many writers use to generate ideas for writing. In brainstorming, a writer jots down as many details and ideas on a subject as come to mind.

Cause   A cause is a reason why something happens or an explanation of why some **effect** occurs. Writers explain why an effect (or result) comes about by explaining its causes. See chapter 8, "Cause and Effect," for further discussion.

Chronological Order   See **Order**.

Class   In **classification** and **division**, a writer can classify or divide items if they are of the same type—that is, if they belong to the same class.

Classification   Classification is the process of sorting a group of items into categories on the basis of some characteristic or quality that the items have in common. As a **mode** of **development**, classification is used by writers to organize and develop information included in a **paragraph** or **essay**. Classification is sometimes combined with **division** to develop a **topic** or **thesis**. See chapter 5, "Classification and Division," for further discussion.

Cliché   Clichés are words or phrases that have become so overused they have lost their expressive power. Examples of clichés are "rosy red," "silly goose," "bull in a china shop," and "works like a horse."

Coherence   Coherence refers to the logical flow of a piece of writing. Writing is coherent when the **main idea** is clearly stated and the connections between the supporting **details** and the main idea are obvious. (See also **Unified/Unity**.)

Collaboration/Collaborative Writing   Collaboration or collaborative writing is the working together of two or more persons in developing and producing a piece of writing.

Comparison/Compare   When making a comparison, the writer discusses the similarities of objects or ideas. Writers sometimes combine comparison with contrast in developing their **main idea**. See chapter 6, "Comparison and Contrast," for further discussion.

Conclusion   In writing, the term *conclusion* is used to refer to the sentence or **paragraph** that completes the composition. Within the conclusion, the writer may restate the **main idea** of the composition or sum up its important points.

   In reading, the term *conclusion* refers to the idea the reader can draw from the information in the reading selection. Drawing a conclusion involves making an **inference**—that is, deriving an idea that is **implied** by the information stated within a composition.

Connotation   Connotation refers to the feelings or qualities a reader associates with a word. In **persuasion**, writers often use the connotations of words to appeal to their readers. (See also **Denotation**.)

Contrast   When making a contrast, the writer discusses the differences among objects or ideas. Writers sometimes combine contrast with **comparison** in developing an idea. See chapter 6, "Comparison and Contrast," for further discussion.

Deductive Order   In deductive order—also called general-to-specific order—the writer presents the argument or discussion by beginning with a general statement, such as the **topic** of a paragraph or **thesis** of an essay, and proceeding to the specific information that supports the statement.

Definition   A definition explains the meaning of a word or term. Writers frequently use a variety of methods for defining the words and terms they use. They may use a dictionary definition, a **synonym**, or an **antonym**. They may also use any combination of the **modes of development** explained in this text.

An **extended definition** is one composed of several sentences or paragraphs. It is often used to define complex objects or concepts. See chapter 9, "Definition," for further discussion.

Denotation   Denotation refers to the exact definition, or dictionary definition, of a word. (See also **Connotation**.)

Description   In a description, the writer discusses the appearance of a person, place, or object. In descriptions, writers use words and details that appeal to the senses in order to create the **impression** they want the reader to have about what is being described.

Details   Details are specific pieces of information—examples, incidents, dates, and so forth—that explain and support the general ideas in a composition. Writers use details to make their general ideas clearer and more understandable to the reader.

Development   Development refers to the detailed explanation of the main—and usually more general—ideas in a composition. The **main idea** (or **topic**) of a paragraph is developed by providing specific information in the sentences within the paragraph. The main idea or **thesis** of an **essay** is explained or developed through **paragraphs**.

Dialogue   Dialogue is conversation, usually between two or more persons. It is used by writers to give the exact words spoken by people and is always set off by quotation marks. The writer usually uses a new paragraph to indicate a change of speaker. Dialogue is commonly found in **narration**.

Division   In division, the writer breaks down or sorts a single object or idea into its components or parts and then gives detailed information about each of the parts. Division is sometimes used in combination with **classification**. See chapter 5, "Classification and Division," for further discussion.

Draft   A draft is the first version of a piece of writing. Preparation of a draft follows prewriting in the writing process. A draft requires rewriting, revising, and editing. (See also **Edit, Prewriting, Revising,** and **Rewriting**.)

Edit   Editing is the final step in the writing process and involves checking the piece of writing for accuracy of spelling, sentence structure, grammar, and punctuation. (See also **Draft, Prewriting, Revising,** and **Rewriting**.)

Effect   An effect is the result of certain events or **causes**. An effect may be the result of one or more causes. Writers often combine cause and effect to explain why something happens. See chapter 8, "Cause and Effect," for further discussion.

Essay   An essay is a written composition based on an idea, which is called its **thesis**. An essay usually consists of at least three **paragraphs**. In the paragraphs, writers usually introduce and state the **thesis, develop** or explain the thesis, and **conclude** the essay. See chapter 1, "The Basics of Writing: Process and Strategies," for further discussion.

Event   An occurrence or happening that a writer wishes to portray, often as part of a **fictional** or **nonfictional narrative**.

Example   An example is a specific illustration of a general idea or statement. Writers may use one or more examples and may extend a single example over an entire essay in order to illustrate and support their ideas.

Extended Definition   See **Definition**.

Extended Example   An extended example is described in several sentences or paragraphs. It is used as a way of providing additional support for a **topic sentence** or **thesis statement**. See chapter 4, "Examples," for further discussion.

Fact(s)   Any thing or things known with certainty. Writers often present facts as a way of showing they are **objective** about a subject. (See also **Opinion**.)

Fallacy   A fallacy is an error in the writer's reasoning or logic. Types of fallacies include the post hoc (meaning "after this, therefore because of this"), hasty generalization, non sequitur (claiming an effect that does not follow from the cause), false analogy, circular argument, argument to the man (argument ad hominem), bandwagon, either-or, and begging the question. See chapters 8, "Cause and Effect," and 10, "Argumentation and Persuasion," for further discussion.

Fiction/Fictional Narrative   A paragraph or an essay that presents a story or event that did not occur or that differs significantly from a real or true event is called fiction. (By contrast, see **Nonfiction/Nonfictional Narrative**.)

Figure of Speech   A word or phrase used to compare unlike things to create an image or **impression**. Examples are "He fought like a tiger" and "A little girl is sugar and spice." (See also **Metaphor** and **Simile**.)

First Person   See **Person**.

Formal Definition   A formal definition assigns the word or term being defined to the **class** or **classification** of items to which it belongs and then describes the characteristics that distinguish it from other items in that class.

Freewriting   Freewriting is a **prewriting** exercise that involves writing without stopping for a set period of time, often five to ten minutes. Freewriting is an effective way to start writing and to generate ideas.

General Idea/General Statement   A general idea or statement is broad and sweeping and therefore must usually be explained with more specific information. The **main idea** of a **paragraph** or an **essay** is a relatively general idea, involving only the main features of the thought. In a paragraph or an essay, the general ideas and statements must be supported by more specific information.

Hyperbole   Hyperbole is a statement that is an exaggeration of a condition or situation.

Image   An image is a "vision" or impression created by descriptive or sensory details.

Imply/Implied   To imply is to hint at or indicate indirectly. Writers sometimes only imply their ideas rather than state them directly. An implied idea requires the reader to draw **conclusions** or make **inferences** in order to determine the idea.

Impression   The effect, feeling, or image that an author tries to create through description.

Incidents   Incidents are the more specific, detailed happenings that make up a particular event. The **narration** of an event will include an account of the specific incidents that occurred as part of the event.

Inductive Order   In inductive order—also called specific-to-general order—the writer presents the argument or discussion by beginning with specific supporting information and proceeding to the **general statement**, such as the **topic** of a **paragraph** or **thesis** of an **essay**.

Infer/Inference   An inference is a **conclusion** drawn by the reader based on information known or **implied**. Writers sometimes imply their ideas rather than state them. Readers must make inferences and use the information that is known or stated to determine the writer's ideas.

Inform   Inform means to relate or tell about something. Writers often use process as a **mode of development** to inform their readers, although any of the modes discussed in this text can be used to inform.

Instruct   Instruct means to teach or educate. Writers often use **process** as a **mode of development** to instruct their readers.

Introduction   The introduction of a **paragraph** or **essay** is at its beginning. The introduction of an essay is often where the writer places the **thesis statement**. (See also **Body** and **Conclusion**.)

Irony   The use of a relationship that is contradictory or unexpected. Writers often use irony to amuse, sadden, instruct, or anger their readers.

Main Idea   The main idea of a composition is the general concept, broad **opinion**, or argument on which the composition is based. The main idea of a **paragraph** is called the **topic**. The main idea of an **essay** is called the **thesis**.

Metaphor   A metaphor is a **figure of speech** that compares unlike items by attributing the qualities or characteristics of one item to the other. A metaphor compares the items without the use of the words *like* or *as*. (See also **Simile**.)

Mixed Method   The mixed method of **comparison** and **contrast** explains similarities and then differences, or differences first and then similarities. (See also **Alternating Method** and **Block Method**.)

Mode of Development   The mode of development refers to the kind of information used to **support** and explain the **main idea** of a paragraph or essay. Writers commonly use, either singly or in combination, the modes discussed in this text: **narration, description, examples, classification** and **division, comparison** and **contrast, process, cause and effect, definition,** and **argumentation** and **persuasion.**

Narration/Narrative Writing   Narration is a **mode of development** used by writers to tell a story or give an account of a historical or fictional event. See chapter 2, "Narration," for further discussion.

Nonfiction/Nonfictional Narrative   A paragraph or essay that presents a story or event that actually happened. (By contrast, see **Fiction/Fictional Narrative.**)

Objective   A paragraph or essay that presents the **facts** without including the writer's interpretation of those facts is said to be objective. (By contrast, see **Subjective.**)

Occasion   An occasion is a set of circumstances under which a particular piece of writing occurs. The writing assignments in this text are occasions for writing **paragraphs** and **essays.**

Opinion   An opinion is a belief or conclusion that may or may not be based on fact. Writers often use opinion as a way of presenting a subjective description of an event or object. (By contrast, see **Fact[s].**)

Order   Order refers to the sequence in which the information in a composition is organized or arranged. Information is commonly organized in chronological order, order of importance, or spatial order. In **chronological order**, the information is arranged according to time. In **order** of **importance**, the information may be arranged from the least to the most important—or from the most to the least important. In **spatial order**, the information is presented from a particular vantage point: the door to a room, front to back, floor to ceiling, and so forth.

Order of Importance   See **Order.**

Paragraph   A paragraph is usually a set of two or more sentences that help explain an idea. The major use of a paragraph is to mark a division of the information within a composition. Another use of the paragraph is to set off **dialogue**. In this text, a paragraph is considered as a unit. The first word of a paragraph is usually indented a few spaces from the left margin of the printed page.

Parallelism   Parallelism refers to the use of the same grammatical structure in successive sentences. Writers use parallel sentence structure to stress or emphasize the relation of or the connections among the pieces of information in the sentences.

Person   Person is indicated by the personal pronouns used in a composition. Writers use the **first person** (*I, we*) to represent themselves as participants or firsthand observers of their subject. They use the **second person** (*you*) to address the reader directly. They use the **third person** (*he, she, it, one, they*) to provide the reader with a less limited and more objective view of the subject than may be possible by using first or second person. (See also **Point of View.**)

Personification   Personification is a figure of speech that attributes human qualities or abilities to animals or objects.

Persuasion   Persuasion is a **mode of development** in which the writer appeals to the reader's emotions in an attempt to convince the reader to accept the writer's **opinion** or judgment. The writer's **thesis** may or may not be controversial. (See also **Argumentation**.)

Point-by-Point Method   See **Alternating Method**.

Point of View   Point of view refers to the way writers present their ideas. Point of view is determined by the **person, time**, and **tone** used in a composition. Person is indicated by personal pronouns. Time is determined by the words that indicate when the action discussed in the composition takes place (past, present, or future). Tone refers to the attitude that writers take toward their subjects. The tone may be serious, humorous, formal, informal, cynical, sarcastic, ironic, sympathetic, and so forth.

Prewriting   Prewriting may involve **freewriting** and **brainstorming**. The purpose of prewriting is to get the writer started on defining the **main idea**. (See also **Brainstorming, Draft**, and **Freewriting**.)

Process   Process is a **mode of development** used by writers to explain the method of performing a task, making or preparing something, or achieving a particular result. See chapter 7, "Process," for further discussion.

Purpose   Purpose refers to a writer's reason for writing. Writers usually want to **inform** and to **instruct**.

Quotation Marks   Quotation marks are a pair of punctuation marks (" ") used to indicate the beginning and end of **dialogue** or information cited verbatim from a source.

Revising   The process of evaluating, reworking, and **rewriting a draft**, keeping **audience, purpose, thesis, development**, and, finally, mechanics (sentence structure, punctuation) in mind.

Rewriting   Rewriting involves reworking and clarifying the **draft** of a piece of writing. (See also **Draft, Edit, Prewriting**, and **Revising**.)

Rhetorical Question   A rhetorical question is one that is not expected to be answered or to which the answer is obvious.

Second Person   See **Person**.

Sentence   A sentence is a group of words that expresses a thought. A sentence usually contains a word or words that express who is doing an action or is being acted upon (the subject of the sentence) and a word or words that express the action that is taking place (the *verb* of the sentence). The first word of a sentence begins with a capital letter. The end of a sentence is marked by a period (.), a question mark (?), or an exclamation point (!).

Simile   A simile is a **figure of speech** in which unlike items are compared. A simile is usually introduced by *like* or *as,* as in "He worked *like a horse* on the project" or "The chicken was as tasteless *as a piece of cardboard.*" (See also Metaphor.)

Spatial Order   See **Order.**

Subjective   Subjective writing is that in which the writer's own feelings about the topic are expressed. (By contrast, see **Objective**.)

Support   Support refers to the information—specific details, **examples**, and so forth—used to develop or explain the **general idea** in a composition.

Symbol   A symbol is a person, place, or object that represents something other than itself, usually something immaterial or abstract.

Synonym   A synonym is a word or phrase that has the same meaning as another word or phrase. Writers sometimes use a synonym to clarify an unfamiliar word or phrase used in their compositions.

Thesis   The thesis is the **main idea** of an essay. The thesis may be stated directly (see **Thesis Statement**) or only implied (see **Imply/Implied**).

Thesis Statement   The thesis statement is the sentence or sentences in which the **main idea** of an **essay** is stated. The thesis statement is generally placed at or near the beginning of an essay.

Third Person   See **Person.**

Time   Time refers to the period (past, present, future) when the action discussed in the composition took place. Time is indicated by action words (verbs) and such words as *tomorrow, yesterday, next week,* and so on. (See also **Point of View.**)

Tone   Tone refers to the attitude writers take toward their subjects. The attitude in a composition may be formal, informal, serious, humorous, and so forth. (See also **Point of View.**)

Topic   The **main idea** of a **paragraph** is called its topic. The topic of a paragraph may be stated directly (see **Topic Sentence**) or only implied (see **Imply/Implied**).

Topic Sentence   The topic sentence is the sentence (or sentences) in which the **main idea** of a **paragraph** is stated. The topic sentence is commonly placed at or near the beginning of a paragraph, but it may appear at any point in the paragraph.

Transitions   Transitions are words and phrases such as *for example, on the other hand, first, second,* or *to illustrate* that help the reader identify the relationships among ideas in a composition.

Unified/Unity   A **paragraph** or **essay** must be unified to be effective, which means each must deal with a single idea, and the information included in the paragraph or essay must be related to that idea. (See also **Main Idea** and **Coherence**.)

Credits

Chapter 2

John Updike: "The Movie House," from *Five Boyhoods* (Doubleday) edited by Martin Levin. © 1962, renewed 1990 by Martin Levin. Reprinted by permission of Martin Levin. **Russell Baker:** "Learning to Write," from *Growing Up* by Russell Baker. Copyright © 1982 by Russell Baker. Reprinted by permission of Don Congdon Associates, Inc. **Connie Schultz:** "Daughter's Doll Teaches Mom Lesson on Race." © 2000 by *The Plain Dealer*. All rights reserved. Reprinted with permission. **Sarah Smith:** "A Little Nebraska," previously published by the Center for Great Plains Studies, University of Nebraska-Lincoln, in *Plains Song Review*, vol. 4, 2002, pp. 53–54. Reprinted by permission of the author.

Chapter 3

Stephen King: "The Attic." Reprinted with the permission of Scribner, a Division of Simon & Schuster, Inc., and Arthur Greene, from *On Writing: A Memoir of the Craft* by Stephen King. Copyright © 2000 by Stephen King. All rights reserved. **James Baldwin:** "My Father," from *Notes of a Native Son* by James Baldwin. © 1955, renewed 1983, by James Baldwin. Reprinted by permission of Beacon Press, Boston. **Deems Taylor:** "The Monster." Copyright 1937, 1965 by Deems Taylor. Permission Curtis Brown Associates, Inc.

Chapter 4

David Mazie: Excerpted with permission from "Keep Your Teen-Age Driver Alive," *Reader's Digest*, June 1991, pp. 85–86. Copyright © 1991 by the Reader's Digest Assn., Inc. **Peggy Robbins:** "The Kickapoo Indian Medicine Company." Reprinted with permission, *American History Magazine*, May 1980. Copyright by Weider History Group. **Jeff Glasser:** "Boomtown U.S.A.," *U.S. News & World Report*, vol. 130, (25), June 25, 2001, p. 16. Copyright 2001 by *U.S. News & World Report*, L.P. Reprinted with permission. **E. B. White:** "Democracy (July 3, 1944)." Reprinted by permission. © E. B. White. Originally published in *The New Yorker*. All rights reserved. **Diana Crane:** "The Social Meaning of T-shirts," from *Fashion and Its Social Agendas*, University of Chicago

Chapter 5

Chapter 6

Chapter 7

Chapter 8

Eliot Wigginton: "Moonshining as a Fine Art," from *The Foxfire Book* by Eliot Wigginton. Copyright © 1968, 1969, 1970, 1971, 1972 by The Foxfire Fund, Inc. Used by permission of Doubleday, a division of Random House, Inc. **Jonathan Schell:** Excerpt from *The Fate of the Earth* by Jonathan Schell. Copyright © 1982 by Jonathan Schell. Originally published in *The Fate of the Earth*. Reprinted by permission of the author and Janklow & Nesbit. **Patrick Steptoe:** "Wanted Children," from *A Matter of Life* by Patrick Steptoe. Reprinted by permission of Random House UK. **Eileen Simpson:** "Reading for Pure Pleasure," from *Reversals: A Personal Account of Victory over Dyslexia.* © 1998 by Farrar Straus & Giroux, LLC. Used by permission. **Brian Manning:** "The Thirsty Animal," *The New York Times*, October 13, 1985. Copyright © 1985 by Brian Manning. Reprinted by permission.

Chapter 9

Jo Goodwin Parker: "What Is Poverty?," from *America's Other Children: Public Schools Outside Suburbia* by George Henderson. Copyright © 1971 by University of Oklahoma Press, Norman. Reprinted by permission of the publisher. All rights reserved. **Isaac Asimov:** "What Is Intelligence Anyway?," from *Please Explain* by Isaac Asimov. © 1973 by Isaac Asimov. Reprinted by permission of Houghton Mifflin Harcourt Publishing Company. All rights reserved. **Tiffany Kary:** "Total Eclipse of the Son," *Psychology Today*, January/February 2003. Reprinted with permission from *Psychology Today.* Copyright © 2003 by Sussex Publishers, Inc. **Rick Reilly:** "Earning Their Pinstripes," *Sports Illustrated*, September 23, 2002, p. 92. Reprinted by permission of *Sports Illustrated.*

Chapter 10

Gil Crandall: "Letter to R. J. Reynolds," from *Reader's Digest*, vol. 125, July 1984, pp. 64–65. Reprinted by permission of the author. **Anna Quindlen:** "Frightening—and Fantastic," *Newsweek*, September 18, 2006, p. 72. Reprinted by permission of International Creative Management, Inc. Copyright © 2006 by Anna Quindlen. **Jesse Scaccia:** "Hang It Up," *The New York Times,* op-ed, May 23, 2006. © 2006 by *The New York Times.* Reprinted by permission. **Helen C. Vo-Dinh:** "Excuses, Excuses," from "My Turn," in *Newsweek,* August 15, 1983. Permission of the author. **Roger Sipher:** "So That Nobody Has to Go to School If They Don't Want to," *The New York Times*, December 19, 1977. © 1977 by The New York Times Company. Reprinted by permission. **Robert Voas:** "Keep the Drinking Age at Twenty-One," *Christian Science Monitor*, Perspectives, January 12, 2006. Reprinted by permission of the author. **Nathalie Fiset:** "Facts about Global Warming You Should Know," from www.bestglobal warmingarticles.com. Reprinted by permission of the author. **Jon Birger:** "What If Global-Warming Fears Are Overblown?," from *Fortune*, May 14, 2009. © 2000 by Time Inc. All rights reserved.

Chapter 11

Roger Hoffman: "There's Always the Dare" *The New York Times*, March 23, 1986. Copyright © 1986 by Roger Hoffmann. Reprinted by permission of the author. **Leonard Pitts Jr.:** "I Won't Twitter My Life Away," from *The Miami Herald*, March 4, 2009. © *The Miami Herald*, 2009. **Magdoline Asfahani:** "Time to Look and Listen," from *Newsweek*, December 2, 1996. All rights reserved. Reprinted by permission.

Index